American Air Rifles

James E. House

Published by

 **krause publications**

700 East State St., Iola, WI 54990-0001
715-445-2214
www.krause.com

Please, call or write us for our free catalog of antiques and collectibles publications.
To place an order or receive our free catalog, call 800-258-0929. For editorial comment and further information,
use our regular business telephone at (715) 445-2214.

Library of Congress Catalog Number: 2001096283
ISBN: 0-87349-368-0

Printed in the United States of America

DEDICATION

To Victoria and Olivia, whose generation will determine the fate of the shooting sports.

ACKNOWLEDGMENTS

I hope you can imagine how enjoyable it has been to collect the information presented in this book. I also hope that this book adds to your enjoyment of airguns. While this book has been a labor of love, it is necessary to acknowledge the assistance and encouragement of several individuals in the process. Special thanks are accorded Joe Murfin, Denise Johnson, and Robert Spears of the Daisy Manufacturing Co. and to John Goff and Kirby Kaiser of the Crosman Corp. Thanks to Brett Daniels of the Wal-Mart photo lab, who was a great help in producing the photos. I would also like to express my appreciation to Ross Bielema and Don Gulbrandsen of Krause Publications for helping the initial dream to become a reality. This project was begun in Lost Cabin Campground in the Big Horn Mountains of Wyoming. My companion then and in every phase of this project was my wife, Kathy. Her assistance with photography, as well as data collection and organization have been invaluable.

TABLE OF CONTENTS

INTRODUCTION

To many people, an air rifle symbolizes a more carefree time when adventure was an everyday occurrence. As in my case, an air rifle may have been an almost constant companion for you. I had two air rifles in my youth, a break-action, single-shot Daisy and a Benjamin multi-pump, both BB guns.

Sad to say, I do not know what happened to either of them. No matter, because I graduated to "real" guns and bows. But I didn't really graduate and a change in direction has occurred again, as I have found in the recent past a renewed passion for airguns. Interest in airguns is on the rise, part of which may be due to the ever-tightening restrictions on firearms.

Perhaps we will see a return, at least in part, to the practice of youth using airguns to learn the shooting sports. The makers of airguns provide support for groups that teach youngsters this way.

There is something in human nature that makes us want to return to our past. The current national epidemic of interest in antiques reveals it. In fact, old airguns, ammunition containers, targets, literature, and related items have themselves become highly collectible. Perhaps we did have it better back then.

But air rifles are not just for kids. There is a considerable emphasis on "precision, adult" air rifles. However, for some reason, those descriptions have become synonymous with "spring-piston, imported" airguns. What has happened to those classic American air rifles over the years? Are they not "serious" air rifles that are capable of fine performance? If so, no one seems to write about them because almost all of the publications deal primarily with imported air rifles. Of course some of the imported models are beautiful, precision instruments, but are no American airguns worthy of being

Youngsters who learn to shoot safely with airguns may continue to enjoy the shooting sports for a lifetime.

The author and his wife, Kathy, have discovered the pleasures of shooting air rifles together.

performance of the multi-pump pneumatics. Questions during conversations with technicians and engineers at the air rifle manufacturers sometimes resulted in answers like "Oh, we don't test that" or "Our spec is at least …."

Much of my career as a scientist was spent examining data for accuracy, reproducibility, and applicability. Not having the data on airguns that I wanted meant that such data needed to be determined. Determine it I did. My results provide a fresh insight into the American air rifle and its capabilities that may surprise you.

The extensive work with air rifles described in this book has shown me that one never totally outgrows an air rifle. You may develop other interests that require other types of projectile launchers, but there is still a fascination with

referred to as serious airguns? Where it is legal, hunting and pest control using airguns have become a passion for some airgunners. Would the user of a "serious, adult" air rifle think that you were crazy to suggest that your American air rifle could be so used? Just how capable are the multi-pump pneumatics that so many of us used when growing up?

Looking for printed answers to these questions turned up very little worthwhile information. What did appear was a thinly veiled bias toward the spring-piston imports. There appears to be almost no hard data readily available on velocity reproducibility, accuracy, or

the air rifle. For me, it is almost coming full circle only to find out that there is still a lot to be learned. It is simply a different form of experimentation. If you are like me, you may be searching for something related to your love of shooting and outdoor activities that provides new challenges while helping you discover something from your past. An air rifle may be just that sort of thing, and this book will provide you with solid information and data, much of it available for the first time, on most aspects of using American air rifles. Interestingly, most of that information is also transferable to the use of any airgun.

CHAPTER 1

AIR RIFLES: THEN AND NOW

WHEN YOU WALK through the sporting goods department of a large discount store, you see a variety of types of modern air rifles. You might glance at them and think that airguns came along at about the same time as television, automatic transmissions or computers. Actually, the first air rifle is supposed to date from about 1560 and it is credited to a man named Guter in Nuremburg, Germany. The oldest airgun that still survives dates from 1637. In the earliest air rifles, propulsion was provided by a bellows that was contained in the stock. A crank was used to compress a spring that was held by a sear. When fired, the spring tension was released and the spring expanded against the bellows to compress the air and launch a dart. Later air rifles of the 1700s had separate air reservoirs that could be pumped to a pressure of 400 to 600 pounds per square inch.

Some of these guns could launch a half-ounce ball 150 to 200 yards.

Early air rifles that used compressed air were made with one of three types of reservoirs for holding the compressed air. One type of reservoir consisted of a removable hollow butt section that could be pumped up and then attached to the action and barrel. This type of gun was developed in the late 1600s. A second type of compressed air reservoir consisted of a cylinder located around the barrel. Development of this type of airgun took place in the 1600s by Georg Fehr and in the early 1700s by Johann Lorenz Kolbe in London. Kolbe, a German immigrant, worked as an instrument maker, but also made air rifles. One of his designs was a repeater that looked like a flintlock rifle.

The third type of reservoir consisted of a detachable, hollow sphere that could be

A BB gun for Christmas has been the dream of beginning shooters for many years, including the author's brother, Larry, in the early 1950s.

pumped to high pressure and attached to the bottom of the piece ahead of the trigger guard. This type of rifle was popular in central Germany, and it was copied in England. It was developed in Germany in the mid-1700s and in England toward the end of the 1700s. The compressed air in the reservoir provided power for several shots before the sphere had to be recharged. Some of these types of guns were employed in the United States, and they were made in large calibers, such as .36, .40, .50 and even larger. Until the mid-1800s, these guns used round balls, which were relatively inaccurate and ballistically not very efficient. For a time after that, cylindrical pellets with felt bases were used. Pellets with a shape similar to that in current use were patented in the 1870s.

Meriwether Lewis of the historic Lewis and Clark expedition of 1804-1806 took along an air rifle. For many years, there was uncertainty about who made the rifle, but in recent years it has been established that it was built for him by Isaiah Lukens of Philadelphia. The rifle had a hollow buttstock that held compressed air. The uses of this gun were mentioned 16 times in the journals of Lewis and Clark. Apparently, the air rifle was an amazing device to the Native Americans they encountered. It also was used to kill at least one deer. Also in the early 1800s, the armies of Napoleon were subjected to sniping by Austrians using repeating air rifles.

After the development of air rifles with pressurized reservoirs, the spring airgun appeared. In the 1830s, a single-stroke airgun was invented and this type was widely used. Shooting galleries that used single-stroke, breech-loading spring air rifles were popular in the mid-1800s. In 1869, Charles Bunge developed a repeating rifle with a revolving cylinder. The internal reservoir air pistol known as the Kalamazoo target pistol was invented by E. H. Hawley of Kalamazoo, Mich. It was produced from 1869 to 1880. In 1874, Henry M. Quackenbush invented a spring-piston air rifle that involved pushing the barrel rearward to compress a coil spring that was behind a movable piston. The piston was held in place by the sear until the piece was discharged, allowing the piston to spring forward and rapidly compress the air, which expelled the projectile. He also developed a rifle that made use of a lever under the stock to compress the spring.

In 1871, Benjamin Haviland and George P. Gunn received patents for spring-piston air rifles that utilized the hinged barrel as a compressing lever. The operation of these rifles was similar to that of modern break-action rifles.

Any compressed gas can be used as a propellent. Of course, the gas must be nontoxic and it must not corrode metal parts. One gas that meets these requirements and is widely employed in guns is carbon dioxide (CO_2). In recent years, many airguns, especially pistols, have been marketed that make use of a 12-gram cylinder of carbon dioxide.

The author's father, 91, holds a Benjamin Model G from the 1920s.

The Daisy Manufacturing Co. moved from Plymouth, Mich., to Rogers, Ark., in 1958, so this Daisy popgun was made before 1958.

Crosman commemorated its 75th anniversary with walnut-stocked Model 2100 and 2200 rifles featuring this inlay.

While such guns are not the subject of this book, the use of a detachable cylinder containing compressed carbon dioxide was pioneered by Paul Giffard in the late 1800s. This device was patented in 1889, and Colt acquired the rights for this type of gun. More than 600 CO_2 guns were produced in France. Giffard then established the Giffard Gun Co. in London, where more than 5,000 additional CO_2 guns were built.

About this time, the multi-pump pneumatic (the so-called "pump up") airguns appeared. In 1882, Walter Benjamin of St. Louis invented an air rifle that utilized an in-line pump in a cylinder located below the barrel. Various models of this type of gun were produced by Whissler Instrument Co. of St. Louis. The Benjamin Air Rifle Co. was formed in 1927 when A.P. Stack purchased the original company.

The Sheridan Co. of Racine, Wis., began production of pneumatic air rifles about 1948. The development work was done by E.N. Wackerhagen and Robert Krause. The name was decided as they saw a street sign on Sheridan Avenue. Gen. Phillip Sheridan is ultimately the source of the name, since both Fort Sheridan and Sheridan Avenue were named in his honor. My wife bought me a polished brass 50th Anniversary Sheridan in Sheridan, Wyo., for a Christmas present. Of course, Sheridan, Wyo., also was named in Gen. Sheridan's honor. My Sheridan from Sheridan is a special rifle.

In 1982, the Benjamin and Sheridan companies merged to become the Benjamin Sheridan Co., which has since become part of the Crosman Corp. Benjamin and Sheridan have produced some of the most successful multi-pump pneumatic airguns in the world. The current models will be dis-cussed in some detail later in this book.

The history of the Daisy Manufacturing Co. can be traced back to 1886 when Clarence J. Hamilton met with representatives of the Plymouth Iron Windmill Co. to discuss the production of a metal air rifle of his design. After Lewis Cass Hough shot the gun, he declared, "Boy, that's a daisy!" At first, the air rifles were given to people who purchased a windmill. Of course, the company went on to produce air rifles and the name was changed to Daisy Manufacturing Co. in 1895. The Daisy Co. continued to make airguns at Plymouth, Mich., until the company moved to a new plant at Rogers, Ark., in 1958.

This writer's first air rifle, a break-action BB gun in the 1940s, was produced at the original plant site. Daisy introduced the lever-action spring air rifle in 1901, and the pump- or slide-

In addition to BB guns, Daisy made a large number of toys like the double-barreled cork gun from the 1930s shown here.

action model in 1915. Throughout most of its history, the Daisy Co. has been owned by the Hough family, and although it was owned by the Victor Comptometer Co. (1967-1970), Heddon and Sons (1971-1974), and the Kidde Corp. (1978-1983), the Hough family again regained the company in 1983. Although best known for its production of spring-air BB guns (more than 9 million of the Red Ryder model alone have been sold), Daisy has produced millions of multi-pump pneumatic rifles, and some of the models will be discussed in considerable detail throughout this book.

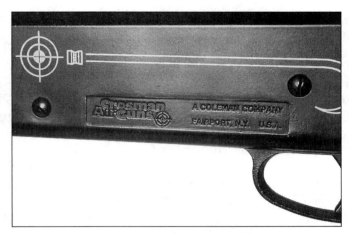

This Crosman 2200 was made in the late 1980s as indicated by the stamping, "A Coleman Company, Fairport, N.Y."

Along with the developments described above, the Crosman Co. began production of pneumatic air rifles about 75 years ago. Crosman's first air rifle was a .22 caliber model that used a pump contained under the barrel, and it was pumped from the muzzle end. The Crosman family originally had a seed company. They were approached by William McLean to manufacture an air rifle that was patterned after one brought from Europe by McLean's employer. That gun is believed to have been an air rifle made by Paul Giffard.

In 1923, the Crosman Rifle Co. went into business, but in 1924 it was taken over by the Crosman Seed Co. Later, Frank Hahn acquired possession of the company, and it was renamed as the Crosman Arms Co. located in Rochester, N.Y. After Hahn's death, Philip Hahn, his son, was president of Crosman during the period of

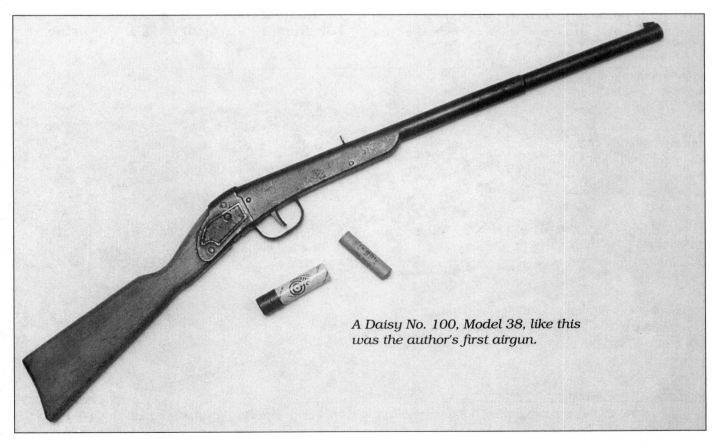

A Daisy No. 100, Model 38, like this was the author's first airgun.

growth from 1940 to the late 1960s. In 1971, Crosman Arms Co. was purchased by the Coleman Co., the huge supplier of camping equipment. With the sale of the Coleman Co. to MacAndres & Forbes, the airgun company that became Crosman Products Inc., was formed. Worldwide Sports and Recreation purchased Crosman Products, Inc., in 1988 and in 1992 the Benjamin Air Rifle Co., now known as the Benjamin Sheridan Corp., was obtained by Crosman. The Crosman Corp. was formerly located at Fairport, N.Y., but is now located at East Bloomfield, N.Y.

Some of the Crosman models have become American legends. For example, the Model 760 Pumpmaster has been produced for more than 30 years and more than 8 million have been sold. Performance of this model and that of other Crosman multi-pump models will be considered in later chapters. Although the Crosman Co. purchased the Benjamin Sheridan Co. in 1992, the production of the fine Benjamin and Sheridan air rifles of previous designs continues.

Break-action air rifles carrying the Winchester name appeared from 1969-1975. These rifles were made in Europe for marketing in the United States. In 2001, rifles bearing the Winchester name are again available and are being marketed by Daisy. Savage Arms Co. also has a series of break-action rifles that are made in Europe. In recent years, several CO_2-powered pistols have been made that resemble the Colt 1911, Beretta 92, Walther, and other pistols. In general, they are made in Europe and are marketed by one of the U.S. companies.

In this section, a very brief history of the airgun has been presented. Only a few of the major developments and developers of airguns have been considered in this introduction with its emphasis on American air rifle development. A much more complete and scholarly history of the early development of the airgun is available in the book by Eldon G. Wolff, *Air-Guns*, from Southwest Sports, P.O. Box 2021, Benton, AR. A very worthwhile history of the airgun can also be found in J.I. Galan's *Air-Gun Digest*, 3rd Edition, from Krause Publications, Iola, WI (800-258-0929).

It must be mentioned that airgunners everywhere have been well supplied by the American airgun manufacturers. Their fine airguns have trained generations of shooters and provided an enormous amount of recreation.

Collecting

The rack of old magazines on a table caught my eye as I walked through the antique mall. In the rack there were several issues of Boys' Life from 1968. Being still a boy at heart, I

Among the author's most prized Daisy memorabilia is this complete BB gun cleaning kit. Complete kits are worth $75 to $100.

Pellet containers are popular items for collectors.

picked up a copy and began slowly to flip the pages. When I saw some of the ads in the magazine, I bought it.

The back cover was an ad for Daisy airguns, and inside there was a full-column ad for the Sheridan Blue Streak. Also in the issue there were ads for Crosman and Benjamin air rifles. Some of the airguns advertised in that magazine from 1968 are still available with only slight changes. Before times changed, boys thought a lot about such things, and the

scouting magazine reflected it. The old magazines showed that there was a great deal of interest in guns and shooting.

I got my first BB gun at 6 years of age. At the time, I was not strong enough to cock one of the lever-cocking models like the Daisy Red Ryder. Fortunately, Daisy made a Number 100, Model 38 that was cocked by break action, and it sold for $1.75. I could put it across my knee and pull on the barrel with one hand and on the stock with the other and cock it. It was loaded by dropping a single BB down the barrel. That little gun was my constant, treasured companion for several years. As I got older, I graduated to a Benjamin Model 310 multi-pump BB rifle. At that time, a cousin had a Crosman Model 100 in .22 caliber. Experiences with air rifles provided an introduction to shooting sports that eventually led to small bore competition at the college level.

Since becoming a serious airgun shooter and moderately active collector, I have seen two of the break-action models like my first airgun. A specimen in good condition now sells for $75 to $150, but I got mine for $90. That is a healthy sum for a gun that sold new for less than $2 in the early 1940s! Ah, the law of supply and demand also works in collecting airguns.

While the description of current airguns given in Chapter 2 will focus on their characteristics and uses, there is another facet of airguns to consider. If you have much of an

Air rifles such as the Benjamin Model G , top, and the Daisy No. 100, Model 38, are highly prized by collectors. These rifles are worth $150 and $100, respectively.

Special-issue guns like this Roy Rogers and Trigger commemorative will be highly collectible in the future. The issue price is $70.

It is doubly rewarding when a pellet tin contains the original pellets as in the case of this Sheridan can. Such full cans are worth $10 to $15.

interest in antiques and visit antique stores and flea markets, you will discover that all types of older airgun memorabilia are highly collectible. Old pellet cans and boxes of all types are of interest as are the older guns themselves. You may be able to find a Daisy Targeteer .118 caliber pistol, and I once found a Daisy PowerLine 880 with a gold colored metal receiver. Close inspection of the barrel showed that the latter was the Ted Williams Model 790 marketed by Sears. Many of the old Crosman, Daisy, and Benjamin airguns can be

found, but do not be surprised when you see that they may cost as much as a new gun or more. This is not a book about collecting airgun items, but rather it is intended as a user's guide to American air rifles. Consequently, we will leave most of this interesting and growing subject to another book.

The famous Daisy Red Ryder BB gun was introduced in 1938. While in an antique mall in Billings, Mont., last year, I came across a Daisy Red Ryder in a booth. The dealer had gone to the trouble to write out on a card

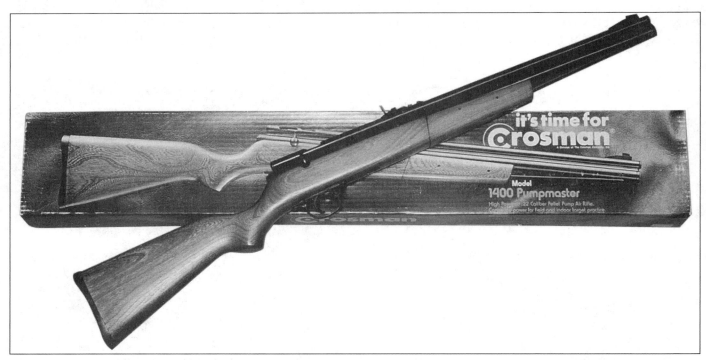

This Crosman Model 1400 was found in its original box and it is still a good shooter. This gun is worth about $100 to $125 in this condition.

attached to the gun that it was an original Model 1938 Red Ryder. It was labeled as "very rare" and the price was $125. Naturally, I looked at the BB gun. On the top, it said, "Daisy Manufacturing Company, Rogers, Arkansas." Since Daisy moved from Plymouth, Mich., to Rogers, Ark., in 1958, the BB gun was definitely not a rare 1938 model. I looked at the serial number (BB guns did not carry serial numbers until comparatively recent times) and I could tell that the gun was only a few years old. I explained all this later to the owner and the price quickly dropped and the note disappeared.

The owner of the BB gun explained that he had obtained it from his grandfather and thought it was old since it was a Model 1938. All Red Ryder guns are known as the Model 1938, but not all are old. The lesson here is to examine any collectible airgun with a critical eye. Study the available literature and learn about the variants of models that interest you. There have been more than a dozen variations of the Crosman 760 alone. Some had wood stocks, some had metal receivers and some had nickel plated barrels.

There are several books that you should study before you set out to assemble a collection of airguns. Four of those reference works are the following. The history of the Benjamin air rifles is presented in D.T. Fletcher's *The St. Louis & Benjamin Air Rifle Companies*, Portland, OR, 1999. A similar book dealing with Crosman air rifles is Fletcher's *75 Years of Crosman Airguns*, Portland, Ore., 1998. These books describe all of the early models of the air rifles and the history of the companies. They also show a very large number of the advertise-

BBs have been made by many companies. These are worth $1 to $15, depending on age.

ments for the older models and factual data for them. Sheridan air rifles are described in Ronald E. Elbe's *Know Your Sheridan Rifles & Pistols*, Blacksmith Corp. Publishers, 1993. The history of the Daisy Manufacturing Co. can be found in Cass Hough's *It's a Daisy!* All of these books contain a wealth of information for the airgun collector.

As you examine airguns and read about them, you will pick up numerous tidbits of information like that provided by knowing that Daisy moved from Michigan to Arkansas in 1958. Similarly, Crosman moved from Rochester, N.Y., to Fairport, N.Y., in 1952. I have Crosman 2100 and 2200 models that are stamped "Crosman ... A Coleman Company, Fairport, N.Y." Without reference to serial numbers, the guns can be dated to the period 1971 to 1988 because that is the period when Coleman owned Crosman and the company was located in Fairport. For the last several years, Crosman air rifles have been made in East Bloomfield, N.Y. If a Crosman air rifle carries the manufacturing site as East Bloomfield, N.Y, it was made in the last dozen years. On Sheridan air rifles, the location of the safety can provide a clue as to the age of the piece. Late rifles have the safety located on the trigger guard in front of the trigger. Earlier models have the safety

Discussions of airguns caused the pastor and his wife to bring out their old Marksman and its original box.

The fact that Daisy produced only 2,500 of the Roy Rogers and Trigger model means that it will be difficult to find years from now.

This complete package of 1952 Daisy targets was found in an antique mall. A collector paid $40 for this sealed package.

Although this book is not about BB guns, I could not pass up this collectible Daisy Targeteer, complete with box and oil. It is valued at $50.

behind the receiver, as it is on some double barrel shotguns. One of my Sheridan Blue Streak rifles that was bought new in 1989 has that type of safety. Very early models have a rotary safety with a tab on either side of the receiver. Pushing down on one raises the other and places the safety "on" or "off." I recently added a Sheridan with this type of safety that was made in the early 1980s. From 1948 to 1963, Sheridan rifles had rotary safeties with disks placed vertically in the center of the rear part of the receivers. There are many other types of information, but the details are too numerous to deal with adequately in a general book. The more specialized works dealing with history and collecting should be consulted.

If you begin to collect air rifles, you will soon find that you may want to specialize. There are several ways to do this: by brand, time period, all variations of a particular model that has been produced for a long time, etc. By specializing, you will find it much easier to recognize the markings and design characteristics that enable you to date the piece and verify its authenticity.

Sources for Collectibles

While I am not a serious collector of airguns, I am frequently asked where I find the guns, targets and pellet cans that I collect. Two of the most common sources are antique malls and flea markets. Many of the dealers in antiques and collectibles obtain their merchandise from estate sales and garage sales. Some dealers who specialize in glassware or furniture may care little about the old airgun that was in the batch of stuff that they got at an auction. You may get a good buy on some airgun items from such dealers, but don't necessarily bet on it.

One of my sayings is, "The most expensive place to buy a hammer is in a hardware store." You can buy a hammer more cheaply at a store that doesn't specialize in hammers (hardware). The same is true of airgun memorabilia. If the dealer specializes in airgun items, as in a couple of antique malls that I frequent, prices will generally be higher than from a dealer who just happens to have a couple of older items. However, the specialized dealer will be more likely to have numerous items from which to choose.

Stores sell merchandise that is usually contained in boxes. One specimen is removed from the box and left in the rack or on the wall as a display model. In a few cases, I have found earlier versions of air rifles that have been on the shelves for several years as display models. Newer variations appeared, but the older items were left for display and not sold. The Daisy 880 used to be made with a metal receiver and a hooded front sight. I have spotted two of these more desirable Daisy rifles on walls in stores where they had been for years. When I saw them, I recognized them as more desirable specimens and asked to buy the display model. In this way, I obtained the two older Daisy Model 880 rifles, several cans of pellets, and a few other items. Examine the merchandise carefully because you might find something that has been discontinued and soon will be a collectible.

Another source that has yielded several of my airguns is pawn shops. People pawn anything of value and airguns are sometimes forfeited. In most cases, pawn shop operators will not invest much in an airgun, so don't pay the asking price. My oldest Sheridan air rifle, a Crosman Mark I .22 caliber CO_2 pistol, a Daisy BB pistol, and an older Daisy 880 with a metal receiver were obtained in this way.

While I have not had a great deal of success in adding to my airgun collection from this

This Daisy replica of the Colt Peacemaker is a BB gun. It was found in a pawn shop with holster, box, and instructions. It is worth $25 to $75, depending on condition.

source, gun shows are another possibility. Sometimes a dealer who has a few airguns to sell will bring them to display along with his other merchandise.

If you want to collect airguns or cameras, you need to decide whether you simply want a particular model to display or whether you want a working model. I try to get working models, but I do not always succeed. My old Sheridan Blue Streak looked good, and I got it for a good price. Only after I got home and allowed it to stand pumped up for 30 minutes did I find that it would not hold air. Since it was in good condition otherwise, I decided to have it rebuilt. That work was done by the outstanding airgunsmith Jim Coplen, 5522 N.W. Clearwater Road, Rochester, MN 55903, for a reasonable sum. After I got it back, I found that it not only held air, it shot just as fast as my new Sheridans. Even with the work done on the

A booth in an antique mall had this 1960s catalog, which contains a wealth of information for the collector. It is worth $15 to $20.

gun, I got a fine shooting Sheridan for considerably less than a new gun would have cost and added a variation of the Sheridan rifle that I did not have. After all that, I decided to rework the stock and forearm. The result was an air rifle that performs like a new one and looks better.

In all fairness, the pawn shop operator who sold me the Sheridan did not know that the gun had a problem since he had never shot it. When I was in the shop some time later, I was looking at an expensive box of field target pellets. On hearing that the Sheridan needed to be repaired, he told me to just keep the box of pellets. They did not sell for as much as the repair bill, but the concern was appreciated. If you want to shoot collectible airguns (as I do), ask to do some testing before you buy the gun or ask for return privileges if it does not work properly. This does not apply to really old guns, however, since they are more likely to be looked at, not shot.

Almost anything related to airguns can be found on the Internet. There are numerous

A collector of Crosman guns would find this CO_2-powered, .22 caliber Mark I irresistible. They are valued at $85 and up.

sites that are devoted to airguns and related items. Use caution in buying in this way since the merchandise cannot be examined prior to purchase. While I have never purchased an airgun over the Internet, I know people who have and they have been very satisfied with the results. The vast majority of Internet merchants describe their merchandise accurately.

Airguns are fascinating. Their development parallels other technological advances in both design and materials used in fabrication. One could become a collector of airguns and air-

Sears formerly marketed airguns, targets, and ammunition under the J.C. Higgins label. They sell for $2 to $3 each.

gun supplies just to see how they mirror other aspects of American life in the time periods. If only those old guns could talk! What tales they would tell of hours spent roaming woods and fields, plinking cans in the back yard, dispatching pests, and hunting small game. The guns would also tell of youthful owners who grew up and left them behind in basements, closets, and attics. While I have models similar to my first two airguns, like millions of others, I do not know what happened to my first two. I wish I had them instead of the replacements that I have collected. However, not having the originals makes me appreciate their replacements even more. Collecting airguns and other memorabilia is a noble pastime.

A pawn shop in Montana was the source of this vintage Crosman Model 357 in .22 caliber. It is worth up to $50, depending on condition.

Not all collectibles related to airguns involve shooting-related items! This recently made die-cast truck sells for $40 to $50.

This old Daisy target was a combined bullseye and baseball game with instructions on the back. These targets bring $5 to $6 each.

These old targets show that Winchester-Western was in the airgun business and that Sheridan was located in Racine, Wis. They usually sell for $2 to $3 each.

CHAPTER 2

AMERICAN MULTI-PUMP PNEUMATICS

Why American Multi-pump Pneumatics?

The American BB gun is an institution unto itself. The low-cost BB gun, however interesting, will not be dealt with in this book. They can be cocked, a BB loaded, and fired. There is no way to vary the power of the gun or design of the projectile. These low-power, single-stroke air rifles, while not exactly toys, are not serious or adult airguns. Thus, they will be excluded from the analysis presented in this book. Moreover, it is not possible to test every pneumatic that has been produced. What will be discussed are representative models of today's airguns in a variety of cost and performance levels. In that way, there is something for everyone, because some users may own a Benjamin or Daisy .22, while others have a Sheridan .20 or a Crosman .177, and so on. Also, several of the current models are virtually identical in performance to earlier models that they replaced, so owners of earlier models also can benefit from the results presented.

Why are only a few of the European break-action, spring-piston rifles discussed? First, this book is intended as a user's guide to American multi-pump rifles. However, in order to give some comparison to the break-action models, three of the break-action type rifles

The American air rifle, made by the millions and enjoyed for generations, provides an excellent way to train new shooters like the author's nephew, Steven.

Some of the advantages of the multi-pump rifles over the break-action type are immediately obvious.

(all imported by American companies) were tested. In this way, the user of a multi-pump rifle can make a comparison with a comparable rifle of the other type.

Perusal of books and catalogs dealing with air rifles shows that the vast majority of the models considered as serious adult, high-performance airguns are imported. Many of these air rifles cost from $150 to $2,000, depending on whether the gun is a field or sporter model or a target model suitable for serious match competition. These guns are indeed works of art and mechanical genius. Some of them are capable of literally putting pellet after pellet in the same hole at 10 meters (33 feet), the usual target distance for air rifles. Many are quite powerful and suitable for pest control and hunting small game as well. But how many of

these guns do you see in your local discount, hardware, or sporting goods store? How many of these elegant air rifles are sold compared to American air rifles? How about the "buy American" philosophy? How capable are American air rifles that cost a fraction of the price of the imports and are so readily available and have been made by the millions?

This book is concerned primarily with multi-pump American air rifles and it is designed to help you get the most from your American airgun. However, in order to provide a comparison of the American and imported break-action rifles, some representative rifles of the latter type will be evaluated. The performance of a pellet has nothing to do with what launched it, and the path of a pellet has to do only with its design characteristics and veloc-

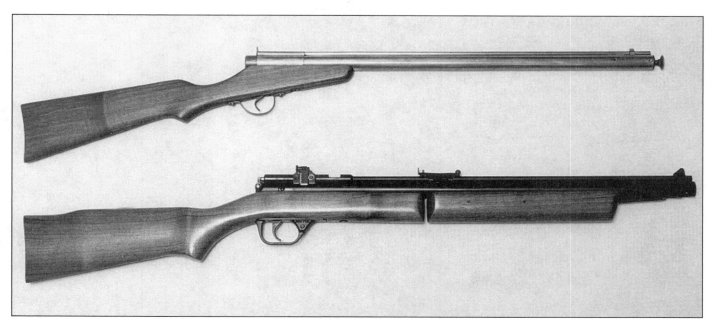

Benjamin air rifles have come a long way from the Model G BB gun, top, to the .22 caliber Model 392.

Pellets are available in .177, .20, .22, and .25 calibers as represented by the Beeman Crow Magnum pellets.

ity. Consequently, much of the information in this book is equally applicable to users of spring-piston airguns, although these guns will not be discussed in as much detail.

The spring-piston airguns require large, heavy receivers and long stocks. Even though they have barrels of 19 to 22 inches long, most of the imported spring airguns are 42 to 45 inches long and weigh 7 to 9 pounds. None of the American-made pneumatics is more than 40 inches long and none weighs more than 6 pounds, with most in the 3 to 5 1/2-pound range. One of the really awesome spring-piston guns, the Webley Patriot in .22 caliber, is more than 45 inches long, weighs about 9 1/2 pounds, and costs more than $400, but it is a beautiful piece.

While in one of the sporting goods superstores, the author was discussing airguns with a none-too-helpful salesman. When he heard the comparisons of size and weight, the salesman responded with, "I don't want to use anything that I have to pump more than once." Well, this writer doesn't want to use an airgun that is longer than and weighs as much as a 375 H&H Magnum! "You pays your money and you takes your choice," as the saying goes.

But keep in mind that tens of millions of American air rifles have been sold and they are competent tools. However, it is unfair to compare a Ford to a Ferrari. That doesn't mean that the Ford doesn't have many good features (especially cost) and that it will not perform most of the tasks required of an automobile just as well as a Ferrari. In the same way, American multi-pump air rifles are capable instruments that can do most things that an air rifle should be expected to do, but they are not made for competitive target shooting.

The underlying idea of this book is that millions of the multi-pump air rifles are sold every year in Kmart, Wal-Mart, Scheel's All Sports,

Sheridan air rifles, like the Silver Streak being used here by the author, have always represented quality construction and high performance.

American air rifles cover the spectrum with these models, from top: the Daisy 880, Crosman 2100B, Daisy 22X, Sheridan Silver Streak, and Benjamin 392.

Gart Sports, Big R, Farm and Fleet, Fleet Farm, Coast-to-Coast, Cabela's, Gander Mountain, Bass Pro Shops, and sporting goods stores in towns of all sizes across the United States. They constitute the vast majority of adult airguns produced and millions of them are used for serious airgun pursuits if not for competition.

In general, many of the expensive spring-piston rifles are not as readily available without ordering and they are somewhat more specialized in their intended uses. Thus, the remainder of this book is devoted to providing information related to the performance and characteristics of the multi-pump air rifles of current American manufacture and a few break-action rifles for comparison. However, almost all of the models in current production have been produced for more than a decade and at least one model, the Crosman 760 Pumpmaster, has been produced for 34 years as of this writing. In general, current production means guns that have been produced for many years and will likely continue to be produced for many more.

The most popular airgun caliber is .177 (4.5 mm), although the .22 (5.5 mm) is also common. The .177 and .22 calibers are sometimes referred to as No. 1 Bore and No. 2 Bore, respectively, particularly in Britain. Less common is the .20 (5 mm) and much less common still is the .25 (6.35 mm, sometimes called No. 3 Bore). In fact, no American-made, multi-pump pneumatic is currently available in .25 caliber. It stands to reason that the selection of ammunition available varies directly with the popularity of the caliber (the number of guns that use the ammunition). There is an incredibly wide selection of pellets in .177 caliber available and a comprehensive selection of pellets in .22 caliber. There are also several types of .20 caliber pellets available. In many instances, the identical type of pellet is available in all three calibers. Some types of .177 and .22 caliber pellets are available in the sporting goods departments of the large discount chain stores. Most sporting goods stores will stock several types in these calibers and

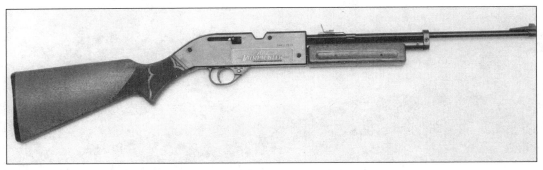

The Crosman 760 is an American legend. More than 8 million have been produced in a 35-year period.

usually one or two types of .20 caliber pellets. In a general way, the prices of pellets reflect the popularity of the calibers, with .177 pellets usually being the least expensive.

American Air Rifles Today

The airgunner of today has a wide range of multi-pump pneumatics from which to choose, but several points should be made before presenting a discussion of current air rifles. First, we have already decided not to include the spring airguns that are designed to shoot BBs. Most of them do not fall into the category of adult air rifles and most are charged with a single stroke (lever, slide) rather than by multiple pumps. They are not sufficiently powerful for hunting and pest control. The second point is that some of the lower-priced pneumatics are designed to fire either BBs as repeaters or .177 pellets as single-shot guns. These guns will be discussed as only pellet guns. The accuracy and performance of these dual-ammunition guns are superior when pellets are used. Consequently, their use as BB guns will not be discussed in this book.

Although price does not necessarily indicate quality, the old saying "You get what you pay for" is generally applicable to airguns. On the other hand, you may be surprised to find that

an air rifle capable of fine performance is not that expensive. Again, this is not a catalog of pneumatic airguns, but most of those currently available have been made for years and will very likely continue to be produced, so they have been included in the evaluations.

The pneumatic air rifles currently available can be found in a wide variety of markets, and prices vary rather widely. Hopefully, the data and discussions presented in this book will take some of the mystery out of the process of selecting and using an airgun. Once you decide what type of rifle meets your needs, expectations and price range, shop around. You may be able to save enough on the purchase price of the gun to buy some accessories and ammunition. For purposes of evaluation, the air rifles to be discussed will be grouped according to the approximate price categories: under $50, between $50 and $100, and over $100. These prices reflect the usual selling prices, not the fictitious list prices. Models in the first two categories come with grooved receivers for easy mounting of telescope sights.

For Under $50...

It is surprising how much pneumatic air rifle can be had for less than $50. In this low-

The Crosman 66B represents good performance at a modest price.

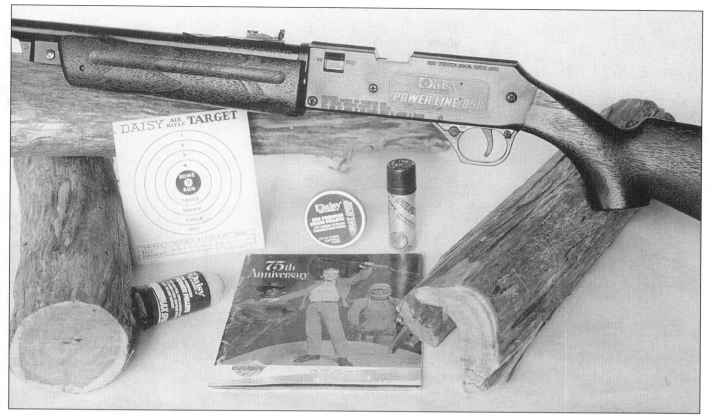

The Daisy 856 gives outstanding performance for an inexpensive rifle.

end category, there are several models from which to choose, all .177 caliber. They are generally less powerful than models in the higher price brackets. However, one of the useful features of multi-pump pneumatics is that the power can be varied at will by the number of pumps. NEVER pump a pneumatic airgun more than the maximum number specified by the manufacturer. To do so is to risk serious damage to the air compression system or a blown seal. Each pump gives very little increase in velocity as the maximum number of pumps is approached, and you may actually achieve greater accuracy when the number of pumps is a couple less than the maximum. A gun that produces 675 feet per second with the maximum of 10 pumps will produce 630 to 640 fps with eight pumps. You will never detect the difference in general use.

Air rifles in the under $50 price range are constructed with a heavy emphasis on plastics. All have molded plastic receivers and plastic stocks and forearms. If this emphasis on polymeric materials sounds offensive, you had better not examine your automobile very closely unless it is a classic! Also, there is a large market for composite (i.e. plastic, although "composite" may sound better) stocks to replace the ones made of wood on all types of firearms, and an increasing number of fine guns are being sold that way. Today's plastics are in some ways superior to either metal or wood for some uses, and the results of the tests described in Chapter 5 will show that the inexpensive guns are at least competent if not cosmetically appealing. All of these inexpensive air rifles have rifled steel barrels, most often encased in a sleeve of plastic and/or metal.

The first rifle in the under $50 category is a true American icon, the Crosman 760B Pumpmaster. This gun has been in production for more than 30 years and more than 8 million have been sold. The author bought his at the Wal-Mart store in Billings, Mont., for $24.94 with no sales tax! The gun may have a plastic stock and forearm and may not have racy lines, but it works. How well it works will be shown in later chapters, but it drives .177 caliber pellets at velocities up to 570 fps.

Some Current Multi-pump Pneumatic Air Rifles

Make	Model	Caliber	Velocity fps	Length inches	Weight pounds	Stock
Under $50						
Crosman	760B	.177	570	33.5	2.75	Plastic
Crosman	66BX	.177	645	38.5	2.94	Plastic
Daisy	856	.177	630	37.4	2.75	Plastic
Daisy	880	.177	665	37.75	3.2	Plastic
$50 to $100						
Crosman	2100B	.177	725	39.75	4.81	Plastic
Crosman	2100W	.177	725	39.75	5.31	Walnut
Crosman	2200B	.22	595	39.75	4.75	Plastic
Crosman	2200W	.22	595	39.75	5.31	Walnut
Daisy	22X	.22	550	37.75	4.50	Hardwood
Daisy	990[a]	.177	630	37.4	4.1	Plastic
Over $100						
Benjamin	392	.22	685	36.25	5.5	Walnut
Benjamin	397	.177	800	36.75	5.5	Walnut
Crosman	2175W[b]	.177	725	39.75	5.5	Walnut
Crosman	2275W[b]	.22	595	39.75	5.5	Walnut
Sheridan	CB9	.20	675	36.5	6.0	Walnut
Sheridan	C9	.20	675	36.5	6.0	Walnut
Sheridan	C9PB[b]	.20	675	36.5	6.0	Walnut

[a] This unique dual-powered model can be used as a multi-pump pneumatic or with CO_2 cartridges. It does not appear in the 2001 Daisy catalog.
[b] These anniversary models were made during 1998 and may no longer be available.

Also in the under $50 category is the Crosman 66BX Powermaster, which moves .177 caliber pellets out the muzzle at up to 645 fps. This handsome gun is also highly effective. Daisy has two models that can be obtained at most retailers for under $50. They are the PowerLine Model 856 that lists a top velocity of 630 fps and the PowerLine Model 880 that shoots .177 caliber pellets at velocities up to 665 fps. Both of these guns have been made for many years and production of both models runs in the millions. Although large numbers of the dual-ammo version of the Daisy PowerLine 856 are still available, beginning in 2001, this model is a pellet rifle only.

Some of the models from Crosman and Daisy are available with different options of sights and stock colors. These

Because it is light and accurate, the Daisy 856 is ideal for plinking by the author's wife, Kathy.

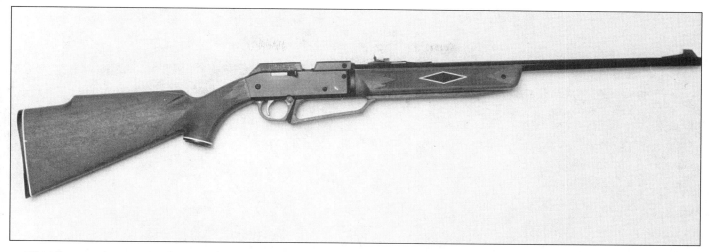
The first multi-pump Daisy air rifle was the .177 caliber Model 880 that was introduced in 1972. Production has been several million and several modifications have appeared over the years.

variations generally are designated with additional numbers or letters in the model numbers. For example, the Daisy Model 856F has a highly visible fiber-optic front sight, while the Crosman Model 664X is the Model 66 with an optional 4-power scope. All of these guns are dual-ammunition models that fire both BBs and .177-caliber pellets. Most are somewhat shorter and lighter than the more expensive guns, which makes them easier for young shooters to handle. They are capable, however, of considerable power and fine accuracy for the usual plinking, informal target shooting, and pest control. A 9-year-old nephew called it "shooting practice" after a serious session at the pop-can range in the woods. Data on all of the current multi-pump pneumatic air rifles is shown in the table.

For $50 to $100

The category of rifles costing $50 to $100 includes quite a range of models, and includes both .177 and .22 caliber guns. All have die-cast metal receivers, and the most popular models are discussed here in no particular order.

First, we have the Crosman Model 2100B in .177 caliber that fires pellets at up to 725 fps. This is a full-size or adult airgun that is available with a plastic stock and forearm (Model 2100B) as well as with a walnut stock (Model 2100W). There is also a 75th Anniversary commemorative model with a walnut stock and forearm and an inlaid medallion (Model 2175W). The models with wood stocks gener-

ally run a bit less than $100. Also in this group is the Crosman 2200B Magnum, which fires .22 caliber pellets at up to 595 fps. Like the 2100 versions, the 2200 is also available with a plastic stock and forearm (Model 2200B) or a walnut stock and forearm (Model 2200W). There is also a 75th Anniversary model (2275W). The Models 2100 and 2200 have been available since the late 1970s and for good reason. The Model 2200B is currently

Still popular almost 30 years after its introduction, the Daisy 880 is still the first multi-pump for many airgunners like Adam.

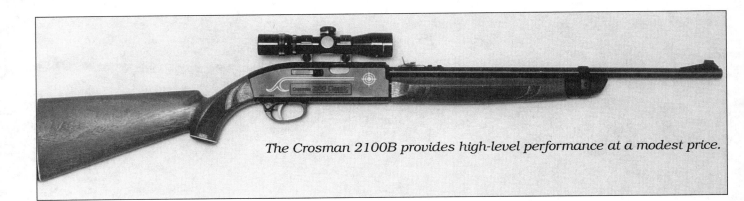

The Crosman 2100B provides high-level performance at a modest price.

With its high velocity, the Crosman 2100B is a good performer in the field.

in its fourth variation to appear since it was introduced in 1978. These are fine rifles that are capable of doing almost anything that anyone would want to do with an air rifle and at a price that does not require sacrificing the retirement plan. The models with walnut stocks are beautiful air rifles that ought to be available at more dealers.

Daisy Manufacturing Co. recently introduced its Power-Line Model 22X. This trim little gun sends .22 caliber pellets along at velocities up to 550 fps. It comes with a hardwood stock and forearm and a metal receiver, but it is otherwise very similar to the PowerLine Model 880 in .177 caliber. Although the list price is $73.95, the Model 22X in the author's rack cost $59.96 with no sales tax in Montana (the state has no sales tax), and it is a lot of gun for the money. Daisy also has the PowerLine 990 in .177 caliber, which is a unique dual-power (multi-pump and CO_2) model having the same performance as the Model 856. The Model 990 is being phased out in 2001, but it is still available from some dealers. Most of the rifles in this category are more powerful than the lower-priced models, but lower power can be selected by using fewer pumps.

The Crosman 2100W provides the performance of the 2100B in a more elegant gun with a walnut stock and forearm.

Daisy's newest multi-pump rifle is the Model 22X in .22 caliber.

For over $100

The air rifles in this price class are constructed more classically of metal and wood. The Crosman Models 2100W and 2200W and the 75th Anniversary models (2175W and 2275W) are really of this type but they were discussed with the $50-to-$100 class because

Although it is a .22 caliber, the Daisy 22X handles as easily as the .177 caliber rifles.

they are simply variations of the Models 2100B and 2200B — models with plastic stocks and forearms that sell for less than $100.

In the over-$100 class, there really are three other basic guns, although some can be had in a couple of other variations. First are the Benjamin (actually now Benjamin Sheridan) Model 397 in .177 caliber and the Model 392 in .22 caliber. These are 5 1/2-pound guns with walnut stocks and forearms. The metal work is brass that has been given a black finish. The Model 397 shoots .177 caliber pellets at up to 800 fps while the Model 392 shoots .22 caliber pellets at up to 685 fps. The .177 caliber rifle is also available with a nickel finish as the Model S397. These are serious adult air rifles having considerable power. They have been manufactured in their basic form (although model numbers have changed) for many years. They are reliable, accurate, and popular.

The next gun in this category is the Sheridan (actually now the Benjamin Sheridan) Model CB9 Blue Streak, which is a .20 caliber. The .20 caliber pellet weighs about the same as one in .22 caliber, but because it is smaller in diameter, it penetrates well and retains its velocity slightly better than the .22 caliber. The Sheridan shoots a .20 caliber pellet at velocities up to 675 fps, so it is quite a powerful airgun. In addition to the Blue Streak, there is a Model C9 with a nickel finish, called the Silver Streak. Finally, in

1998, a 50th Anniversary Model C9PB appeared. Fifty years indicates good things about the gun. The C9PB has a highly polished brass finish that is coated to prevent tarnishing. The Sheridan has had a very extensive and loyal following and it has always been a favorite for pest control and with those who use an airgun for taking small game (where legal).

All of the Benjamin and Sheridan models come drilled and tapped for mounting a receiver (peep) sight made by Williams. The one drawback to the Benjamin Sheridan guns is that mounting a telescopic sight on them is somewhat less convenient. Their receivers are not shaped so that they have the usual 3/8-inch grooves for mounting a scope directly to the receiver. Mounting a scope is done by using a two-piece intermount that clamps to the barrel. The top of each half has a groove. When the two pieces are clamped in place, a scope mount made for grooved receivers can be used. Scope mounting is only a minor handicap, but a scope must be mounted rather far forward ahead of the receiver. The rifle's bolt action also requires that the scope be mounted in front of it. Therefore, a short scope having short eye relief cannot be used.

Incidentally, some of the imported spring-piston guns give a backward-and-forward recoil motion that requires a specially designed airgun scope that can withstand that type of recoil. It will be discussed in more detail later, but the mount also must be strong to take this punishment.

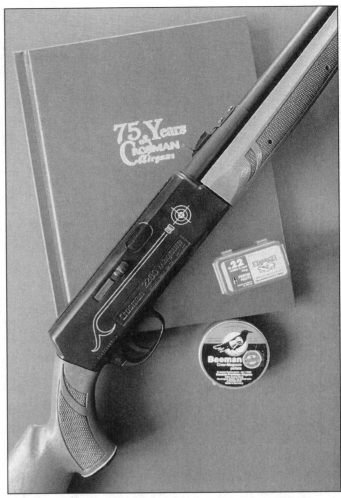

The Crosman 2200 Magnum is a powerful, dependable air rifle for serious airgunners.

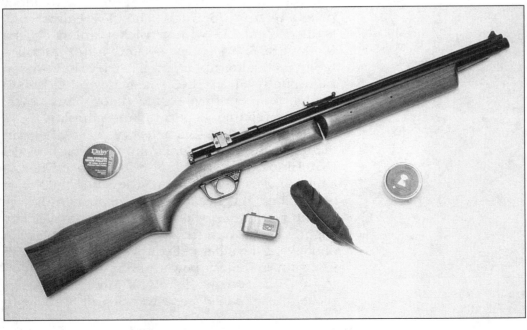

Current Benjamin air rifles have the traditional metal-and-walnut construction, and they give outstanding performance.

Small-game hunters could do a lot worse than the Crosman 2200 topped with a good scope.

These models of American airguns grouped in the three price categories constitute the most popular and successful multi-pump pneumatic air rifles of current manufacture.

The issue now is how to select one or more models.

Selecting an Airgun

Suppose you are a complete beginner and you want to select a pneumatic air rifle. Or perhaps you want to move up from the little Crosman 760 that you have had for 20 years to a more potent air rifle. These processes may be a little confusing at first, but consider a few points related to the new air rifle that you select.

(1) What do you want to do with it? Do you want to shoot pop cans? Do you want to shoot paper targets? After becoming proficient, do you want to hunt small game?

(2) How much do you want to spend?

(3) What accessories do you plan to buy?

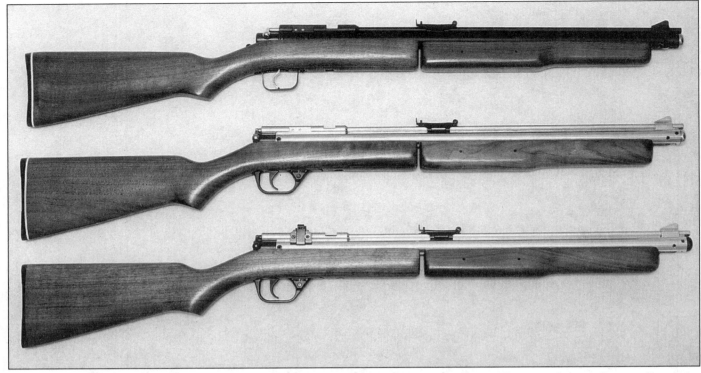

For more than 50 years, Sheridan air rifles have been known for their excellent workmanship and performance. From top are the CB9 Blue Streak, C9 Silver Streak, and C9PB Polished Brass 50th Anniversary models.

If you want to shoot pop cans and paper targets, a .177 caliber is all you need. The .177 caliber pellets are available in a wide variety of types, and they are inexpensive and widely available. The guns are usually quite accurate. To get started, one of the under-$50 models like the Crosman 66B or the Daisy PowerLine 856 or 880 may be all you need. These entry-level guns have plenty of power and accuracy for plinking and could also be used on pests up to the size of rats and starlings.

If you have already been using an air rifle of this performance level, you are probably looking to move up to a more sophisticated gun. Also, if you plan to do pest control on larger vermin, you will want a gun with more power like the Crosman 2100 or the Benjamin Sheridan 397.

Suppose you know that eventually you would like to use the excellent Beeman Crow Magnum hollow-point pellets (the name tells what they were designed for) and hunt crows and small game. Opinions differ on this, but the .20 and .22 caliber guns are generally more effective than the .177 caliber guns on game. One theory is that the higher velocity of the .177 caliber pellet gives it better penetra-

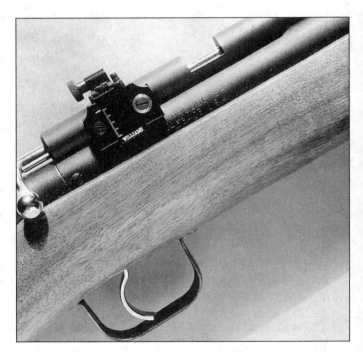

The Williams receiver sight enables the shooter of a Benjamin or Sheridan air rifle to shoot accurately without a scope.

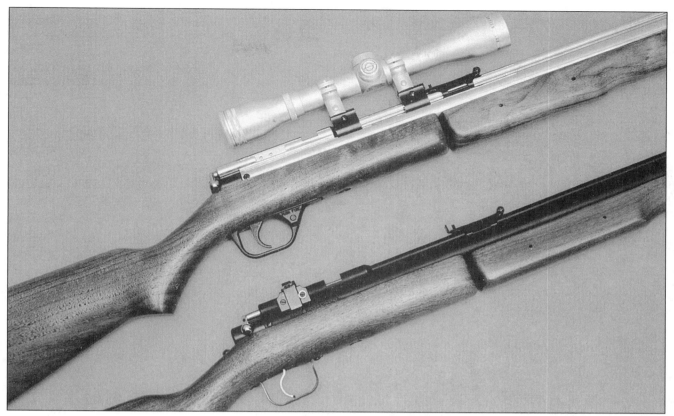

While it is possible to mount a scope on a Benjamin or Sheridan rifle, an intermount that clamps to the barrel is required. A peep sight is also a good choice.

tion, while another is that the much greater weight and larger diameter of the .20 and .22 caliber pellets give them much greater "smash." Both theories are partially correct, but only partially (see Chapter 10). Air rifles used for dispatching any game should have considerable power, but ordinary airguns do not even approach the power of a .22 short. Yes, the imported .25-caliber, spring-piston rifles are very effective as air rifles go, but they are not the subject of this book. A .22 short fires a 29-grain bullet at approximately 1,100 fps, while a powerful .22 caliber air rifle fires a 14.3 grain pellet at 650 to 700 fps. That is an enormous difference in power.

The cost of Benjamin and Sheridan guns is more than $100, but a very competent Crosman or Daisy can cost as little as $40 to $70. Additionally, consider the availability and ease of using accessories. For example, to mount a scope on a Benjamin or Sheridan air rifle requires an intermount costing about $15 to $20. Also, these rifles generally require a full-sized scope with a tube of 1 inch or larger,

because of the mounting system. All of the other multi-pump pneumatics will accept the small-tube airgun scopes, as well as larger scopes with the proper base to fit their grooved receivers.

With all things considered, it is hard to beat the Crosman 2100B or 2200B or the Daisy PowerLine 880 or 22X. They are all in the $40 to $75 range and have the power and accuracy required for punching pop cans, paper targets, and small pests and game, but you should choose your pellet wisely (see Chapter 10) and develop your skill. On the other hand, if spending $100 to $150 for the air rifle doesn't offend you, get a Benjamin or Sheridan in .177, .20, or .22 caliber or one of the beautiful walnut-stocked Crosman models. But if very young shooters need to be trained with the same gun, something smaller and lighter needs to be selected since the Benjamin, Sheridan and the walnut-stocked Crosman guns weigh 5 1/2 to 6 pounds. They also are more difficult to pump than the Daisy rifles.

Actually, the best solution may be a low-cost, lightweight model for plinking and training

For almost any plinking activity or for hunting and pest control, the Sheridan is a superb choice.

young shooters, and a larger, higher-powered model for more serious uses. You will probably get hooked and want more than one anyway!

Much of the remainder of this book is devoted to showing the results obtained from exploring the capabilities of the current American air rifles.

CHAPTER 3

SIGHTS, SIGHTING, AND SAFETY

On a rifle, the sights are on top of the barrel. Depending on the type of sights, the bore may be anywhere from 1/2 to 1 1/2 inches below the line of sight. The sights are adjusted so that the barrel is tipped upward slightly when the sights are aligned on the target. In that way, at some range the path of the pellet will meet or cross the line of sight at the distance for which the rifle is sighted in. This will be true regardless of the type of sights used. The trick is to adjust the sights so that you can align them on the target and have the pellet strike at the desired point. Types of sights suitable for use on airguns will be reviewed in this chapter and the subject will be dealt with more fully in Chapter 8.

Air rifles are powerful shooting devices, many of which are suitable for hunting small game and controlling pests. While they provide much enjoyment and recreation, they are not toys in any sense of the word. As it always must be, safety is a concern in the shooting sports. In this chapter are a few basic rules and observations regarding safety.

Open Sights

All the air rifles listed in the table shown in Chapter 2 come with the usual open sights. Most have a front sight that when viewed along the barrel appears as a square-topped post. The rear sight is some sort of notch in a metal blade that can be moved up or down to adjust for elevation. All but one of the guns, the little Crosman 760B, have rear sights that can also be moved to the left or right to adjust for windage. One type of adjustable rear sight consists of a metal blade with a notch in it,

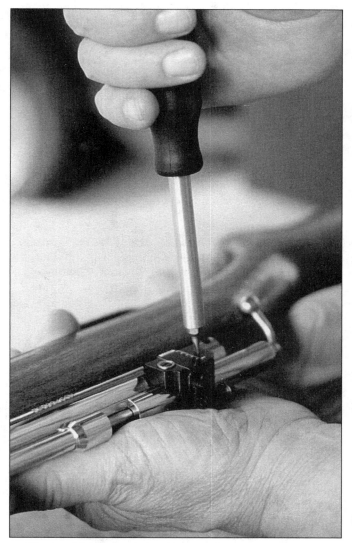

The sights on an air rifle go a long way toward determining its effectiveness.

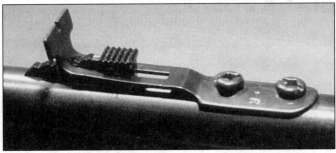

The open rear sights on American air rifles are sturdy and easily adjusted. Shown here, from top, are the sights on the Daisy 22X, Crosman 66B, and Benjamin 397.

that is held in place with a screw. The metal blade can be moved by loosening the screw. The figures show how the sights should be aligned. After shooting three or more shots to see where the pellets strike the target, the group can be moved toward the center of the target (the point of aim) by moving the rear sight in the same direction that you want to move the pellet's point of impact. If the group is too low, raise the rear sight. If you want to move the shots to the right, move the rear sight to the right. Simply follow the directions in the owner's manual.

The adjustment of the sights on an airgun sounds like a trivial matter. In some cases, it is, but there are some complications. Paper targets come with a standard size black area or bullseye (the bull for short). Furthermore, for a given competition, the targets are always at one distance, often 10 meters (33 feet). Sighting the gun for this type of shooting consists of adjusting the sights so that a consistent sight picture can be obtained and the pellets strike the target at that point of aim. The most common way is known as the 6 o'clock hold.

The front sight is centered in the rear sight notch and the gun is moved until the bull is almost sitting on the post. Some shooters leave a tiny sliver of space between the top of the front sight and the bull. If the front sight rides up on the bull and covers part of it, it is difficult to see how high the front sight is because you have black (the front sight) on black (the bull). The height of the rear sight is adjusted until the shots hit

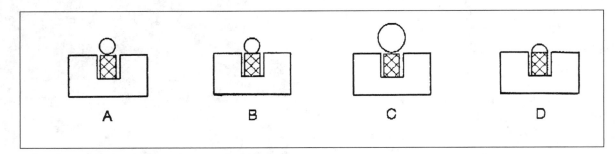

A   B   C   D

Figure A shows the sight picture for a correct 6 o'clock hold.

Figure B shows the front sight riding up an undetermined amount on the bull's eye.

Figure C shows the 6 o'clock hold on a larger bull than in Figure A. If the gun is sighted to hit the center of the bull in Figure A, the shots will hit below the center of the larger bull.

Figure D shows the arrangement where the shots hit at the top of the post. With this sighting, the shots hit on the target where the top of the post rests, and regardless of the size of the bull, they will still be centered.

Break-action rifles typically come with dial-adjustable rear sights like that shown on the Beeman S1.

the center of the black, and you are ready for consistent shooting.

But what if the distance changes? What if the target is not a standard size or is not circular? With a 6 o'clock sight arrangement, the projectiles rise to meet the line of sight at the center of a standard circular target at one distance.

For shooting at targets at different distances or of different sizes and shapes, a more practical arrangement is to adjust the rear sight so that the shots hit where the top of the post is held. The sight picture (alignment of front and rear sights) does not change. With the sights adjusted to hit a point of aim at the center of the bull, the sight picture is as shown in the accompanying figure. No matter what size the bull is, when the top of the front sight is across its middle, that will be the point of impact. The simplicity of this arrangement is an advantage, because when the front and rear sights are properly aligned, the top of the front sight is placed on the target at the desired point of impact. You can switch from a circular target to a starling, to a sparrow, to a pop can, to a rat, and in each case simply put the top of the front sight where you want the pellet to hit. It would be a little difficult to use a 6 o'clock hold on a pop can at one distance and a sparrow at a different distance. While having pellets hit at the point of aim is a better arrangement for field shooting, the 6 o'clock hold is the standard procedure for formal tar-

The quick and easy-to-use open sights are suitable for general plinking.

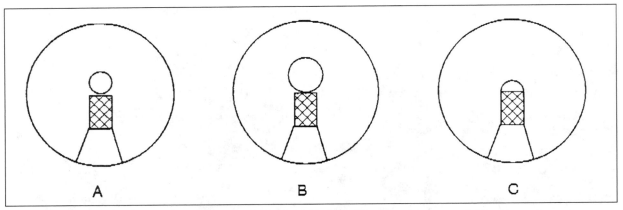

Figure A shows the sight picture for a 6 o'clock hold using a peep sight.

Figure B shows a 6 o'clock hold on a larger bull. If the gun is sighted correctly, as in Figure A, the shots will hit below the center of the larger bull.

Figure C shows the sight picture when the gun is sighted to hit at the center of the bull. Shots will be centered regardless of the size of the bull.

Williams receiver sights are available for mounting on grooved receivers as on this Daisy 880, top, as well as for the Benjamin and Sheridan rifles, bottom.

get shooting when targets of uniform size and shape are being shot at a given distance.

Peep Sights

Even with the best notch and post sights, aiming is not as accurate as it might be. The next step up in aiming accuracy is provided by the aperture (sometimes known as the receiver or peep) rear sight. Generally, a square-top post front sight is still used. The peep sight consists of an opening or aperture which the shooter looks through at the front sight. When looking through a small opening, the human eye instinctively positions itself so that it is looking through the brightest point, which is the center of the opening. With this in mind, the shooter looks through the peep sight, not at it. The top of the front sight is positioned in the center of the peep sight aperture and the gun is moved until the target rests on the front sight in a 6 o'clock hold. If so desired, the sights can be adjusted so the shots hit where the top of the post rests when the top of the post is centered on the target. As described above for open sights, this arrangement is easier to use for targets of irregular shape or targets at different distances.

The peep sight is fully adjustable for elevation and windage, usually by click adjustments in the better models, or by loosening screws and tightening them when the aperture has been moved the desired amount. The peep sights shown represent two types, both made by Williams. The first type attaches in the 3/8-

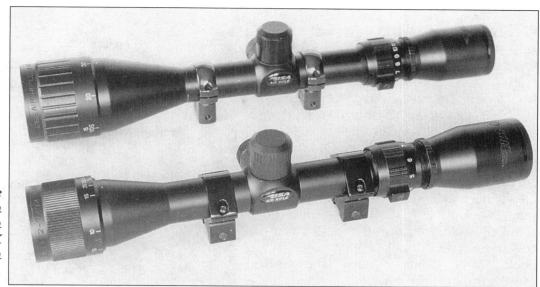

The most accurate aiming device is an airgun scope. Shown here are the BSA 2-7X and 3-12X models with focusing objectives.

inch scope-mount grooves on top of the receiver. Thus, this type of sight can be used on many air rifles because most of them have 3/8-inch grooves on top of the receiver for quick scope attachment. Note that this type of receiver sight comes in different heights. Some of the sights are so high that it is impossible to sight in the rifle unless a higher front sight is used. Be sure to match the height of the receiver sight with that of the front sight.

The second receiver sight shown fits only the Benjamin and Sheridan air rifles. These rifles come with threaded holes for attachment of the Williams receiver sight made especially for these models. While it might not seem that a peep sight represents much of an advantage over the usual open sights, this is not true. In fact, sophisticated receiver sights reduce the sighting error drastically. Such sights are used on match rifles for high-level competition where scopes are not allowed.

When an open or aperture sight is used, the rear sight is closest to the eye, the front sight is farther away, and the target is much farther away. The human eye cannot focus on three objects at different distances. The aperture sight is much better than the open rear sight because the eye does not have to focus on it, but rather simply looks through it at the brightest point, the center of the aperture. Thus, more accurate aiming is possible with the peep sight. Well-made peep sights are not cheap and most cost as much as a

This target was shot to test scope adjustments by shooting three-shot groups at 10 meters and changing the scope 50 clicks between groups. Three shots were fired at the center of the bull, and changes were 50 clicks up, 50 clicks right, 50 clicks down, then 50 clicks left.

moderately good scope. One advantage of receiver sights is that they do not significantly change the bulk, weight, or profile of the gun since they are very compact. I find the receiver sight particularly well suited to the Benjamin and Sheridan rifles.

Scope Sights

The sighting error is reduced even further when a scope is used. In that case, there are only two objects to consider: the reticle (usually crosshairs or a dot of some sort) and the target. Furthermore, the optical properties of the scope are designed so that the crosshairs and the target appear at the same distance. It is not a question of whether to focus the eye on the target or the reticle, since both are in sharp focus. The shooter simply places the crosshairs at the desired point on the target and squeezes off the shot.

Since air rifles have short-range capabilities, a scope of about 4-power (written as 4X) is adequate. If one is so inclined, a variable power on the order of 2-7X is not bad, either.

The addition of a BSA 2-7X scope to this Daisy 880 turned it into an outstanding performer.

One thing to keep in mind is that a scope is designed so that the reticle does appear not to change position as the eye moves across the axis of the scope at only one fixed distance. If you hold your arm extended and look first through one eye and then the other, objects beyond your arm appear to change positions. This is known as parallax. Scopes designed for use on centerfire rifles are usually made so that the parallax is removed at 100 yards. Scopes made for use on .22 rim-fire rifles usually have no parallax at 50 yards. Since air rifles are used at short range, it is better to use a scope that is designed for .22 rifles than one designed for centerfire rifles. If you mount a scope designed for use on a centerfire rifle on your air rifle, you will note the apparent movement of the crosshairs on the target as you move your head from side to side. It is possible to use scopes of this type on air rifles, but it is necessary to position the eye

This Crosman red dot sight can be attached to any airgun with a grooved receiver.

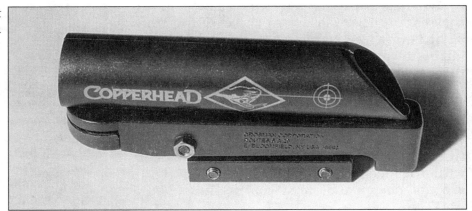

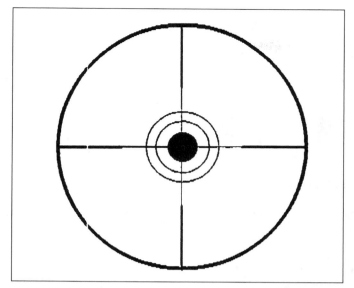

The simplest of all sight pictures. Just place the crosshairs on the center of the bull.

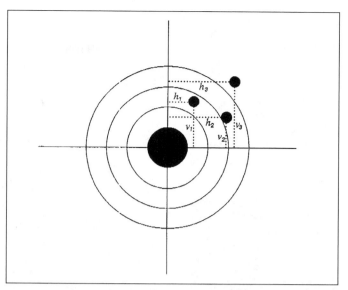

To determine where a three-shot group is centered, determine the distance from the center of each pellet hole to the horizontal axis and add the three values. The total of the three values divided by 3 gives the average height of the group. Determine the distance from the center of each hole to the vertical axis, add the values and divide by 3. This gives the average distance that the pellets hit to the right. Adjust sights accordingly.

in as nearly the same spot as possible for each shot. Also, some of the scopes designed for use on centerfire rifles are rather large and may look out of place on an air rifle.

Regardless of the type of sights on the rifle, the goal is to make the point of aim using those sights to coincide with the point of impact of the pellets. How do you determine the point of impact? First, shoot at least three shots at the target. For purposes of illustration, let us assume that all of the shots are slightly high and to the right. An average point of impact can be determined by measuring the total amount that the three shots hit high by adding the heights of all the shots above a horizontal line through the center of the bull and dividing by three. Similarly, the average position that the group lies to the right can be found by adding the distance to the right of a vertical line through the center of the bull for each shot, then dividing the total by three.

Having determined the center of the three-shot group, the sights can be adjusted accordingly. The process can be repeated until the center of the group obtained is at the desired point on the target. This may be directly in the center or it may be slightly higher so that the pellet will hit a target anywhere along the path of the pellet out to some other distance (see Chapter 8). The rear sight must be moved in the direction that the point of impact needs to

The way that a .20 caliber Sheridan blasted a hole through this 5/8-inch board shows that air rifles are not toys.

Before, during, and after shooting sessions, keep the muzzle pointed in a safe direction.

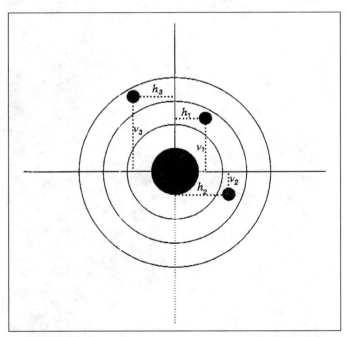

To determine where this group is centered, add the distances as before, except distances below the horizontal axis and to the left of the vertical axis are considered as negative values.

go. If the gun shoots low, raise the rear sight. If the point of impact is too far to the right, move the rear sight to the left. This principle applies to both open and aperture sights.

Other Sights

In addition to the types of sights discussed, two others have become rather popular. The first of these is the so-called red dot sight. These devices attach to the grooved receiver of an air rifle the same as a scope mount. A red dot sight makes use of a small battery that projects a red dot on a plastic lens. The sight has a switch that turns the red dot on and off to conserve battery power when not in use. The lens has etched on it one or more circles and crossed lines that enable the shooter to position the red dot in the center. Then, by moving the rifle, the glowing red dot can be positioned on the target. When aligned on the target, the red dot covers part of the target.

One of the problems with red dot sights is that on some models, the dot has a fixed size. It may cover 1 inch of the target at 10 yards but 2 1/2 inches at 25 yards. This does not allow for nearly as precise aiming as a scope, which has a crosshair that may cover only 1/10 inch at 25 yards. I feel that the coarse nature of the red dot sight does not allow highly accurate aiming. Newer and more expensive models, however, may feature adjustable dot sizes or small dots for more precision.

Moreover, the circles and crossed lines on the plastic lens are sometimes difficult to see under some lighting conditions. Finally, the sight adjustment on the inexpensive red dot sights designed for airguns is made by loosening two screws and moving the sight sideways or up and down. The adjustments are not repeatable, accurate click adjustments that correspond to precise movements of the point of impact. More expensive red dots are adjusted just as scopes, with precise, repeatable clicks.

Another type of sight that is becoming more frequently seen is the laser sight. This sight also mounts on a grooved receiver. It consists of a battery-powered laser that projects its beam on the target. The direction of the beam is also adjustable so that the gun can be sighted in. I am even less excited about this type of sight than I am the red dot sight. In fact, I do not own any laser sight nor do I plan to.

Lasers are capable of causing serious eye damage. It doesn't take much exposure to do a great deal of harm. It is interesting that with all of the accessories available directly from a company like Crosman, it is the laser sight that is not available by customer order. These lasers should not be in the wrong hands.

Like some red dot sights, the laser beam covers a large enough part of the target to make accurate aiming at 25 yards virtually impossible.

In all fairness, the red dot and laser sights are actually more often used on air pistols. They can be fun to use for a time, but a serious air rifle shooter generally should stick to the other types of sights. The red dot and laser sights allow for quick target acquisition at short distances and are better suited for "action" shooting. The inexpensive ones (less than $20) are not designed for deliberate, accurate shot placement.

Safety

Playing catcher on a baseball team involves a certain amount of common sense. Don't stand close enough to the batter to get hit when the batter swings. Don't look into the

Select a safe backstop when testing airguns.

dugout when a baseball is coming toward you at 90 mph. Wear proper protective equipment. Shooting is a lot like this.

In many sports, such as tennis or golf, there is a proper etiquette. There are certain things that you simply do not do. The shooting sports have an etiquette that not only describes proper procedures and form, but also creates a safe atmosphere for enjoying these fascinating skill sports. Airguns are not toys! They should be treated exactly as firearms are.

There are a few basic rules that must be followed for shooting to be done safely. Safety is not a sometime thing in the shooting sports. It must be so ingrained as to become automatic. There is no room for an "it is only an airgun" attitude. Airguns are guns! Seeing a target hit at 50 yards, seeing a 1-inch board completely penetrated, or seeing an airgun used on pests will quickly dispel any notion that airguns are toys. The airgun shooter must follow exactly the same safe practices as the user of a firearm.

Safe gun handling and shooting involve, but are not necessarily limited to, the following aspects, which I offer with some personal comments to drive home the points.

1. Treat every gun as if it were loaded. In fact, assume that every gun is loaded.

As a young man, I once asked to look at a used Colt Model 1911 .45 auto in a gun shop. The shop owner handed it to me and I looked it over. Just to see what it looked like inside, I pulled back the slide and out came a loaded round. In fact, the magazine contained several rounds. The dealer nearly fainted. It seems that the dealer had made a trade for the empty gun a few days before and when it came in, he put it in the glass case. What he didn't know was that the man trading it had loaded it before coming back to complete the trade and had forgotten to unload it. Instances such as this are rare, but they can be tragic.

2. Never allow a gun to point in an unsafe direction. Do not allow the muzzle to cover anything that could not be shot. I had a cousin die when a .45 auto accidentally discharged as a fellow officer was drawing a loaded gun. The muzzle was allowed to point in an unsafe direction. Practice drawing with a loaded gun was bad enough, but had it been outdoors on a safe range the shot would have gone in a safe direction.

3. Always wear eye protection. Elasticity is the tendency of a deformed object to be restored to its original shape, as in the case of a stretched rubber band. It takes energy to deform an object. In some materials, the energy is stored and that energy is released as the object goes back to its original shape. If a projectile does not penetrate far enough to stick in the target, it will be propelled back toward the shooter by the elasticity of the highly compressed target.

A BB fired from a low-powered BB gun will almost always bounce back from a board as it is sent back toward the shooter by the compressed wood. If a steel BB hits a metal plate, the BB and the steel surface are compressed slightly. These stresses cause the BB to be launched back toward the shooter at high velocity. On the other hand, a lead pellet striking

This type of pellet trap can be used to stop pellets safely. It should never be used for BBs.

Never cross a fence while holding a gun.

a steel plate (such as an animal silhouette) becomes greatly deformed. It is literally flattened and splatters. There is much less tendency for it to be propelled back toward the shooter. Particleboard and plywood are particularly bad because they contain glues and resins that are very elastic. I once shot a target that I had placed on a piece of particleboard and the lead pellet came back and parted my hair. Don't do it! Never shoot at a flat, hard surface, especially with steel BBs. In fact, ricochets are much more likely with low-powered BB guns shooting steel BBs than they are with higher-powered airguns shooting lead pellets.

4. Do not shoot over water. I have seen multiple ricochets as pellets have skipped on water. Also, they may change directions because of ripples or waves on the surface. This practice is so dangerous that it is explicitly forbidden in the game codes of most states. Recently, my brother and I were shooting at dirt clods in a field that had been prepared for planting. Frequently we saw dust go up near the intended target and then again 40 to 50 yards beyond. The pellets were ricocheting across soft ground.

5. Do not cross fences, streams, or other obstructions with a loaded gun. There is no way to control the direction of the muzzle if you stumble, fall or slip. I have seen several instances in which the gun went one direction and its user went another.

6. Keep your airgun unloaded and "on safe" until you are ready to begin actual shooting. Transporting a loaded gun (even an airgun) is unlawful in most states. When you are at the shooting location and all participants are ready, loaded guns are expected. Hunting and field shooting are somewhat different because a loaded gun must be ready. Just follow all of the other rules when in the field.

7. Keep your airgun stored so that it is not accessible to unauthorized people. When I was quite young, I picked up a revolver from beside the bed in the home of a relative. Since it was small, I thought it looked like some type of toy gun. When I looked at it from the side, I saw the cartridge heads at the rear of the cylinder. Even though I was only about 6 or 7 years old, I had been around guns enough to know that I should carefully put it down and leave. Some-

Before a shot is fired, take time to explain clearly how the air rifle works as the author's son, Keith, is doing with Victoria and Olivia.

times, the outcome is not so pleasant. Do not believe that because we are discussing airguns, it is not possible for a tragedy to occur.

8. Obey all range commands instantly. Shooting a gun is not the same as playing basketball. In basketball, a shot almost always goes up as a whistle is blown, just in case it might go in and be counted. When shooting any type of gun, you NEVER fire a shot if someone says "Don't shoot." On an organized range, the command is "cease fire," and that means instantly. It does not mean "after this last one." Something may have happened that you don't see but makes firing unsafe. Obey all range commands instantly. Not doing so will get you disqualified in a formal match and you may lose your range privileges in any case.

As I have written this brief discussion of safety, I have thought back over almost 60 years of shooting. I have witnessed a few accidents and dozens of near misses. All types of guns made currently have more safety features than those made several years ago. I have a .22 caliber break-action air rifle made about 35 years ago that has no safety at all. I have another made in early 2001 that has a safety that goes on automatically as you cock the gun. All modern air rifles have safeties, even BB guns. Never trust a mechanical safety. Always employ safe gun-handling practices. The best safety device is the one under your cap.

While this book is not concerned with BB guns, some readers may use them. Emptying the BB reservoir does not mean that the last BB is out of the barrel. I checked the BB reservoir of a collectible BB gun in an antique mall. It was empty, so to see if the gun worked, I cocked it and placed the muzzle on my heavy leather shoe. Imagine my surprise when I found a BB in a dent on the leather when I pulled the trigger. This may sound reckless, but it was the only safe direction in the store. The BB gun was known to be a low-powered model and with the muzzle against leather, there was nowhere for the BB to go. Even so, I made sure that my toes were not against the top of the shoe. Actually, I always suspect that used BB guns in antique malls may hold that last BB in the barrel. I wanted to be the one to remove it safely before someone not as familiar with BB guns came along and shot someone across the antique mall. When I explained that, the worker promised to be more careful with any BB guns brought in.

All of the safety devices in the world will not make shooting safe if the shooter is not safe. I have seen enough during my many years in the shooting sports that you will get no quarter from me if you treat the subject of safety lightly. Gun-related accidents have been declining steadily in recent years, but further improvement is needed and possible. You owe it to yourself, your shooting companions, and the sport to do everything possible to be a safe shooter.

Having given a brief description of air rifles, sighting equipment, and safety, we now turn our attention to the other aspect of airgun performance, the ammunition. There is a considerable array of pellet types available. After giving an introduction to that important topic, we will progress to describe the performance of the multi-pump American air rifles.

Trigger locks are becoming increasingly popular, even for airguns.

CHAPTER 4

PELLETS

If you are at all interested in rifle shooting, you know there is a large number of bullet types intended for different purposes. Some are sharp-pointed, some are round-nosed, and some are flat-pointed. Some have full metal jackets for penetrating very thick skin and heavy bone. Others have very thin jackets and are designed to fragment when hitting as little resistance as that given by a crow.

The designers of airgun pellets have not been idle. However, since pellet guns are not used on thick-skinned animals with large bones, some design parameters are not applicable. You probably already know that pellets are made of lead, and they are relatively soft, although some are made of alloys and are harder than if they were made of pure lead. However, there are pellets that are pointed, round-nosed, flat-nosed, and hollow-pointed. Moreover, there are numerous other differences in design involving the number and placement of bands and in the depth of the hollow portion of the base.

The airgun shooter has an enormous range of pellets from which to choose.

Pellets come in a wide variety of shapes that indicate their intended uses. These pellets are, from left, the Crosman Copperhead wadcutter, Gamo Hunter, Daisy Pointed, and Beeman Crow Magnum.

In order for airgun pellets to fit the barrel tightly and form a gas seal, the base must expand under relatively low pressure. That means they must be soft, which is why lead is a suitable material. In addition to forming a gas seal at the base, many pellets also have bands nearer the front of the pellet. With all of the variables that are incorporated in the construction of pellets, the knowledgeable air gunner should have an understanding of the types of ammunition available, their intended uses, and how they perform. The right ammunition may make an airgun perform better and will almost certainly increase its versatility.

General Pellet Shape

The most common airgun pellets have a shape known as diabolo. That name was adapted from the name of a somewhat similarly shaped wooden object that was used many years ago in a throwing game. It is believed to have originated in Greece, and the game eventually became popular in Europe. Pellets having the diabolo shape have been made for about 100 years.

The diabolo shape is generally referred to as an hourglass shape. The forward end or "head" and the base or "skirt" of the pellet are of larger diameter than the midsection. The skirt is essentially hollow. The reason for this is that airguns operate at much lower pressure than firearms. The base of the

pellet must be soft and expandable for it to enlarge and fit the bore tightly and engage the rifling. However, only the head and skirt are in contact with the barrel so friction is reduced, allowing maximum speed down the bore.

Although the general shape of a pellet has been described as being diabolo, there are many variations, especially in the shape of the head. Pellets are available that have flat points (wadcutters), round points, hollow points, and sharp points. As expected, these pellets have considerably different ballistic characteristics (see Chapter 8). Suppose that a particular air rifle has a muzzle velocity of 750 fps and that the paths of pellets having different shapes but the same weight are compared. The path of a flat-pointed pellet will be more curved than that of a pointed one. Generally, the round- and hollow-pointed pellets will have trajectories that are more curved than pointed pellets, but somewhat flatter than flat-point pellets. This is not always true when specific

Loading your air rifle with the right ammunition will enhance its accuracy and effectiveness.

types and brands of pellets are compared. The subject of pellet flight will be dealt with more fully in Chapter 8.

Uniformity of Pellets

While sometimes used interchangeably, the terms accuracy and precision describe two different things. The word "accuracy" describes how close the value for some quantity is to its prescribed or intended value. "Precision" refers to how repeatable the event or measurement is. For example, an archer may shoot a group of arrows in a small cluster (high precision) while the group may be far from the center of the target (poor accuracy). Another way to describe the terms accuracy and precision is to consider five bullets. If the bullets are supposed to have a nominal weight of 50.00 grains but the actual weights are 48.00, 48.01, 47.98, 48.02, and 48.01 grains, the bullets have high precision in their weights (the weights are close to the same value) but their weights show poor accuracy (the actual weights are not close to the specified nominal value).

One factor that is paramount to airgun performance is pellet uniformity. If pellets of the same type and brand have different weights or dimensions, they have poor preci-

For field shooting and hunting, the ammunition chosen is quite different from that used on paper targets.

sion, and they may not give small groups when fired at a target.

In order to study the weight uniformity of pellets, it is necessary to have a very accurate scale. Because pellets weigh much less than typical bullets, the differences in weight will be quite small. Therefore, some of the powder scales used by handloaders of ammunition are not sufficiently accurate to critically examine the weights of pellets. To obtain the results described here, a laboratory analytical balance that weighs in grams to four decimal places was used. While not every type of pellet that is available was studied, a variety of pellets from different manufacturers were weighed and the weights in grams were converted into grains using the relationship that a gram is equivalent to 15.432 grains.

Weighing only one pellet of each type is like analyzing the passing effectiveness of a quarterback who has thrown only one pass. One pellet is not statistically valid because the one selected

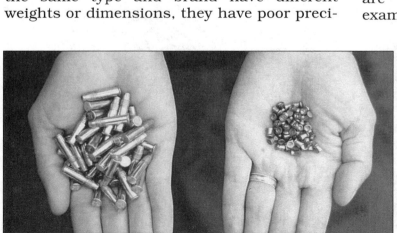

Space requirements for carrying and storing pellets are minimal as shown by the difference between 50 .22 cartridges and 50 pellets.

This is a selection of pellets from Gamo that shows excellent weight uniformity. They are, from left, the Match, Hunter, Master Point, and Magnum.

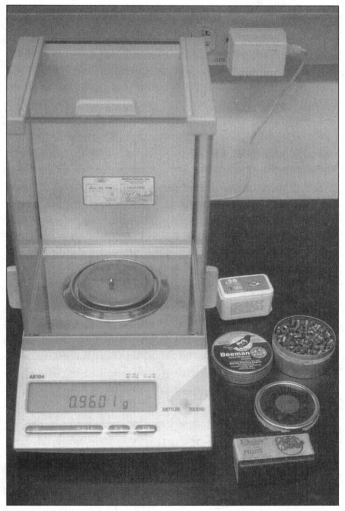

This laboratory balance was used to weigh samples of many types of pellets to determine weight uniformity.

could be an especially heavy or light specimen. Therefore, 20 pellets of each type were weighed in order to obtain a sufficiently large sample for the results to be statistically valid.

One way of showing the spread in a series of data is to determine the average value and show the highest value, the lowest value, and the standard deviation (SD). The standard deviation is a calculated quantity that is obtained by adding the squares of all the deviations from the average value. That sum is divided by the number of values minus one, and the square root of the result is taken. You need not be concerned with a derivation of the formula but it can be written as below.

In this formula, a is the average pellet weight, w_1 is the weight of pellet 1, w_2 is the weight of pellet 2, etc., and w_N is the weight of pellet N, where N is the number of pellets in the sample. This may sound rather complicated, but if one is to show any difference between brands or types of pellets, this statistical analysis is essential. Fortunately, almost any electronic calculator with some degree of sophistication (a "scientific" calculator) enables this type of calculation to be made quickly.

The table shows the actual weights of each of the 20 pellets in the sample for four different types of .22 caliber pellets. In each case, the first 20 pellets out of the container were used and no attempt was made to do any sorting or selecting. This table shows the type of data that was collected for 50 types of pellets

$$SD = \sqrt{\frac{(w_1 - a)^2 + (w_2 - a)^2 + (w_3 - a)^2 + \cdots + (w_N - a)^2}{N - 1}}$$

Weights of 20 Individual Pellets of Four Types in .22 Caliber

Crosman Wadcutter	Crosman Pointed	Daisy Pointed	Dynamit Nobel Meisterkugeln
14.33	14.37	15.59	14.30
14.44	14.34	15.75	14.16
14.46	14.36	15.74	14.27
14.46	14.34	15.73	14.22
14.35	14.33	15.69	14.38
14.20	14.32	15.74	14.18
14.33	14.26	15.78	14.19
14.23	14.39	15.74	14.22
14.26	14.34	15.78	14.28
14.22	14.40	15.62	14.30
14.23	14.38	15.51	14.21
14.31	14.40	15.69	14.19
14.31	14.31	15.54	14.30
14.34	14.42	15.68	14.50
14.32	14.35	15.64	14.10
14.31	14.29	15.62	14.22
14.30	14.30	15.73	14.21
14.37	14.32	15.65	14.35
14.37	14.37	15.72	14.37
14.31	14.40	15.69	14.27
Ave. Wt.: 14.32	14.35	15.68	14.26
Std. Dev. 0.07	0.04	0.08	0.09

Ave. Wt. is the average weight; Std. Dev. is the standard deviation.

(23 types of .177, seven types of .20, and 20 types of .22 caliber).

Because the analytical balance weighs to four decimal places, the .177 caliber pellets, which weigh less than 10 grains, have weights and standard deviations that can be given to three decimal places. The four-digit accuracy of the balance allows only two decimal places for the .20 and .22 caliber pellets because two digits are required before the decimal point.

This table shows clearly how much variation one might find in the weights of the four types of .22 caliber pellets. It should be noted that of these four pellets, only the Dynamit Nobel Meisterkugeln, a well-known match pellet, is in any way a "premium" pellet. The others are just what you would go to your local "Mart" and find on the shelf. It is interesting that the standard deviations for the Crosman Wadcutter and Daisy Pointed pellets are about the same as the match pellet, while the Crosman Pointed pellet's uniformity is even better.

However, weight is only one consideration in pellet accuracy. The results of a thorough testing of how they actually shoot in multi-pump air rifles as well as discussions on ballistics, penetration, and energy transfer will be presented in later chapters. For a particular type of shooting, it might be desired to use a specific type of pellet. For example, for hunting or pest control you might want to use a hollow point or a pointed pellet. This decision should not be made on uniformity of weights, and pellets from the next lot might give different results. The uniformity of a particular type of pellet is not necessarily an indication of its performance. While the individual weights for 20 pellet samples of the four selected types were shown for illustration, it is not necessary to give this much detail for every type of pellet. However, the average weight, highest weight, lowest weight, and the standard deviations have been determined for 20 pellet samples of 50 different types of pellets in .177, .20, and .22 calibers, with the results shown in this table.

The data speaks for itself in regard to weight uniformity. Interestingly, the average weights of some pellets are almost exactly the weights specified by the manufacturers. Others deviate considerably from the nominal weight published for that type. Regardless of the weight given by the manufacturer, the four-decimal-place analytical laboratory balance used in this work is certified for accuracy and tells it

Weight Determinations for 20-Pellet Samples of Various Types

Pellet	Weight in Grains			
	Average	High	Low	Std. Dev.
.177 Caliber				
Beeman Crow Magnum	8.280	8.347	8.228	0.036
Beeman Copper Point	7.409	7.451	7.361	0.023
Beeman Flathead	8.341	8.509	8.197	0.089
Beeman Hollow Point	7.191	7.306	7.111	0.060
Beeman Silver Sting	8.383	8.457	8.285	0.046
Crosman Domed	7.864	7.963	7.761	0.066
Crosman Pointed	7.968	8.083	7.852	0.066
Crosman Premier (L)	7.941	8.034	7.725	0.076
Crosman Premier (H)	10.50	10.60	10.44	0.04
Crosman Wadcutter	7.930	8.032	7.843	0.061
Daisy Pointed	7.143	7.318	6.981	0.079
Daisy Wadcutter	7.756	7.881	7.583	0.100
D.N.* Meisterkugeln	8.225	8.312	8.060	0.054
D.N.* Superdome	8.346	8.503	8.248	0.068
D.N.* Supermag	9.356	9.460	9.268	0.082
D.N.* Super-H-Point	7.277	7.350	7.219	0.046
D.N.* Superpoint	7.924	8.117	7.647	0.145
Eley Wasp	7.521	7.562	7.469	0.022
Gamo Master Point	7.839	7.907	7.779	0.037
Gamo Hunter	7.378	7.412	7.301	0.028
Gamo Magnum	8.287	8.376	8.190	0.059
Gamo Match	7.510	7.532	7.464	0.021
Marksman Laserhawk	3.187	3.233	3.113	0.038
.20 Caliber				
Beeman Crow Magnum	12.99	13.16	12.76	0.10
Beeman H & N Match	10.32	10.39	10.20	0.05
Benjamin Diabolo	14.26	14.39	14.11	0.09
Benjamin Cylindrical	14.28	14.41	14.10	0.09
Crosman Domed	14.28	14.40	14.09	0.07
Crosman Premier	14.32	14.44	14.18	0.09
Sheridan Cyl. (new)	14.31	14.44	14.16	0.09
.22 Caliber				
Beeman Crow Magnum	18.47	18.68	18.25	0.10
Beeman Kodiak	21.41	21.74	21.21	0.16
Beeman Silver Jet	14.24	14.40	14.04	0.10
Beeman Silver Sting	15.74	15.85	15.52	0.10
Benjamin Diabolo	14.24	14.37	14.13	0.07
Crosman Pointed	14.35	14.42	14.26	0.04
Crosman Premier	14.34	14.44	14.26	0.06
Crosman Wadcutter	14.32	14.46	14.20	0.07
Daisy Pointed	15.68	15.78	15.54	0.08
D.N.* Meisterkugeln	14.26	14.50	14.10	0.09
D.N.* Superdome	14.49	14.57	14.38	0.05
D.N.* Superpoint	14.69	14.86	14.60	0.07
D.N.* Super-H-Point	14.32	14.56	14.20	0.10
Eley Wasp	14.43	14.52	14.39	0.03
Gamo Hunter	15.33	15.44	15.22	0.07
Gamo Magnum	15.41	15.51	15.25	0.07
Gamo Master Point	16.32	16.44	16.15	0.07
Gamo Match	13.88	13.95	13.78	0.05
Ruko Magnum II	15.54	15.65	15.46	0.06
Ruko Match	13.86	13.97	13.77	0.05

(*D.N. is RWS-Dynamit Nobel)

Dimensions range widely for pellets of different types. The dimensions of many types are shown in the tables.

like it is. I have become somewhat dubious of the weights printed on some pellet containers.

However, it must be emphasized that weight uniformity is only one factor in the overall performance of any pellet. How well it shoots is an entirely different matter, and the selection of a pellet for a particular application in a specific gun should be made on how well it performs, not how uniform the weight is. Also, the next lot of a given pellet from a particular manufacturer may be more or less uniform. One factor to keep in mind is that the match-quality pellets from some manufacturers are segregated so that all pellets in any container are made by the same set of tools. This includes the outstanding "made in America" Crosman Premier pellet that is available in .177 caliber in two weights (7.9 and 10.5 grains), and in both .20 and .22 calibers, with a weight of 14.3 grains.

Because of their softness, it is more difficult to obtain highly accurate dimensions for pellets. Also, the head and skirt are normally designed to have different diameters. For some pellets, the head rides on the rifling while the skirt engages the rifling so the head and skirt are of different dimensions. If you examine a large number of pellets closely, it is not uncommon to find some pellets with deformities, particularly in the skirt region. Some serious air gunners pass their pellets through a sizing die that assures uniform diameter. The sizing process also restores the rather fragile skirt region to a circular shape.

The head diameter, skirt diameter, and overall length for many types of pellets were determined to three decimal places, using a dial caliper. As mentioned before, it is much more difficult to determine dimensions accurately than it is to determine an accurate weight. The dimensions given in the table represent averages for the determinations on five individual pellets of each type.

The next two chapters will describe the results obtained with many of these pellets in

A Summary of the Dimensions of 49 Types of Pellets

	Average Dimension in Inches		
Pellet	**Head Diameter**	**Skirt Diameter**	**Length**
.177 Caliber			
Beeman Crow Magnum	0.178	0.185	0.238
Beeman Copper Point	0.175	0.184	0.260
Beeman Flathead	0.176	0.184	0.222
Beeman Hollow Point	0.176	0.186	0.215
Beeman Silver Sting	0.177	0.186	0.268
Crosman Domed	0.176	0.180	0.223
Crosman Pointed	0.175	0.183	0.226
Crosman Premier (L)	0.177	0.180	0.223
Crosman Premier (H)	0.178	0.182	0.264
Crosman Wadcutter	0.175	0.181	0.213
Daisy Pointed	0.175	0.185	0.217
Daisy Wadcutter	0.176	0.185	0.206
D.N.* Meisterkugeln	0.176	0.186	0.216
D.N.* Superdome	0.176	0.189	0.252
D.N.* Supermag	0.177	0.186	0.228
D.N.* Super-H-Point	0.176	0.184	0.220
D.N.* Superpoint	0.176	0.187	0.270
Eley Wasp	0.176	0.185	0.206
Gamo Master Point	0.178	0.185	0.275
Gamo Hunter	0.176	0.187	0.230
Gamo Magnum	0.175	0.187	0.270
Gamo Match	0.175	0.186	0.204
.20 Caliber			
Beeman Crow Magnum	0.199	0.204	0.284
Beeman H & N Match	0.199	0.204	0.230
Benjamin Diabolo	0.197	0.202	0.297
Benjamin Cylindrical	0.198	0.200	0.273
Crosman Domed	0.197	0.200	0.298
Crosman Premier	0.200	0.201	0.298
Sheridan Cyl. (new)	0.197	0.200	0.273
.22 Caliber			
Beeman Crow Magnum	0.217	0.225	0.309
Beeman Kodiak	0.217	0.223	0.333
Beeman Silver Jet	0.216	0.224	0.311
Beeman Silver Sting	0.217	0.224	0.341
Benjamin Diabolo	0.215	0.222	0.269
Crosman Pointed	0.216	0.222	0.278
Crosman Premier	0.217	0.220	0.269
Crosman Wadcutter	0.215	0.222	0.251
Daisy Pointed	0.215	0.226	0.350
D.N.* Meisterkugeln	0.215	0.225	0.251
D.N.* Superdome	0.216	0.225	0.298
D.N.* Superpoint	0.216	0.225	0.341
D.N.* Super-H-Point	0.215	0.226	0.272
Eley Wasp	0.217	0.230	0.246
Gamo Hunter	0.215	0.224	0.296
Gamo Magnum	0.214	0.225	0.349
Gamo Master Point	0.215	0.225	0.352
Gamo Match	0.214	0.226	0.258
Ruko Magnum II	0.215	0.224	0.348
Ruko Match	0.214	0.223	0.262

(*D.N. is RWS-Dynamit Nobel)

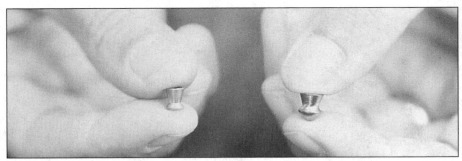

The larger .22 caliber pellets, right, are much easier to handle than those in .177 caliber.

American guns. Chapters 8 and 10 will explore in greater detail their flight characteristics and their terminal performance. One fact that becomes apparent during the weighing and measuring of the hundreds of pellets whose weights and dimensions are summarized in the tables is that the .20 and .22 caliber pellets are much easier to handle!

Wadcutter Pellets

The most popular pellet style is the flat point or wadcutter. This pellet cuts a clean hole in paper targets, and it hits with authority on small critters. Penetration is generally somewhat less than for pointed or round-nosed (domed) pellets, but it is adequate for smaller game and pests. One advantage of the wadcutter-shaped pellet on live targets is its rapid energy transfer and larger wound channel (see Chapter 10). As will be discussed in greater detail in Chapter 8, the wadcutter pellet loses its velocity more rapidly than do the other types because its flat nose design results in greater air resistance. While it would not be the best choice for shooting at greater distances, the Wadcutter is a good all-around selection.

For target shooting, the wadcutter has traditionally been the first choice. Most of the match pellets (Gamo Match, Dynamit Nobel Meisterkugeln, Beeman H & N Match, etc.) are of the wadcutter design. However, the Crosman Premier domed pellet has an enviable reputation as a first-class target round, especially for field target shooting. If you examine several brands of wadcutter pellets, you will find that there is a great difference in the size of the hollow region inside the base. Most wadcutters are hollow almost all the way to the underside of the flat head. One exception is the Crosman wadcutter, which has a much shallower hollow area inside the base. Therefore, it is a pellet that has its mass in the forward region and the head area is very sturdy. It has given surprising penetration on a number of targets I have shot.

In addition to the true wadcutter with a very flat head, there are numerous modified wadcutters that have some rounding or beveling of the edges. While a shape such as this gives a little better ballistic efficiency, most of the pellets of this shape are substantially hollow. Accordingly, they do not give penetration equal to that of a true wadcutter that is made with a more solid head. They are, however, good for general use.

Round Head Pellets

In recent years, round head or domed pellets have become quite popular and for good

Two popular wadcutter pellets are the Crosman Copperhead, left, and the Gamo Match.

These domed pellets are, from left, the Crosman Premier in .177, .20, and .22 calibers.

reason. They combine several desirable attributes of other designs. Pellets having the round nose shape do not always have a perfectly smooth, round head. A few have a rounded head but have rings or ridges running around the head hear the body of the pellet. Just as all wadcutters are not perfectly flat, not all domed pellets are perfectly round, although some are.

Domed pellets are readily available in grades for general shooting as well as in a match grade. For example, Crosman has recently expanded the popular Copperhead line to include a domed pellet in .177, .20 and .22 calibers. An interesting feature of these pellets is that their configuration is the same as the Crosman Premier pellets in the same caliber. This is a very desirable feature, since it means that the domed Crosman Copperhead pellets will give essentially the same trajectory as the Premier. Of course, the Premier pellets in a given lot are made using one set of dies, which results in higher uniformity, but the Copperhead pellets are quite good and they have excellent uniformity. Although the details will be covered in more detail in Chapter 8, the domed pellets give excellent ballistic performance. In fact, the Crosman Premier has become very popular for use in field shooting competition because it is ballistically efficient and

has target accuracy. It is also widely used in hunting small game and pests because it shoots flat and penetrates well.

Another excellent choice in a domed pellet is the Benjamin Diabolo, which is available in .177, .20 and .22 calibers. This is a personal favorite in .22 caliber. It is a sturdy pellet, meaning that the hollow base does not extend very far. This results in a large, solid, round nose, which allows the pellet to give excellent penetration. Even the skirt area is thick enough that it does not collapse on impact. The round nose gives a reasonably good signature on paper targets and it gives very effective energy transfer on live targets.

The newer Benjamin Sheridan cylindrically shaped pellet in .20 caliber is essentially a domed head with a thick waist. The original Sheridan .20 caliber pellet was a real cylinder with no waist and a domed top. The gas seal was accomplished by a thin flange around the base. It was, for all practical purposes, a bullet with a slightly hollow base. It was well-known as a pellet that gave excellent penetration.

Outstanding imported pellets of the domed variety include the Dynamit Nobel Superdome, the Gamo Hunter, and the Eley Wasp. These pellets provide good ammunition for your airgun. Only shooting them in your gun will determine if they show any advantage over the Crosman or Benjamin pellets.

This excellent selection of .20 caliber pellets is, from left, the Beeman H&N Match, the Beeman Crow Magnum, the Crosman Copperhead Domed, the Crosman Premier, and the new Sheridan Cylindrical pellets.

These pointed pellets are, from left, the Gamo Magnum, Beeman Silver Jet, Gamo Master Point, Dynamit Nobel RWS Superpoint, Crosman Copperhead pointed, and the Daisy pointed.

Pointed Pellets

There are numerous pointed pellets on the market in all three popular calibers. It might be thought that these pellets would be about the same in their ability to retain their velocity or to penetrate a firm target. A close examination of several pointed pellets shows that some of them have bases that are hollow almost up to the head. These pellets have a large, hollow inner region that is literally a cone-shaped cavity. Owing to their thin walls, such pellets tend to have the base move forward on impact so that the thin section "rivets". Some of these pellets recovered after striking a firm target show a considerable amount of riveting. On the other hand, the Crosman Copperhead pointed pellet has a hollow area that is much more shallow inside the skirt area and the head area is

Older .20 caliber Sheridan pellets had a flange around the base of a cylindrical body.

The entire forward section of the Crosman Copperhead pointed pellet is solid because the cavity in the skirt area is shallow.

Fired from a Daisy 880, the Beeman Crow Magnum penetrated a 5/8-inch board and expanded well in the process.

This Crosman Copperhead pointed pellet penetrated a 5/8-inch board with little deformation.

Two of the most popular hollowpoint pellets are the Beeman Crow Magnum, left, and the Dynamit Nobel RWS Super-H-Point.

entirely solid. These pellets tend to be more compact than most other pointed types and they give deeper penetration (see Chapter 10).

Hollowpoint Pellets

There are not too many types of hollow-pointed pellets. The Beeman Crow Magnum and the Dynamit Nobel RWS Super-H-Point have become popular for hunting and pest control. When traveling at sufficiently high velocity, these pellets hit with real clout. I have had considerably more experience with the Beeman Crow Magnum and it has become one of my favorite pellets. Although the details of the tests will be described in Chapter 10, expansion of this pellet is impressive. Even if the velocity is not sufficient to cause much expansion, the rather flat, open point causes rapid energy transfer to the target. A hollowpoint is a good choice unless your type of hunting demands the deepest possible penetration or unless your

particular airgun does not shoot hollow-points accurately, which is unlikely.

In this chapter, we have given a brief over-view of a large number of the pellet types that are readily available. It is remarkable how good they really are. Until I examined in detail their uniformity and construction, I was not sufficiently aware of this fact. In fact, work with a multitude of modern pellets caused me to examine more closely several types of old pellets that I have collected. The difference between pellets today and those made 30 to 40 years ago is enormous. By today's standards, the older pellets are quite crude. Today, there is a pellet type available for almost any imaginable purpose, and most of them will perform quite well in virtually any airgun.

CHAPTER 5

EVALUATION OF .177 RIFLES

In Chapter 2, the American multi-pump pneumatic airguns were described in a brief survey. These are current models that are widely available, and most of them have been produced for a considerable number of years. Most of them also have been produced by the millions. Since this book is meant to be a user's guide to these air rifles, it is necessary to present some factual information on their performance. This chapter will deal with the .177 caliber rifles, while Chapter 6 will present the results of work with .20 and .22 caliber rifles.

In addition to testing the American multi-pump rifles, the performance of three break-action rifles also will be evaluated. The users of both multi-pump and break-action rifles will have a basis for a comparison of the two types. While this book is not primarily concerned with break-action rifles, it is useful to show this type of comparison.

Evaluations Conducted

The decision was made to test all the air rifles in four areas. First, the uniformity of pellet velocity was to be determined with five different types of pellets. Velocities were measured by means of a Competition Electronics ProChrono chronograph, and the average velocity and standard deviation were calculated. It was decided that two pumps fewer than the maximum recommended by the manufacturers would be used as the power level for the velocity uniformity test.

Second, the decision was made to determine the accuracy at 10 yards using a variety of pellets in each gun. Pellets were selected to

Evaluating air rifle performance meant measuring velocities, as the author is doing here with the Daisy 880.

Testing the accuracy of a large number of air rifles involved a lot of work at the bench.

include some inexpensive general purpose ones as well as some used for target and field shooting. Ideally, accuracy should be determined as the number of pumps varies from two up to the maximum specified by the manufacturer, using all possible types of pellets.

In the interest of completing the work in a lifetime, it was decided to limit the number of pellet types used in each gun to five and the number of pumps to one level, that being two less than the maximum. After selecting the pellets for use in each gun, velocity uniformity and accuracy were evaluated. For all of the accuracy testing except with the Crosman 66,

a BSA 3-12X airgun scope was mounted and it was used at 12 power. With each of the five pellet types, five three-shot groups were shot at 10 yards, and the size of each group (distances between centers of the widest shots) was determined with a dial caliper.

Third, I studied the velocity produced as the guns are pumped from two to the maximum number allowed. This was done to see how the velocity increase per pump varied. Fourth, the velocity produced with all of the pellet types available was determined when the guns were pumped the maximum number of times allowed. This series of tests gives a good over-

Several variations in the Crosman 760 have appeared in the 35 years of its production. More than 8 million have been made.

view of the performance of each model. The complete sets of data for each rifle model are shown in tables given in Appendix A.

However, lest there be any question about the objectivity of the results presented, let it be clear from the beginning that all of the guns and ammunition were bought by the author from regular retail stores. No manufacturer supplied anything used in the tests. There is absolutely no "payback" in the results presented. Bear in mind that a different specimen of the same model of gun may give somewhat different results, just as in the case of firearms. However, the results obtained set a standard of what to expect from each model, and the data shown is not readily obtainable elsewhere. Now, let the results speak for themselves.

The Crosman 760B Pumpmaster

Introduced in 1966, this air rifle is a true American icon. My sample of the Crosman 760 was bought for $24.94 with no sales tax in Montana. Well, since most "precision" air rifles cost upward of $200, this one ought to give 6-inch groups at a range of 6 feet! Having shot Crosman air rifles for many years, I knew better than that. This little gun comes with open sights; the rear sight is adjustable for elevation only. Out of the box, it shot low and very slightly to the right at 10 yards. Moving the rear sight ramp two steps made it print close enough to the point of aim that it was devastating to pop cans, and it would do well on pests at that distance and farther. The Crosman 760 was tested for velocity uniformity with five types of pellets. The standard deviation ranged from 2 to 8 fps with those pellets. The complete results obtained are shown in Appendix A.

Data such as that shown in Appendix A is invaluable, but it is virtually never available. The data shows that the Crosman 760 had an average standard deviation of 6 fps with five-shot strings of the five pellets tested. This is quite respectable for such an inexpensive rifle.

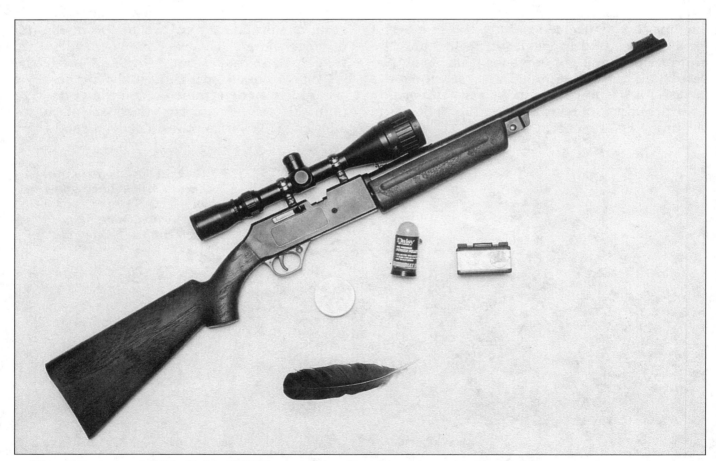

The performance of this Daisy 856F was outstanding for an inexpensive rifle.

This should dispel the myth about the lack of shot-to-shot uniformity from even the inexpensive multi-pump guns. As you examine the results of similar tests with the other pneumatics, you will observe that uniformity of velocity is a common trait.

The trigger pull on this and other Crosman models is a little disconcerting at first. You pull, the trigger starts to move and about a quarter of an inch later, it fires without any increase in force required. Although it is long and mushy, the trigger action is not bad when you get used to it. Just hold the sight picture and keep pulling.

In order to see what the Crosman 760 was capable of in terms of accuracy, the BSA 3-12X scope was mounted. I must admit, that big scope on the little 760 presented a rather cosmic appearance. After a few preliminary shots to get the point of impact near where the crosshairs rested, it was time to get serious. The complete results of the accuracy tests are shown in Appendix A.

The average size of all 25 groups obtained at 10 yards with the Crosman 760 is only 0.34

inches. The results show that the 760 performed somewhat better with the light Crosman Premier than with any other pellets tested. Would I select the 760 for "serious" uses? No, because I would want a more powerful rifle for hunting or plinking at longer ranges. However, if I had only a Crosman 760, I would use the Crosman Premier pellets and limit my shots at pests to rather short range. I would mount a compact scope and make like a bounty hunter on smaller pests.

The price of this gun is an unbelievable bargain. I can't imagine buying this much fun for so little money. Its performance clearly shows that the Crosman 760 is a perfectly acceptable choice for plinking and pest control.

The Daisy PowerLine 856F

Introduced in 1985, this gun replaced the Daisy Model 860 that I used regularly to shoot dime-sized or smaller groups at 10 meters before giving the gun to my son. That older Daisy would really shoot, but unfortunately it was never tested from a benchrest! The current Daisy 856 is usually available in the $30

Because of its ease of pumping, the Daisy 856F quickly became a favorite with the author's wife, Kathy.

The opening at the rear of the loading port of the Daisy 856 and 880 is where BBs enter when the rifle is used as a BB repeater. It is possible for a pellet to slide into this opening if the barrel is elevated during loading.

to $40 range, and the one tested is a Model 856F, the F signifying that it has a red fiber-optic front sight of high visibility. Despite its low price, this is a competent air rifle of moderate power. It is somewhat larger than a Crosman 760 and represents the real entry level in adult air rifles.

There are three areas in which the Daisy 856 (and the 880 described later) excel. These are in the areas of pumping ease, trigger pull, and open sights. The Daisy models, especially the 856, are very easy to pump. Moreover, after a slight take-up motion, the trigger let-off is crisp, and the open rear sight has a flat top with a square notch that nicely accommodates the rectangular front post. In my opinion, these features make the Daisy 856 easier to shoot accurately than comparable Crosman models. In fact, my Daisy 856 performed so well that my wife commandeered it! Testing the Daisy PowerLine 856F for reproducibility of velocity gave the data shown in a table in Appendix A.

While the Daisy PowerLine 856 is an inexpensive gun, it performed admirably in regard to velocity uniformity. The average standard deviation is only approximately 3 fps for five-shot strings with five pellets. This is an outstanding performance from a gun that regularly sells for about $30 to $35 in discount stores. In fact, the velocities are so reproduc-

ible that the variation may be due in part to not having the path of the pellet across the chronograph screens exactly the same for each shot.

There is nothing to criticize in terms of shot-to-shot reproducibility from this multi-pump pneumatic. It has already been mentioned that a previously owned Daisy 860, since replaced by the Model 856, was exceptionally accurate. Therefore, it was with some degree of anticipation that the accuracy tests were conducted with the Model 856. With the 3-12X scope attached, the group sizes obtained with this rifle are summarized in the table shown in Appendix A.

The data shows that the accuracy of the Daisy 856 is sufficiently high that it would be easy to hit any appropriate target about as far as the power level of this gun would justify shooting at it. The overall average group size with the five pellets tested was only 0.24 inches, and accuracy was very nearly the same for all of the pellets tested. As you examine the data for all the rifles, you will see that this was not always the case. What more can you ask from an air rifle that sells for as little as $29.96 in some stores? With its accuracy potential, the 856 is entirely suitable for pest control as well as being an outstanding choice for plinking. The Daisy 856 would be my first choice as an inexpensive air rifle for teaching gun etiquette to youngsters.

The Daisy PowerLine Model 856 is also an excellent choice for a beginning "adult" air rifle, although it weighs only about 3 pounds. Its predecessor, the Model 860, was my first serious pellet gun. As the data shows, the PowerLine 856 is capable of excellent accuracy and unless you have sharp eyes, a modest scope is certainly warranted. The power level of this gun makes it suitable for pest control as well, since eight pumps produces an average velocity of approximately 600 fps.

It is unfortunate that Daisy changed the die-cast metal receiver of the Model 860 to a molded plastic one for the Model 856. It gives the gun a feel and appearance that make it seem inexpensive (which it is!), but a metal receiver like that used on the earlier model would have been more esthetically appealing. However, other models of air rifles have changed similarly over the years, but they perform just as well as earlier models that contain more metal.

The Daisy PowerLine 856 and 880 models can be used as BB repeaters. The BB port is on the left side of the receiver. An opening at the rear of the loading ramp allows BBs to enter as the bolt is cycled when using the gun as a BB repeater. This opening can allow a pellet to drop back into the BB-loading mechanism if the muzzle is tilted upward while the bolt is in its rearward position. A pellet lodged somewhere in the BB-feeding port can be difficult to extract. When loading the Daisy 856 and 880, I withdraw the bolt fully to the rear, then push it forward slightly to cover part of the BB port while keeping the muzzle pointed down. In this way, there is no possibility for a pellet to slide back into the BB port.

Beginning in 2001, the Daisy 856 is being marketed as a pellet rifle only. The BB repeater feature is being eliminated. In my opinion, this does not detract from the desirability of the Daisy 856 at all. It is a fine pellet rifle and should be used in that way to take advantage of its power and accuracy. Just for the record, I managed to get my old Daisy 860 back from my son. It cost me a new Daisy 22X to do it, but it shows how much I like that old Model 860!

The Crosman 66BX Powermaster

This handsome, well-made air rifle was introduced in 1983. Millions have been sold and for good reason, because it is a fine air rifle at a modest price. Several versions are available that have different color stocks and/or sight combinations. Like the Daisy PowerLine 856 and 880, the Crosman has a plastic receiver, stock, and forearm. To me, the most attractive model is the Model 66BX with the brown stock and forearm that has white spacers at the buttplate, grip cap, and front end of the forearm.

The Crosman 66 has very good open sights. However, the trigger pull is rather long, but it is smooth and light, even if it is not crisp.

The Crosman 66BX was tested for velocity uniformity using five types of pellets with the results from the chronograph shown in a table given in Appendix A.

Uniformity of velocity with the Crosman 66BX was not quite on a par with some of the other rifles, but it was still very good for such an inexpensive air gun. The average standard deviation was approximately 6 fps for five shot strings with five different pellet types when eight pumps were used.

The Crosman 66BX was tested for accuracy using five types of pellets. Because there is very little step-down from the receiver to the barrel, it was not possible to mount the BSA 3-12X scope with its large forward bell on this rifle. As a result, a Weaver V22 scope was mounted and used at 6X for accuracy testing. Because this scope is intended for use on .22 rimfire rifles, there is some parallax at 10 yards.

Measurements for the groups obtained are summarized in the table shown in Appendix A. The overall average group size was only 0.32 inches. The smallest average group size was with the Dynamit Nobel RWS Meisterkugeln pellet (0.27 inches) and the largest was with the Dynamit Nobel RWS Superdome (0.36 inches).

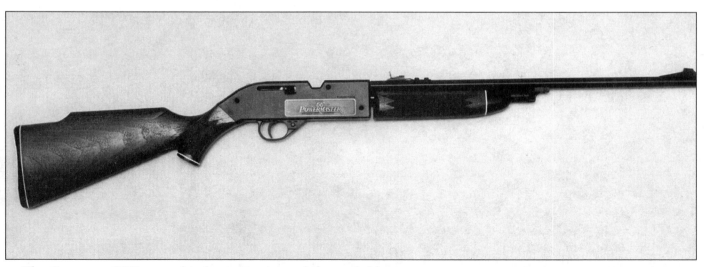

The Crosman 66B proved to be accurate and dependable.

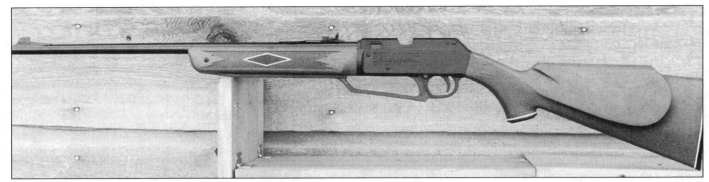

The Daisy 880 has been produced since 1972. It was the first multi-pump rifle produced by Daisy and it has been extremely popular.

The data shows that the performance of the Crosman 66BX is quite acceptable for a gun in its price range. There is no doubt that the groups would have been slightly smaller if the 3-12X BSA airgun scope could have been used. In my testing program, the Crosman 66BX gave performance that is about equal to that of my wife's Daisy 856. The trigger pull of the Crosman 66BX is much like that of the Crosman 760B described earlier. It takes some getting used to, but overall, this is a very easy-to-use air rifle that handles well and is pleasing to the eye.

The Daisy PowerLine 880

This mainstay of the Daisy line has been in production since 1972. It has not endured for this period of time for nothing. Millions have been produced and large production runs have also been made with other labels for specific chains of stores (Sears, Western Auto, etc.). It is a serious air rifle, and one of the desirable characteristics of this gun is that it is quite easy to pump, even when 10 pumps are required. A metal receiver like that used on the PowerLine 22X (described in Chapter 6) would make the current Model 880 more pleasing esthetically, and older versions of the 880 were made that way. I have collected three of these older variations of the Model 880 and they shoot very well.

The Daisy PowerLine 880 is a well-respected air rifle that has many nice features. How well it performs in terms of velocity uniformity is shown by the velocities given in the table presented in Appendix A.

With its ease of pumping and good trigger action, the Daisy 880 is a good all-around choice.

The Daisy 880 gave excellent velocity uniformity with an average standard deviation of 3 fps for five-shot strings with five different pellets. In this area, it is comparable to air rifles costing three times as much as the 880. This rifle is a serious contender as a competent, inexpensive air arm.

With the velocity uniformity experiments conducted, it was time to evaluate the accuracy potential of the Daisy 880. Appendix A shows a table of the results that were obtained with five types of pellets selected for use in this gun.

With all five types of pellets used, the groups obtained at 10 yards with the Daisy 880 gave an overall average of 0.48 inch. This is well within the specification for this rifle, but it is not as good as was obtained with other, less expensive rifles. In fact, the Daisy 856 performed better with respect to both velocity and accuracy. This particular Daisy 880 did not seem to like the 7.9 grain Crosman Premier pellet, which shoots very well in almost all of the other rifles. The Daisy 880 belonging to my wife performed even worse with this pellet.

The Daisy 880 gave best accuracy with Daisy and Gamo pellets. The pointed pellets of these brands are very similar and both have deep internal cavities, which may have some effect on accuracy. If you have a Daisy 880, my testing indicates that you should definitely try several types of pellets, as accuracy varies considerably.

The trigger action of the Daisy Power-Line 880 is quite good for an air rifle. After a short motion to take up the slack, the let-off is fairly crisp. The open sights allow for a good, sharp sight picture. As mentioned earlier in the section dealing with the Daisy 856, the Daisy rifles are second-to-none in these areas.

The Daisy PowerLine 880 is a competent air rifle. One individual that I know told me how he hunted rabbits and squirrels with one for years. Personally, I prefer an air rifle with more power for such work, but it is a lot of gun for the money. It is a trim little gun that handles and points well, but in all fairness, neither my Daisy 880 nor my wife's gave any

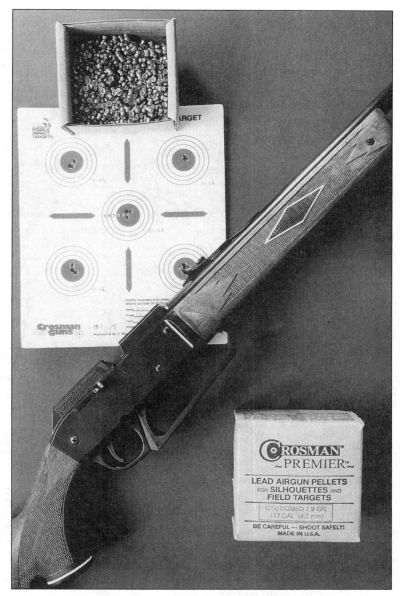

This Daisy 880 from the early 1980s has a metal receiver, and delivers excellent performance.

better accuracy or velocity than the Daisy 856 that changed hands between us. The older versions of the Model 880 with metal receivers that I have are an entirely different matter. One of these gave an average group size of only 0.19 inches at 10 yards with the 7.9 grain Crosman Premier.

The Crosman 2100B

The Crosman 2100B is a sturdy, full-size air rifle that weighs almost 5 pounds. It has been produced for many years, and it represents the most powerful .177 caliber rifle in the $50 to $70 range. Unlike the plastic-

The Crosman 2100B proved to be very fast with a velocity of more than 700 fps with lighter pellets and eight pumps. Its accuracy is superb.

stocked 2100B, the wood-stocked 2100W is not a BB gun, but only a pellet rifle. With its high velocity (up to 725 fps) and its inherent accuracy, this is an air rifle that can handle most anything. The uniformity of velocity obtained with eight pumps was tested using five types of pellets. The results given by the chronograph are summarized in a table shown in Appendix A.

Two aspects of the velocities obtained are important. First, they are quite high, with all of the averages being more than 700 fps when only eight pumps are used. This means that the Crosman 2100 is a powerful air rifle suitable for hunting and pest control. Second, the velocities are very uniform, with the average standard deviation being slightly more than 3 fps for five-shot strings and five types of pellets. This is an excellent performance. This particular specimen may be exceptional, but the 2100 gave considerably more uniform velocities than did the less expensive 760 and 66 models.

The Crosman 2100B used in these tests was bought in the late 1980s. At that time, the recommended maximum number of pumps was 10, but Crosman representatives now recommend that eight pumps constitute a practical maximum. The advertised maximum velocity is 725 fps with 10 pumps, and the data presented in Appendix A shows that with the lighter pellets, this gun will exceed that value with eight pumps. While the full data is not presented, using 10 pumps gave velocities as high as 787 fps with the Daisy pointed pellet, which weighs 7.143 grains.

With a good scope attached, a fast-shooting Crosman 2100B is a good pest rifle.

Having determined that velocities from the Crosman 2100B have excellent uniformity, attention was turned to its accuracy potential. The sizes of the groups obtained are summarized in the table shown in Appendix A.

Most of the groups obtained with the Crosman 2100 were simply a ragged hole. This rifle is extremely accurate with all of the pellets tested, but the Beeman Crow Magnum seemed to be slightly less accurate than the other pellets tested. Accuracy with the Gamo Master Point and the Dynamit Nobel RWS Superdome pellets proved to be on a par with that obtained with the Crosman Premier. By any reasonable measure, this air rifle gave outstanding accuracy with the overall average group size for the five pellets used being only 0.21 inches, which ties it with the Benjamin 397 as my most accurate .177 rifle.

With its high velocity, the Crosman 2100B is very effective for pest control. If pellets are chosen carefully, it can also be used for hunting small game, but a scope should be used to assure accurate pellet placement. The gun is sufficiently accurate that 35- to 45-yard shots should present no problem if a good scope is used (see Chapter 10). It represents an excellent choice as an all-around air rifle.

The Benjamin 397

This gun is a true American classic. The current model is known as the third variation, but the basic model has been made for many years. It weighs 5.5 pounds, and it features a walnut stock and forearm. The metal is black-coated brass, although a nickel-plated Model S397 is available. The manufacturer warns that eight pumps is the maximum for Benjamin and Sheridan guns. Accordingly, velocity uniformity and accuracy testing were conducted with the gun pumped six strokes. The velocity uniformity is documented by the data shown in the Appendix A table.

The velocity uniformity for the Benjamin 397 resulted in an average standard deviation of only 3 fps for five-shot strings using five dif-

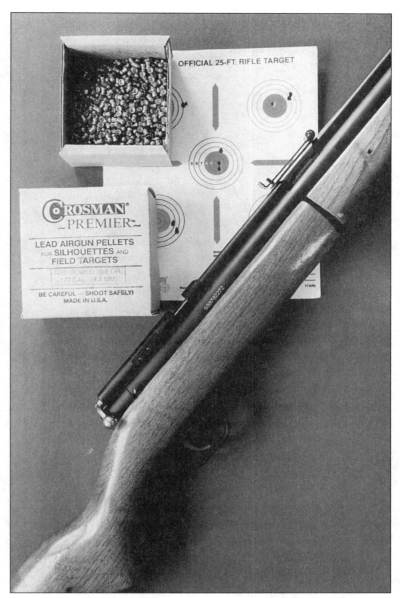

The accuracy of this Benjamin 397 was the best of all the .177 caliber rifles tested. These groups obtained at 30 yards are typical.

ferent pellets. Once again we find that a multi-pump air rifle gives very uniform velocities.

Traditionally, Benjamin air rifles have delivered fine accuracy. In fact, Benjamin advertises "1/2 inch accuracy at 33 feet." After mounting a 3-12X scope, the group sizes shown in the table in Appendix A were obtained.

The groups obtained with the Crosman Premier pellet were all ragged holes. The five three-shot groups averaged only 0.13 inches, and the limit there was my ability to place the crosshairs on the center of a small black

The author's brother, Ron, finds the Benjamin 397 very appropriate for backyard shooting.

dot. Also, my Benjamin 397 has an incredibly heavy trigger pull, and it is anything but smooth. For all five types of pellets used, the overall average group size is only 0.21 inches. This is exactly the same as the overall average for the Crosman 2100. Both are extremely accurate air rifles. However, the Daisy 856 gave an overall average group size of only 0.24 inches. The tests show that the accuracy claimed for the Benjamin is a very conservative claim, especially when the right ammunition is used. With a top velocity approaching 800 fps, this gun is almost in the "magnum" class and it certainly is suitable for pest control and for some hunting. In Chapter 10, the accuracy of this fine air rifle will be described in more detail as the

results obtained at ranges up to 50 yards will be presented.

As is the case with firearms, the tests show that air rifles give considerable variation in accuracy, depending on the ammunition used. This is expected. No doubt that testing a number of specimens of the same model would show there is considerable variation between rifles. This also occurs with firearms. By all means, try several different types of pellets in your particular rifle. It is interesting to note that the Dynamit Nobel RWS Meisterkugeln seemed to work well in all of the rifles tested.

Another interesting fact that emerged from the tests is that when the rifle was sighted in to obtain groups at 10 yards with one pellet, all the other .177 pellets gave points of impact that varied no more than one-half inch at the same distance. The point of impact is not very sensitive to the type of pellet used. As will be mentioned in Chapter 6, this is not the case for the .22 caliber rifles.

Velocity and Number of Pumps

Having determined the velocity uniformity and accuracy potential of each of the .177 caliber rifles, the next phase of the study was to determine how the velocity varies with the number of pumps for one type of pellet fired from each rifle. The velocity data obtained from the chronograph is shown in this table.

The data shows that the velocity increase per pump falls off considerably as the maximum number of pumps is approached. Keep in mind that the Daisy pointed .177 pellet weighs only 7.143 grains, while the Crosman pellets weigh 7.9 grains. Therefore, the Crosman 66 at 10 pumps gave a velocity of 578 fps with a 7.9-grain pellet while the Daisy 856 gives a velocity of 655 fps with a 7.143 grain pellet. The Daisy 856 and 880 and the Crosman 66 are actually very similar in power.

It is interesting to note that the Daisy 880 gives a higher velocity than the Daisy 856 when the number of pumps is six or fewer, but for the guns tested, the 856 gave a higher velocity when seven to 10 pumps were used. The Daisy 856 is an outstanding air rifle in the lower-priced category, and if I knew that I would get another that performs as well as the one tested, I would buy it.

The variation in velocity with the number of pumps is always of concern with multi-pump rifles.

Velocity as a Function of Number of Pumps for .177 Caliber Rifles

Pumps	Velocity in fps for the rifle/pellet combination					
	Crosman 760B/ Crosman Pointed	Daisy 856F/ Daisy Pointed	Crosman 66BX/ Crosman Pointed	Daisy 880/ Daisy Pointed	Crosman 2100B/ Crosman Pointed	Benjamin 397/ Crosman Domed
2	245	334	337	375	423	430
3	304	421	390	459	500	520
4	351	466	468	484	559	589
5	406	521	505	526	607	629
6	450	555	520	561	646	669
7	470	587	547	580	684	695
8	495	619	558	588	704	724
9	513	635	567	602	723	NR
10	526	655	578	620	758	NR

The Daisy 856F that the author is shooting here is one rifle that gave its advertised maximum velocity.

The real heavyweights of the .177 caliber multi-pumps with regard to power are the Crosman 2100 and the Benjamin 397. The data shows that they are almost identical in power as long as the same number of pumps is used. The Benjamin has a maximum of eight pumps, and that number is currently recommended for the Crosman 2100. The latter was also tested to 10 pumps, since that number was listed as a maximum at the time of purchase and it still appears in the owner's manual as the maximum. Clearly, both models are suitable for hunting and pest control (see Chapter 10).

In order to determine how much variation one could expect between guns, a second Crosman Model 66 was obtained. The second gun was the black model with gold trim. Given below are the velocities for the Gamo Match pellet when fired using a number of pumps varying from three to 10.

This shows that there is no significant difference between the two Crosman Model 66

rifles tested, even though they were obtained at different times and were actually different variations of the basic model. However, when the first rifle (the brown Model 66BX) was tested at a later date, the maximum velocities obtained were somewhat higher (approximately 20 fps) than those obtained originally. After it was fired approximately 10 times, the maximum velocity returned to the value previously obtained. As mentioned earlier, my Crosman 66 did not give velocities that were quite as uniform as some of the other models, but it gave excellent accuracy.

Maximum Pellet Velocities

In addition to determining the velocity as a function of the number of pumps, each of the .177 rifles was tested to determine the velocity produced when the rifles were given their maximum number of pumps. In this case, additional insight is obtained when different pellets are used so each of the .177 rifles was tested with its maximum number of pumps

No. Pumps	2	3	4	5	6	7	8	9	10
M66, Black	363	418	473	516	551	572	593	613	626
M66, Brown	353	431	487	532	558	585	603	610	624

with all 23 different types of .177 pellets used. The following table shows the results of this investigation.

The data shown in the table reveals several important characteristics of the rifles. First, the highest velocities are not far from those published by the manufacturers. As will be explored in greater detail later, the maximum velocity depends on the pellet weight. Only the Daisy 856 and the Crosman 2100 gave velocities as high as those specified by the manufacturer. In the case of American air rifles, the pellets used to obtain the maximum advertised velocities are not specified. Additionally, each model has some velocity range within which it is acceptable. In most cases, that window is as large as approximately 10 percent of the specified velocity. In other words, a model that is supposed to give 600 fps is acceptable if it gives 540 to 660 fps. All of the guns meet this requirement with a wide range of pellets.

It should also be pointed out that a second new Daisy 880 was obtained after the evaluations were under way. While the entire set of tests was not repeated with this second gun,

the maximum velocities obtained at 10 pumps were checked against those listed in the table below. For almost every pellet, the maximum velocity obtained with the two guns was within 10 to 15 fps. With a few types of pellets, the velocities were exactly the same with the two guns. The data presented earlier for two specimens of the Crosman 66 also showed that the two guns performed in an almost identical manner. Results such as these indicate that the guns of current manufacture are likely to be uniform from batch to batch.

However, a collectible Daisy 880 manufactured in 1982 (old enough that it has a metal receiver) was added to the collection for a sum of $15. With 10 pumps, that gun gave velocities that were approximately 50 fps higher than the new 880s with every pellet. In fact with the 7.143-grain Daisy pellet, the velocity was 702 fps. Perhaps they were made differently back then. I have also obtained two Daisy Model 880 rifles made in 1993 that have metal receivers and hooded front sights. Both of them give about 50 to 60 fps higher velocity than the new 880s do.

Maximum Pellet Velocities for Each .177 Caliber Rifle With 23 Types of Pellets

| | Velocity, ft/sec | | | | | |
Pellet (Pumps)	Crosman 760B (10)	Daisy 856F (10)	Crosman 66BX (10)	Daisy 880 (10)	Crosman 2100B (8)	Benjamin 397 (8)
Beeman Crow Magnum	504	623	631	592	710	723
Beeman Copper Point	508	649	655	613	732	739
Beeman Flathead	498	617	620	590	703	722
Beeman Hollow Point	538	657	665	619	751	750
Beeman Silver Sting	482	633	609	590	699	720
Crosman Domed	515	622	628	601	717	734
Crosman Pointed	525	626	630	596	712	730
Crosman Premier (L)	490	615	610	607	692	720
Crosman Premier (H)	439	568	566	534	638	649
Crosman Wadcutter	493	628	613	594	698	729
Daisy Pointed	542	656	650	629	742	757
Daisy Wadcutter	527	637	630	609	715	739
D.N. RWS Meisterkugeln	512	622	607	591	699	721
D.N. RWS Superdome	479	620	619	592	700	721
D.N. RWS Supermag	473	599	584	569	660	682
D.N. RWS Super-H-Point	529	646	649	619	745	740
D.N. RWS Superpoint	497	620	630	593	704	721
Eley Wasp	531	646	638	613	736	745
Gamo Master Point	524	621	620	611	722	740
Gamo Hunter	544	643	643	625	735	758
Gamo Magnum	508	614	621	591	703	722
Gamo Match	538	635	639	618	726	745
Marksman Laserhawk	662	797	815	728	904	942
Advertised Maximum	570	630	645	665	725	800

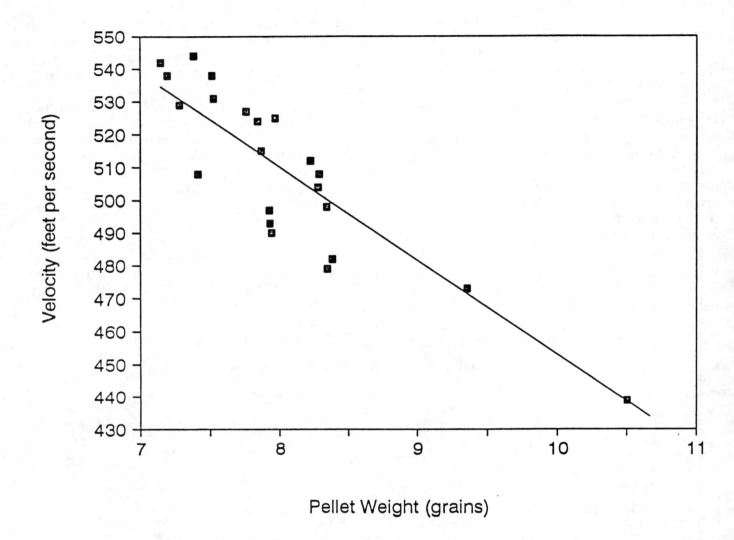

Maxmum velocity vs. pellet weight for the Crosman 760.

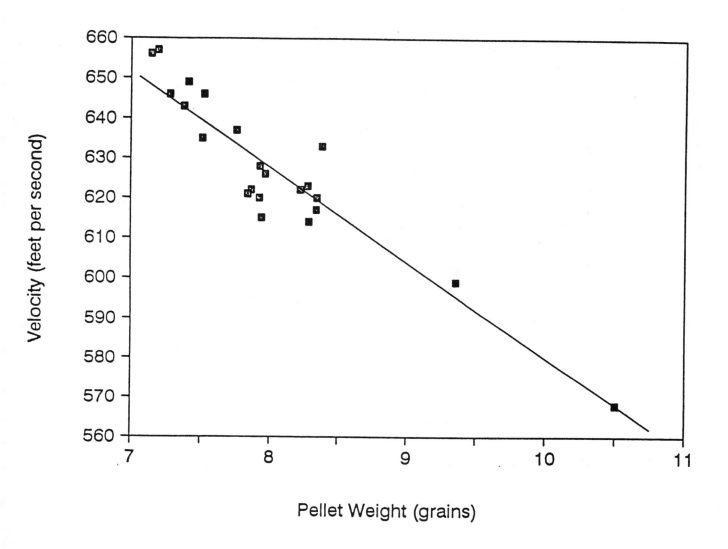

Maximum velocity vs. pellet weight for the Daisy 856.

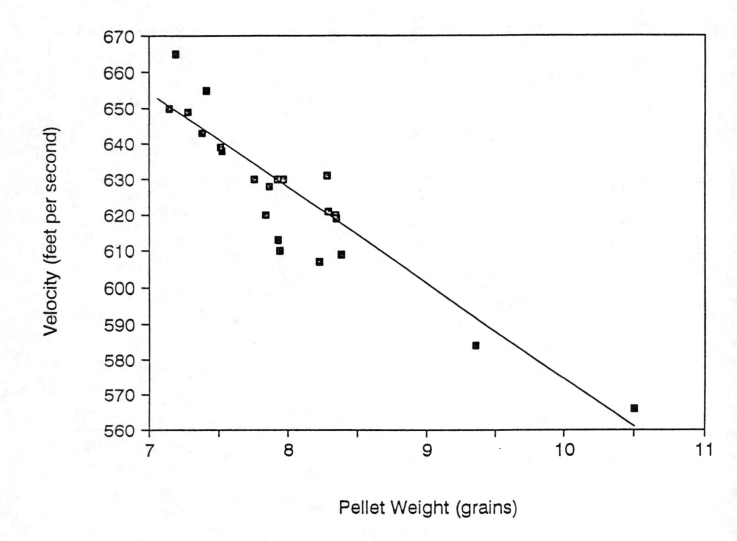

Maximum velocity vs. pellet weight for the Crosman 66.

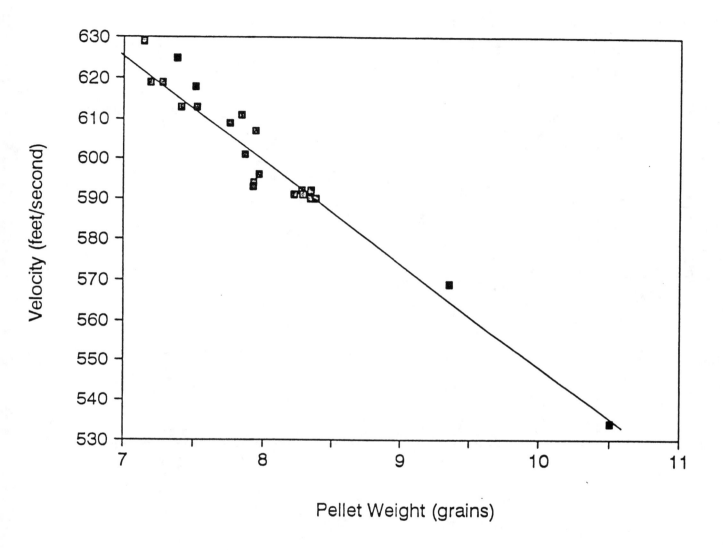

Maximum velocity vs. pellet weight for the Daisy 880.

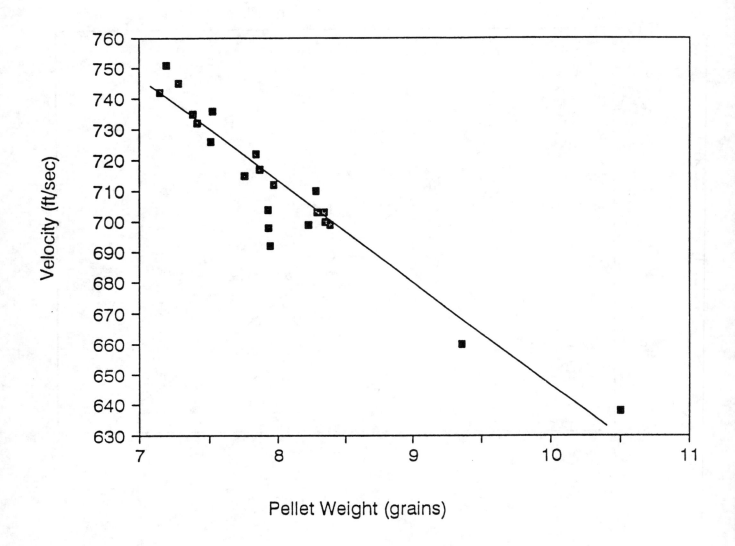

Maximum velocity vs. pellet weight for the Crosman 2100.

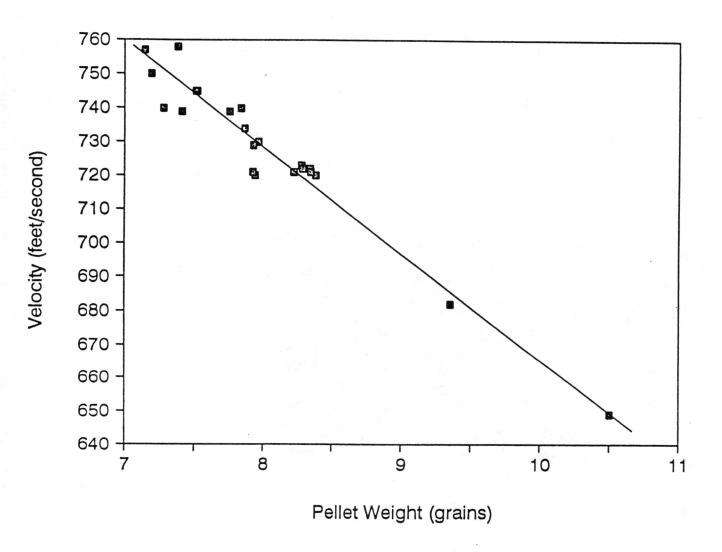

Maximum velocity vs. pellet weight for the Benjamin 397.

I have also added two new Crosman 2100 models, another plastic-stocked 2100B and a walnut-stocked 2100W. Although the whole testing program was not repeated, maximum velocities were determined for these rifles. The new 2100B gave 40 to 50 fps lower velocities than my old 2100B, which is still faster than advertised. However, the new 2100W gave velocities about 70 to 75 fps lower than my old 2100B.

From the data shown in the table, it is clear that pellet weight determines the maximum velocity for a particular rifle. To show this more clearly, a graph has been prepared for each rifle to show the relationship between its maximum velocity and pellet weight. Those graphs are shown previously and reveal that the relationship in each case is very close to being linear. These graphs allow the user to look at the weight of a pellet and read what its maximum velocity will be for a particular rifle model. In addition, the graph can be used to determine what pellet weight should be selected if a known maximum velocity is to be achieved. Suppose a Daisy Model 856 has a maximum velocity specified as 630 fps. Examining the graph for the Daisy 856 shows that it can reach that velocity with a pellet weighing approximately 7.9 grains, a normal weight in .177 caliber.

The Gamo Sporter 500 is easier to cock than most break-action rifles, but it still gives relatively high velocities.

Keep in mind that an air rifle is a mechanical device composed of many parts. Such devices are subject to a certain amount of variation between individual examples. It is entirely possible that if a different specimen of each gun was tested, the results would differ to some extent. However, in some cases, two guns of the same model were tested and the results were almost identical. A third gun might be different, but probably not very much. From my experience, this may not be true for guns made several years apart.

This chapter has dealt with .177 caliber rifles. Chapter 6 will present similar data for the .20- and .22-caliber guns. Some of the general observations presented at the end of that chapter will also apply to the .177 guns. We will now describe the results of testing three break-action rifles in .177 caliber to see how they compare to the multi-pump pneumatics.

Break-Action .177 Caliber Rifles

This book is primarily about American multi-pump air rifles. Even so, the results of their performance need not be considered alone. It is desirable to have a basis for comparison with the performance of some representative break-action models. A frame of reference for the performance of the multi-pump rifles should be provided by presenting similar data obtained using break-action rifles.

In order to provide a comparison of American multi-pump and imported break-action rifles, some rationale had to be followed. One way would be to pick a break action in each of the calibers: .177, .20, and .22. In this way, there would be a break-action rifle to compare to the multi-pumps in these calibers. A second way would be to pick break-action rifles in one caliber, but of different price and performance levels. After all, the multi-pump rifles in .177 caliber fall into different price and performance categories. This procedure would enable a better evaluation to be made of this type of rifle than would the hit-or-miss approach of picking only one rifle in each caliber.

Remember that many of the American multi-pump rifles cost far less than $100 and none approach $200. Probably my favorite break-action rifle is the Webley Patriot. However, this rifle costs more than $400 and it would not be exactly fair to compare it to American rifles that cost from one-fourth to one-third that amount. A better comparison is made when break-action rifles in the price range of $100 to $200 are compared to the multi-pump rifles.

The selection of break-action rifles is greatest in .177 caliber. Accordingly, three break-action rifles in .177 caliber were selected for evaluation using the same procedures as used for the multi-pump rifles. The rifles selected and their actual cost and advertised maximum velocities are as follows; the Gamo Sporter Model 500 ($119.95, 760 fps), the Beeman Model S1 ($179.95, 900 fps), and the Gamo Hunter ($219.95, 1,000 fps). The Beeman S1 and the Gamo Hunter are advertised as being more powerful than the fastest multi-pump .177 caliber, which is the Benjamin 397 (800 fps). Other data for these rifles is listed in the table.

I once read in a magazine the story of two chaps testing one of the popular break-action rifles. The best they could get at 10 meters (33 feet) were groups of around three-quarters of an inch! Compare that with the results shown in Appendix A for the .177 multi-pump rifles. They thought something was wrong with the rifle and sent it back for testing by the factory technician. It was returned along with a test target showing the expected small groups. It seems that the chaps testing the piece could not control the movement that resulted when the heavy piston and spring slammed forward when the rifle was fired. The worst groups obtained with any multi-pump rifle were as good as an expensive break-action gave for those chaps. It is not that the inherent accuracy of the break-action rifle is poor, but it may not be possible for a novice to obtain anywhere near that level of accuracy. One major

Break Action .177 Caliber Rifles Selected for Evaluation

Rifle	Velocity ft/sec.	Length inches	Weight lbs.
Gamo Sporter 500	760	42.5	5.5
Beeman S1	900	45.5	7.1
Gamo Hunter (Camo)	1,000	43.3	6.6

Because of its light weight, the Gamo Sporter 500 is a good choice for a first rifle of this type.

supplier of break-action rifles includes a sheet telling how to get better accuracy with a list of things to do. They include not holding the rifle too tightly, not resting the rifle on anything hard, etc. Break-action rifles take some getting used to. These things jump like a tickled frog when touched off.

Having said that, I confess that my experience with break-action rifles does not approach that with the multi-pump type. However, I have shot everything from BB guns to a .458 Winchester Magnum and I have shot competitively. My last three-shot group at 100 yards with the .458 could be covered with a quarter. My last three-shot group at 100 yards with my .308 Winchester could be covered with a nickel. I consider myself to be a better-than-average marksman and adaptable to almost any type of rifle. While others may be able to achieve better accuracy with the break-

action rifles that I tested, I do not believe that it would be much better.

I have mentioned elsewhere that a scope for use on a spring-piston gun must be specially designed for use on that type of rifle. I used two BSA airgun scopes, a 2-7X and a 3-12X. No problem was encountered with either scope on the break-action rifles. The problem encountered was with the mount. I had available only two ordinary clamp-on mounts and both slid to the rear in spite of all I could do. Many of the more powerful break-action rifles have a scope stop screwed in place on top of the receiver. With this feature, the scope can be mounted with the rear base in contact with the stop. This stop will prevent movement of the base rearward. Having had the problem that I did with conventional scope mounts and rifles having no scope stop, I recommend that for break-action rifles, you get a

Break-action rifles give a strong forward recoil, which tends to slide the scope back, unless a scope stop is present as on this Beeman.

special mount intended for use on that type of rifle and you may want to buy a rifle with a scope-stop provision.

Because of not having a suitable scope mount available, my initial testing was carried out using the open sights on the break-action rifles. Bear in mind that these sights are by no means crude. For all of the rifles they consist of a hooded, square-topped post front sight and a rear sight that has a crisp, square notch. The rear sights on the rifles were easily adjusted by turning large dials that move the rear sight up or down and to the left or right. I had no trouble in sighting in the rifles to hit a 1-inch bullseye at 10 meters. After that, I shot groups with several different types of pellets. To be honest, after having read of all the problems that other shooters have with spring-piston guns, I didn't expect much success.

After initial testing with open sights, the scope mount problem was solved by getting a Beeman mount that is intended for use on break-action airguns. It is a very sturdy device with massive screws for clamping in the mounting grooves. The mount comes with two Allen wrenches, one for tightening the screws that attach the bases to the scope and a larger one for tightening the bases on the rifle. One of the bases also comes

with a pin that can insert into a hole on top of the receiver to serve as a stop. Unfortunately, the Gamo rifles tested do not come with such a hole to accept the pin.

The Gamo Sporter 500

The Gamo 500 is listed as giving a velocity of 760 fps. Velocity testing of all the 760 break-action rifles was carried out at elevations of 5,500 and 8,400 feet. In Chapter 7, the effects of elevation on the velocity produced by multi-pump and break-action rifles are considered in detail. For a multi-pump rifle, there is a loss in velocity of 4 to 6 percent in going from 800 feet above sea level to 5,500 feet in elevation. There is a 4 to 6 per-

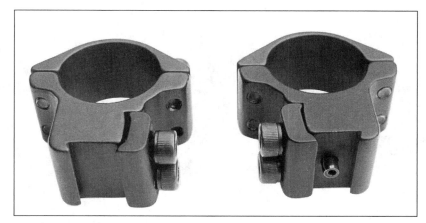

This massive Beeman scope mount was required to prevent scope movement during recoil of the break-action rifles.

Break-action rifles from Gamo like the Sporter 500 represent good value for a moderate price.

cent additional velocity loss in going from 5,500 ft to 8,400 ft. For break-action rifles, the velocity losses appear to be slightly greater than this for each of these changes in elevation. This will be illustrated by analysis of data given in Chapter 7.

Complete velocity uniformity results for the Gamo Sporter 500 are given in tables presented in Appendix A. Average velocities given by the Gamo 500 had an average standard deviation of only about 4 fps, and this is with a new rifle. This is excellent performance. The following table presents the velocities obtained for all three break-action rifles using 15 types of pellets. Velocities obtained at 5,500 and 8,400 feet in elevation are shown.

The velocities show the effect of elevation mentioned earlier and the expected variation with pellet weight.

Three-shot groups were obtained by firing over two leather bags filled with sand resting on the tailgate of the truck. This arrangement was as steady as a rock. Shooting first with the Gamo Sporter 500 with Meisterkugeln

Velocities Obtained for Break-Action Rifles

Pellet	Gamo 500 5500 ft.	Gamo 500 8400 ft.	Beeman S1 5500 ft.	Beeman S1 8400 ft.	Gamo Hunter 5500 ft.	Gamo Hunter 8400 ft.
Beeman Crow Magnum	669	622	745	719	818	745
Beeman Laser Sport	738	665	799	772	864	784
Beeman Silver Sting	671	628	734	718	819	751
Crosman Domed	696	636	768	681	805	740
Crosman Pointed	702	650	761	701	806	753
Crosman Premier (L)	673	630	746	697	819	738
Crosman Premier (H)	572	516	619	609	693	621
Crosman Wadcutter	692	643	777	733	815	748
Daisy Pointed	739	687	823	758	901	834
Daisy Wadcutter	740	680	824	753	864	824
Daisy Power Pellet	616	573	698	604	738	641
D.N. RWS Hobby	752	706	819	770	906	840
D.N. RWS Meisterkugeln	685	634	756	724	838	771
Gamo Hunter	725	660	805	749	865	796
Gamo Master Point	698	648	787	758	844	786
Advertised Max. Vel.	760		900		1,000	

pellets, I obtained groups of 0.31, 0.30, 0.88, 0.94, and 0.72 inches, which give an average of 0.63 inches with a standard deviation of 0.31 inches. The Crosman Copperhead pointed pellet gave groups of 0.48, 0.84, 0.22, 0.50, and 0.89 inch for an average of 0.59 inch and a standard deviation of 0.28 inch. The next pellet tested was the 10.5-grain Crosman Premier. With that pellet, I got groups of 0.48, 0.53, 0.50, 0.63, and 0.41 inch for an average of 0.51 inch with a standard deviation of only 0.08 inch.

From the results given above, it should be obvious that the Gamo Sporter 500 is capable of fine accuracy. Three groups were fired using the Gamo Hunter pellet. They measured 0.38, 0.69, and 0.75 inch for an average of 0.61 inch and a standard deviation of 0.20 inch. Would a scope have made a difference? Of course it would, but I must confess that before the scope mount acted up, the groups I got were just about the same as those given above.

Two things are obvious from the results. First, the Gamo Sporter 500 is an accurate break-action rifle. If the practice was followed of giving the smallest group obtained as the accuracy of the rifle, we would say that the Gamo 500 has an accuracy of 0.22 inch at 10 meters (with open sights!). I have

no doubt that I can do better with a scope in a rugged mount.

Second, the groups obtained with open sights on the Gamo 500 are about equal to the best that I have obtained using similarly sighted multi-pump rifles. At this point, I see no great difference in the accuracy of the two types of rifles as long as the sighting equipment is the same. Keep in mind that the overall average group size obtained with the Daisy 856 was only 0.24 inch at 10 yards when a 12X scope was used.

After getting a suitable scope mount, the BSA 2-7X scope was mounted on the Gamo 500. Five types of pellets were used with five three-shot groups of each type fired. With this arrangement, an overall average for the 25 groups was 0.61 inch. This is almost exactly the same average group size that I obtained in the preliminary accuracy tests. I believe that accuracy at this level represents about the limit of what I can obtain with a rifle that moves and vibrates as the pellet leaves the barrel. From things that I have read, it seems to be about as good as a lot of other people can do. These results are considerably better, however, than those obtained by the two chaps whose best groups were about three-fourths inch at 10 meters.

Of the three break actions tested, the author developed a fondness for the Gamo Hunter.

The Gamo Sporter 500 is a rifle of convenient size and weight. Although it would normally not be considered a hunting rifle, it has considerable power. I believe that it would be a good choice for a rifle of this type intended for general use.

The Gamo Hunter

The Gamo Hunter has a maximum velocity listed as 1,000 fps. As mentioned earlier, break-action rifles lose considerable velocity in going from sea level to higher elevation. The Gamo Hunter was tested at 5,500 and 8,400 feet in elevation. Velocities at sea level would be 6 to 7 percent higher than those obtained at 5,500 feet and 12 to 14 percent higher than those obtained at 8,400 feet.

Complete results of the velocity uniformity tests are shown in tables given in Appendix A. The Gamo Hunter gave uniform velocities, with an average standard deviation of only 4 fps for velocities measured at elevations of both 5,500 and 8,400 feet.

The table given above shows the velocities obtained with all 15 types of pellets used in the tests. Even at an elevation of 5,500 feet, the average velocity with the Daisy Pointed pellet was 901 fps and for the Dynamit Nobel RWS Hobby was 906 fps. These are light pellets, but even pellets of normal weight gave velocities of more than 800 fps. At sea level, these velocities would be considerably higher and the Daisy and Hobby pellets would produce 950 to 975 fps. With a really light pellet, the Gamo Hunter will push 1,000 fps. The Gamo Hunter gives energies that place it in the magnum class, even at an altitude of 5,500 feet. This is a powerful rifle.

The open sights on this rifle also consist of a sharp, square-topped post front and square notch rear. After sighting in, the rifle was tested by firing groups at 10 meters using the Crosman Copperhead pointed pellet. The groups obtained measured 0.75, 0.72, 1.13, 0.38, and 0.75 inch for an average of 0.75 inch with a standard deviation of 0.27 inch.

The Gamo Hunter offers high velocity in a rifle of reasonable size and weight.

While the Beeman S1 is a sturdy, well-made rifle, it represents the upper limit of dimensions that the author is willing to tolerate.

With the Gamo Hunter pellet, five groups averaged 0.59 inch. The smallest was 0.22 inch and the largest was 0.89 inch. Groups obtained using the 10.5-grain Crosman Premier pellet were more consistent, with an average of 0.51 inch and a range of 0.41 to 0.63 inch. Five groups obtained using the Dynamit Nobel RWS Meisterkugeln pellet averaged 0.83 inch.

After attaching a 2-7X scope, full accuracy testing was carried out using five different types of pellets. The smallest average for five groups resulted from the Beeman Silver Sting pellet and it was only 0.37 inch. The smallest group measured only 0.09 inch, while the largest was 0.56 inch. This is excellent accuracy.

One pellet that my Gamo Hunter did not shoot well is the Gamo Master Point. With this pellet, the groups ranged from 0.61 to 1.13 inches, with an average of 0.82 inch. In addition to shooting well with the Beeman Silver Sting, the 10.5-grain Crosman Premier performed well with groups ranging from 0.31 to 0.55 inch, with an average of 0.40 inch. If the

results obtained with the Gamo Master Point are deleted, the overall average group size was only 0.43 inch. I simply cannot shoot this type of rifle more accurately than that.

The Gamo Hunter that I have has a camo stock and it is intended as a hunting rifle. It certainly has the power to be used in that way. In order to see what the rifle would do at longer distances, I conducted accuracy tests at 25 yards using the Dynamit Nobel RWS Meisterkugeln, Gamo Master Point, and Crosman Premier (10.5 grains) pellets. Five groups were fired using each type of pellet. The average group sizes were 1.17, 1.43 and 0.95 inches, respectively, for the three types of pellets. These results are exactly in accord with the accuracy that they gave at 10 yards. This rifle really seems to like the heavy Crosman Premier pellet and it is the one that I would select for most hunting applications.

The Gamo Hunter is a pleasant rifle to shoot and the test results show that it has the accuracy and power to be used in hunting. It is a welcome addition to my airgun battery because it is solid, powerful, and accurate.

The Beeman S1

This rifle is big. It has almost exactly the same size and weight as a .338 Winchester Magnum that I use. It is surprising to see the tiny hole in the barrel of a rifle this size and weight.

The instructions that come with this rifle indicate a break-in period of 1,000 to 1,500 shots. The instructions also say that results may be erratic until the break-in period is complete. I can attest to the validity of that statement. As with the two Gamo rifles, velocities were measured at elevations of 5,500 and 8,400 ft. Before recording velocities shown for the Beeman S1, it was fired approximately 300 times. During that time, great variations in pellet velocities occurred.

After firing a considerable number of times, velocities became more uniform, especially with certain pellets. For example, when fired at an elevation of 8,400 feet, the standard deviations for five shots were only 2 and 3 fps for the Beeman Silver Sting and Crow Magnum, respectively. On the other hand, the standard deviations for the Gamo Hunter and Dynamit Nobel RWS Hobby pellets were 12 (10 shots) and 18 (eight shots) fps, respectively. Velocity uniformity is better now than it was initially, but it is still not acceptable with certain pellets. Others give very uniform velocities. The complete velocity uniformity data is presented in tables given in Appendix A.

Accuracy testing of the Beeman S1 was limited to two types of pellets when the 2-7X scope was attached. At 10 yards, five three-shot groups with the Beeman Laser Sport pellet averaged 0.76 inch (with a spread of 0.67 to 0.81 inch). The 10.5-grain Crosman Premier gave an average group size of 0.60 inch, with a range of 0.48 to 0.73 inch. From these results and those obtained using open sights, it appears that the accuracy of the Beeman S1 is about on a par with the other break-action rifles tested.

CHAPTER 6

EVALUATION OF .20 AND .22 RIFLES

Numerical data form the bases for comparing performances of guns, cars, and quarterbacks. In this chapter, a large amount of data obtained by testing the .20 and .22 caliber multi-pump rifles will be presented. Evaluations of velocity uniformity, maximum velocity, and accuracy were carried out using the procedures described in Chapter 5. Although some of the .177 caliber rifles are suitable for hunting, the .20 and .22 rifles are better choices for such activities, so this chapter will be of particular interest to hunters using air rifles.

The Sheridan CB9, C9, and C9PB

The Sheridan is the only American .20 caliber (5 mm) multi-pump pneumatic and is a true classic that has been made for more than 50 years. It is now known as the Benjamin Sheridan. New variations with slight modifications (e.g., position of the safety) have appeared over the years. One current model is technically known as the CB9 or Blue Streak, but there is also a nickel-plated Model C9 known as the Silver Streak. Both models have rather bulky stocks of good walnut that are amenable to customizing. The most recent Sheridan model is a 50th Anniversary edition known as the C9PB which has polished brass

metal work. Maximum power is obtained with eight pumps, which produces a maximum velocity advertised to be 675 fps. All three of the Sheridan models were tested in this study.

Most .20 caliber pellets weigh about the same as those in .22 caliber, so the power level of these guns is on a par with the Benjamin 392 in .22 caliber. However, since a .20 caliber pellet has a smaller cross-sectional area than

When my brother, Ron, and I are in a serious discussion about airguns, the larger calibers like the Benjamin .22 take center stage.

Sheridan's Silver Streak is a beautiful rifle whose performance equals its looks.

The Sheridan is a convenient size and has enough weight for steady holding.

a .22 caliber, the .20 is slightly more efficient ballistically. Thus, it is not uncommon for a .20 caliber pellet to have greater downrange energy and give deeper penetration than one of .22 caliber if both start with the same muzzle velocity. In some ways, the .20 caliber has some of the advantages of a .22 as well as those of a .177, and it was cleverly designed that way. The data displayed in the table in Appendix B shows the velocity uniformity obtained with five types of pellets fired from a Sheridan Blue Streak Model CB9 that was made in the late 1980s.

A very new Sheridan Silver Streak Model C9 was also tested for velocity uniformity with five types of pellets. The table given in Appendix B also shows the results obtained from the chronograph for the new Sheridan Silver Streak.

From the bench, the Sheridan proved to be an outstanding performer.

605 to 640 fps for the three rifles tested. A table shown in Appendix B gives the velocities obtained when seven types of pellets were used in all three of the Sheridan rifles.

The Sheridan .20 caliber rifles may be pumped a maximum of eight times. The Beeman H&N Match pellet, which weighs only 10.32 grains, gave an average velocity of 704 fps in the three Sheridan models. With some of the lighter .20 caliber pellets, the Sheridan rifles will certainly exceed the manufacturer's claim of 675 fps. Even 10.32 grains is not exceptionally light for a .20 caliber pellet. Some of the break-action .20 caliber rifles are tested with pellets weighing as little as 9.7 grains. With these pellets, the velocity from a Sheridan is comparable to that of break-action rifles in .20 caliber.

The Beeman Crow Magnum in .20 caliber weighs 12.99 grains, so the velocities with that pellet were also high. All of the American-made pellets in .20 caliber weigh very close to 14.3 grains. With those pellets, velocities were in the 605 to 640 fps range. All of these pellets are very sturdy with solid forward sections so they hit hard and penetrate well. An air rifle that generates an energy of at least 12 foot-pounds (16.4 joules) is sometimes designated as a "magnum" rifle. A 14.3-grain pellet traveling at 615 fps generates an energy of 12 foot-pounds, so the Sheridan is right on the threshold of being a magnum air rifle, and its performance proves it.

Accuracy testing at 10 yards was performed with the Blue Streak. The scope mount used on the Benjamin rifles would not clamp tightly on the barrel of the Sheridan Blue Streak or Silver Streak, so firing was carried out with the Williams peep sight attached. Therefore, the groups described do not repre-

Finally, a Sheridan C9PB Polished Brass 50th Anniversary model was fired to determine the velocity uniformity. The same types of pellets were used as in the testing of other Sheridans. A table given in Appendix B shows the velocities obtained with this Sheridan anniversary model.

With three Sheridan rifles evaluated, a reliable picture emerges for these American classics. Velocity uniformity is excellent with an average standard deviation of only 2 to 3 fps for all three guns with five types of pellets. Certainly this speaks well for these rifles, and it would be difficult to imagine more repeatable velocities.

The next phase of evaluating the Sheridan rifles determined the velocity that each gives when it is pumped the maximum number of times (eight). With pellets weighing approximately 14.3 grains, the average velocity is

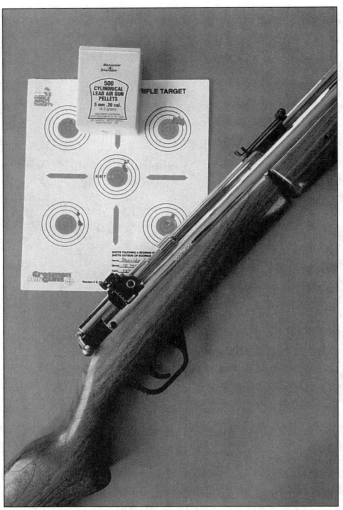

Sheridan rifles are advertised to give 1/2-inch accuracy at 33 feet, but all of mine will do much better.

sent the ultimate accuracy of this rifle, since there is a considerable difference between aiming with a peep sight and with a 12X scope. While an abbreviated accuracy test was performed, the Sheridan cylindrical pellet gave groups that averaged 0.38 inches at 10 yards when the rifle was given six pumps. The average group size using the Crosman Premier pellet was 0.36 inches.

The accuracy of the Sheridan is adequate for almost any type of use. Even with a peep sight, it is not difficult to obtain three-shot groups that are considerably smaller than the 1/2-inch accuracy described by the manufacturer. We will have more to say about the accuracy of Sheridan rifles at longer ranges in Chapter 10, where hunting with air rifles is considered.

In addition to the velocity uniformity and accuracy determinations, the velocity increase with number of pumps was studied. In this case, the new style of Sheridan cylindrical pellet was used and the table shows the results obtained.

From the data obtained, it is evident that the velocities produced by the different Sheridan rifles are quite similar as the number of pumps is varied. In this case, three rifles were tested and duplicate rifles were tested for some of the .177 caliber rifles (see Chapter 5). In all cases, the variation between rifles of the same make and model is negligible.

As will be discussed in more detail in Chapter 10, the Sheridan .20 caliber models are powerful air rifles. Their accuracy and penetration are legendary among American airgunners. The results of the experiments carried out in this study only confirm this reputation. Although .20 caliber pellets are not as widely available as those in .177 and .22 cali-

Cylindrical Pellet Velocity Per No. of Pumps for Sheridan Rifles

Velocity in fps for .20 Caliber Sheridan Rifles

Pumps	Blue Streak	Silver Streak	Polished Brass
2	354	359	372
3	439	415	434
4	473	481	480
5	522	501	524
6	555	557	574
7	580	582	577
8	604	607	610

Sheridan air rifles have long been popular for hunting and pest control.

bers, the selection is extensive and includes target, plinking, and hunting types.

A Sheridan merits serious consideration when an air rifle is being selected, especially if pest control and hunting are planned. Remember, however, that the Sheridan CB9 and C9 get rather difficult to pump after about five pumps. They are adult air rifles and would not normally be selected for training youngsters who have to load and pump for themselves. My old Blue Streak has a decent trigger pull, but the new Silver Streak and Polished Brass models have trigger pulls

that resemble dragging one brick across another. Like anything else, you get used to it or a good gunsmith can be employed to improve the trigger action.

The Daisy PowerLine 22X

Introduced in March 1999, the Daisy PowerLine 22X marks the reintroduction of a .22 caliber air rifle in the Daisy product line. It has a nicely shaped hardwood stock and forearm. Like the Daisy PowerLine 880, the pumping lever is separate from the forearm. The forearm is in two halves and the pumping lever

In its factory form, the Daisy 22X has a pleasing look. I modified mine by slimming the forearm and giving the stock a pistol grip and fluted comb.

works between them. Pumping the Daisy 22X requires very little effort, even when 10 pumps are used. In my opinion, the Daisy PowerLine 22X has lines as pleasing as those of any American air rifle. My gun also has the best trigger pull of all of the air rifles that I tested. After a very short take-up movement, the let-off is remarkably crisp for an air rifle, a characteristic of the Daisy multi-pump air rifles.

Daisy recommends a maximum of 10 pumps for the Model 22X, but only eight pumps were used in determining the velocity

uniformity in keeping with the practice of using two pumps fewer than the maximum. The table shown in Appendix B gives the velocities indicated by the chronograph. The largest standard deviation in velocity was only 5 fps. Eight pumps gave the Daisy pointed pellet 460 fps, while the same number of pumps gave the Gamo Match pellet 490 fps.

Keep in mind that the Daisy pointed pellet is a rather heavy one at 15.68 grains. On the other hand, the Gamo Match pellet is rather light at 13.88 grains. The result is that the lit-

In order to see what the Daisy 22X is capable of, mount a good airgun scope like the BSA 3-12X used here.

tle Daisy with eight pumps gives 30 fps lower velocity with the Daisy pellet. However, the velocity uniformity is excellent, with the average standard deviation being only about 3 fps for strings of five shots. The Gamo pellets, which showed outstanding weight and dimensional uniformity, gave the most uniform velocities, with the standard deviations being only 1 fps. This is fine performance from the little Daisy and it indicates that excellent accuracy might be expected.

The BSA 3-12X scope was mounted on the Daisy 22X and the sizes of the groups obtained at 10 yards are shown in the table given in Appendix B. The Daisy 22X shows outstanding accuracy for such an inexpensive rifle with the overall average group size being only 0.27 inch. The Daisy Pointed and the Gamo Master Point are both pointed pellets that have very large interior cavities and skirt diameters. For some reason, this rifle shoots extremely well with these pellets.

In addition to the groups obtained with the five pellets listed in the table, two other pellets were tested in the Daisy 22X. The Cros-

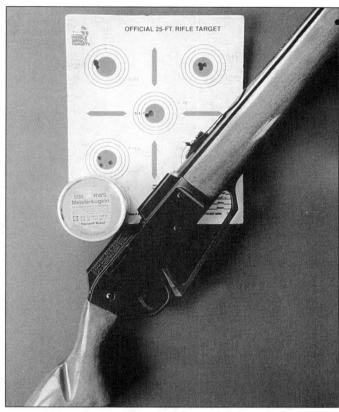

Although it is not expensive, the Daisy 22X is capable of outstanding accuracy.

The Daisy 22X is an ideal choice for a light, trim .22 caliber pellet rifle.

This young shooter has found that the Daisy 22X is easy to pump and shoot.

man Premier, which is a very high quality pellet intended for field target use, gave five groups that averaged 0.71 inch (the smallest 0.49 inch and the largest 0.99 inch). The Daisy really does not like this pellet, which has a skirt diameter of 0.220 inch! To see if there was something strange going on, I tried the Crosman Copperhead wadcutters (skirt diameter 0.222 inch) and got groups ranging from 0.28 to 0.90 inch for an average of 0.59 inch. This is not bad performance, but it shows clearly that you should experiment with different pellets even if you have an inexpensive air rifle. The Daisy 22X seems to give much better accuracy with pellets that have larger skirt diameters such as the Daisy and Gamo pellets (see Chapter 4). As was described in Chapter 5, the Daisy 880 also did not perform as well with the 7.9 grain

Crosman Premier in .177 caliber as it did with several other pellets. It may be that the pellet skirt diameter is crucial in determining the accuracy of Daisy air rifles.

With a maximum velocity approaching 550 fps, the Daisy PowerLine 22X represents a modest power level in a .22 caliber rifle. However, as results presented in later chapters will show, the .22 caliber pellets, especially certain types, hit hard. While this gun might not be a first choice for pest control and limited hunting, it would certainly not be last. In fact, it represents a fine balance of size and weight with power and accuracy. Because of the easy pumping action of the Daisy 22X and its overall size and weight, it would be a good choice for a youngster accompanied by an adult who wants to hunt small game or shoot pests. It is a favorite of my wife, and I have customized the stock and forearm on hers.

With a pellet modified to reduce its weight, the Daisy 22X gave a velocity of 535 fps. It also gave 511 and 514 fps with the Gamo Match (13.88 grains) and Ruko Match (13.86 grains), respectively. With some of the very light .22 pellets that are in the 10- to 11-grain range, the Daisy 22X would easily produce the advertised velocity of 550 fps. After all, this is what is done with the imported spring piston guns to boost their advertised velocities. In accuracy at 10 yards, the Daisy 22X is the equal of any of the .22 caliber rifles tested.

Several changes have been made in this model since it was first introduced. Because the power plant is essentially adapted from that of the Daisy PowerLine 880, the earliest samples of the Model 22X retained the BB loading plunger in the bolt head. This is no longer the case, and several other slight modifications have been made, including a change from a hex-head to a slotted-head bolt for attaching the stock. The latest rifles have a fiber optic front sight like that on the Daisy 856 and 880. The guns with low serial numbers may have some value to collectors, but the later specimens with the improvements are more desirable to shooters.

One additional comment relative to the Daisy PowerLine 22X is in order. If you are at all handy with tools and want to spend a few hours on the project, the gun's appearance can be enhanced by slimming the forearm, shaping the pistol grip, and fluting the comb.

The result is very pleasing to the eye and actually improves handling. A Daisy PowerLine 22X would have been an addition to my airgun battery as a "project gun" without its numerous other desirable qualities.

The Crosman 2200B Magnum

This model represents the author's second addition in the serious air rifle category many years ago. It has never been a disappointment, although that was partially because of chance, as explained below. With a muzzle velocity approaching 600 fps, this .22-caliber gun is definitely in the "magnum" class in terms of performance. Pumping effort required is intermediate between that of the Daisy 22X and the much more difficult-to-pump Benjamin and Sheridan guns.

This fine air rifle evolved from the Crosman Model 1400 that was produced in the 1970s. That gun had an excellent reputation and the fact that the Model 2200 has been produced since 1978 speaks well for it. Rifles of bad design do not remain in production for more than two decades.

When my 2200B was purchased in the late 1980s, Crosman literature recommended a maximum of 10 pumps. Recent conversations with Crosman engineers indicate that a maximum of eight pumps should be observed, even though the owner's manual still lists a 10-pump maximum. Therefore, the Crosman 2200B was tested for velocity uniformity using eight pumps, with the results shown in the table given in Appendix B.

With five types of pellets, five-shot strings gave an average standard deviation of only slightly more than 3 fps. Velocity variations of this magnitude are negligible for all practical shooting situations. Note that even with eight pumps, pellets weighing about 14.3 grains are given an average velocity of more than 540 fps. This gun

The Crosman 2200B is a full-size, sturdy rifle that has been produced for many years. Because it is a powerful rifle, it is suitable for many uses, including hunting and pest control.

My Crosman 2200B has strong preferences in pellets. Excellent accuracy was obtained with the Dynamit Nobel RWS Meisterkugeln pellet, as these groups show.

is intermediate in power between the Daisy 22X and the Benjamin 392, and it is a versatile piece.

In the late 1980s, the Crosman 2200B had a maximum advertised velocity of 595 fps specified at a maximum of 10 pumps. With my gun, ten pumps gave the Dynamit Nobel RWS Meisterkugeln (14.26 grains) a velocity of 590 fps, according to the chronograph. With some of the light .22 caliber pellets, this rifle will top 600 fps if the original 10-pump maximum is employed, so it definitely meets the advertised velocity of 595 fps.

My Crosman 2200 always gave good accuracy. However, I did not experiment with pellet types for many years, so it was with a great deal of interest that I mounted the BSA 3-12X scope on the rifle and started testing. The results obtained with five types of pellets are shown in the table given in Appendix B. The average group size for the Crosman Copperhead pointed pellet was 0.26 inch, while that for the Copperhead wadcutter was 0.46 inch.

The reason that the Crosman 2200 always performed well for me was that for many

The Crosman 2200B is a good choice for small-game hunting and pest control.

good as some other pellets gave, even though it was certainly accurate enough to be very useful for hunting.

My Crosman 2200 seems to be very picky with regard to pellets. With the Crosman Copperhead pointed and Dynamit Nobel RWS Meisterkugeln pellets, it shoots very well indeed. The groups were simply ragged holes. However, it doesn't seem to shoot especially well with anything else that I tried. If you have a Crosman 2200, spend some time evaluating pellet performance. A different specimen might perform better with some other pellet, but for my rifle the choice is simple: Use Crosman Copperhead pointed or RWS Meisterkugeln pellets. That is not really too limiting, because the Copperhead pointed is a good pellet for hunting and the Meisterkugeln is a good choice for general shooting.

The Benjamin 392

The Benjamin 392 is 36.25 inches long and weighs 5.5 pounds. It has a walnut stock and forearm, and most specimens examined have good wood, although some do not have well-matched coloration of the stock and forearm. The maximum number of pumps is eight, which produces advertised velocities up to 685 fps. At least on paper, this makes it the most powerful air rifle tested. With the right pellets, it is deadly on small game, and the Benjamin .22 rifles have been used in this way for generations. Some of the results presented in Chapter 10 will further illustrate the capabilities of this fine gun.

I have always favored .22 caliber air rifles, and the Benjamin 392 will drive .22 caliber pellets at up to 685 fps, which puts it in the "magnum" class. With well-placed pellets of suitable construction, it will handle most air rifle tasks. While it is not much of a factor when the Benjamin 392 is used in hunting, this is an air rifle that gets to be strenuous to pump for many shots of more than five or six pumps.

It should be noted that when certain pellets were being loaded in the Benjamin, some difficulty was encountered. In most cases, the pellet could simply be placed in the loading track and the bolt closed. With other pellets — the Daisy pointed and the Beeman Silver

years, I had only Crosman Copperhead pointed and wadcutter pellets. Those happen to be some of the best performing pellets in that particular gun. Only the Dynamit Nobel RWS Meisterkugeln performed as well (average group size 0.26 inch). Had I experimented with several types of pellets early in my use of this rifle, I might have been disappointed, because even the Crosman Premier gave groups that averaged 0.71 inch at 10 yards. In an attempt to discover other pellets that perform well in this rifle, I shot several single groups. The Daisy pointed group size was 0.85 inch, the Dynamit Nobel RWS Superdome was 0.98 inch, the Beeman Crow Magnum was 1.21 inches, and the Beeman Kodiak was 0.81 inch. In most of my rifles, accuracy of the Beeman Crow Magnum pellet was not quite as

Benjamin air rifles have come a long way since this old Model G from the 1920s, held by the author's father.

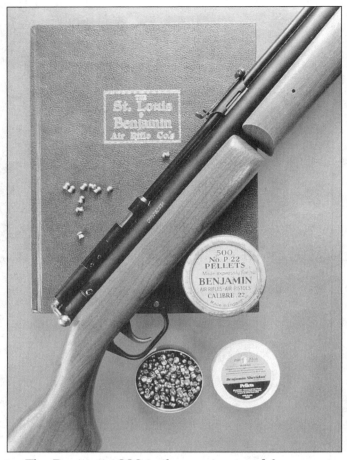

The Benjamin 392 is the most powerful American multi-pump air rifle, and it is an excellent choice for the small-game hunter.

Jet for example — it was sometimes not possible to close the bolt without a great deal of force being applied. It was found that the reason for this was that these pellets have rather square shoulders on the rings around the head and these rings were catching on the sharp, square edges at the rear of the chamber. If the pellets were started in the chamber itself, the bolt could be closed normally. Only pellets having the square-shouldered rings caused any difficulty and all the others could be chambered easily by starting with the pellet in the loading track.

The Benjamin was tested for velocity uniformity using six pumps (since the maximum is eight pumps). The results given by the chronograph are shown in the table for this rifle given in Appendix B for this rifle.

With six pumps, the Benjamin 392 averaged around 600 fps, depending on the pel-

let. However, the average standard deviation is only 2 fps for five-shot strings with five different pellets. That level of velocity reproducibility equals the best found for any of the air rifles tested. Even at the power level from six pumps, the Benjamin 392 is a powerful air rifle that is suitable for hunting and pest control.

The results obtained from testing the accuracy of the Benjamin 392 at 10 yards are shown in the appropriate table in Appendix B. The average group size for five three-shot groups ranged from 0.23 inch (Crosman Copperhead pointed and Daisy pointed pellets) to 0.36 inch (Beeman Crow Magnum pellet). The overall average group size was only 0.27 inch. As was observed for other rifles, the Beeman Crow Magnum pellet appears to be slightly less accurate than some other pellets. It does not seem to give top accuracy in any of the

Just as he did many years ago, the author enjoys being in the woods with a Benjamin.

rifles that I tested. However, it is plenty accurate for its intended uses.

The data shows that the Benjamin 392 is capable of fine accuracy. My rifle has a trigger pull that is much better than that of my .177 caliber Benjamin. All of the pellets fired for accuracy performed well, but the Crosman Premier and the Dynamit Nobel RWS Meisterkugeln did not perform any better than the inexpensive Crosman Copperhead and Daisy pointed pellets. The data shows that the Benjamin 392 is capable of considerably better accuracy than the 1/2 inch at 33 feet indicated by the manufacturer.

In addition to being a potent air rifle, the Benjamin has the accuracy necessary to be a very effective game and pest rifle. This gun is truly an American legend. However, it is really strenuous to pump, especially when a scope is attached. With all things considered, the Benjamin is a superb air rifle. If I had to start disposing of my air rifles, the .22 caliber Benjamin would be among the last to go.

Velocity and Number of Pumps

There is always some question as to what velocity is produced by multi-pump pneumatic rifles as the number of pumps is varied. In performing that evaluation, each of the .20 and .22 caliber rifles was fired with a specific type of pellet using a number of pumps varying from two to the maximum specified for the gun. While it might be desirable to perform this test with many different types of pellets, this introduces another variable, the variation in pellet weight, which will be addressed later. Therefore, a single

Velocity Per Number of Pumps for .22 Caliber Rifles

Velocity in fps for the combination given

Pumps	Benjamin 392, Crosman Pointed	Crosman 2200B, Crosman Pointed	Daisy 22X Daisy Pointed
2	397	336	279
3	468	425	329
4	526	450	369
5	567	472	398
6	597	508	430
7	623	521	442
8	644	544	460
9	NR	562	478
10	NR	580	493

type of pellet was used with each rifle. The velocities produced by using different numbers of pumps are shown in the table.

The table shows that the velocity does not change nearly as much per pump when the maximum number of pumps is approached as it does in the middle of the range. This is widely known, and it is the reason that many users of multi-pump pneumatics rarely pump their guns to the maximum number allowed.

These results show that the Benjamin 392 is a powerful rifle even when only five or six pumps are used. The Crosman 2200B at 10 pumps delivers a velocity that is very close to the published maximum of 595 fps. The Daisy 22X was tested with the Daisy Pointed pellet, which is a heavy one at 15.68 grains. Therefore, with this pellet, its top velocity is below the published maximum of 550 fps. With some of the lighter pellets, the velocity was well over 500 fps.

The tests show clearly that the last couple of pumps accomplish very little as far as increasing velocity is concerned. This indicates that for all practical purposes, using two or three pumps below the maximum number is sufficient for almost all uses.

Maximum Pellet Velocities

There is a persistent question regarding the maximum velocity produced by a pellet rifle when different pellets are used. This question is central to the issue of maximum advertised velocity, but actual data is rarely seen. Therefore, each of the .22 rifles was tested at its maximum number of pumps with all of the types of .22 pellets on hand. The velocities obtained with the various types of pellets are shown in this table.

Examination of the data shown in the table below reveals several interesting features. First, all of the rifles give velocities that are slightly lower than the published maximums for these air rifles. However, in all fairness, the Crosman 2200B was tested at only eight pumps, while the owner's manual gave a maximum of 10 pumps for this gun at the time of its manufacture. With 10 pumps, the Crosman 2200B gave a velocity of 587 fps with the Gamo Match and 592 fps with the Ruko Match. With 10 pumps, the rifle also gave a velocity of 572 fps with the Beeman Silver Jet pellet. Thus, the Crosman 2200B is very close to the published value for the highest velocity (595 fps), and it would certainly meet or exceed that value if some of the very light .22

Maximum Velocities for .22 Caliber Rifles With 20 Pellet Types

Pellet	Velocity in fps		
	Daisy 22X (10 Pumps)	Crosman 2200B (8 Pumps)	Benjamin 392 (8 Pumps)
Beeman Crow Magnum	449	471	557
Beeman Kodiak	409	426	534
Beeman Silver Jet	501	533	638
Beeman Silver Sting	489	509	622
Benjamin Diabolo	506	546	646
Crosman Pointed	509	544	644
Crosman Premier	500	543	626
Crosman Wadcutter	507	543	640
Daisy Pointed	488	508	623
D.N. RWS Meisterkugeln	511	548	647
D.N. RWS Superdome	497	537	638
D.N. RWS Superpoint	499	533	643
D.N. RWS Super-H-Point	510	544	650
Eley Wasp	458	532	617
Gamo Hunter	489	522	632
Gamo Magnum	494	522	632
Gamo Master Point	478	510	616
Gamo Match	511	556	657
Ruko Magnum II	492	522	626
Ruko Match	514	560	659
Advertised Maximum	550	595	685

Excellent accuracy was obtained with the Benjamin 392, but attaching a scope makes it awkward to pump.

pellets were used. Those who market some spring-piston air rifles regularly do this.

Second, with most pellets tested, the Benjamin 392 gives velocities that are a little below the advertised maximum velocity of 685 fps. This is not uncommon, and the difference is slight. When the Gamo Match or the Ruko Match pellets are used, the velocities are 657 and 659 fps, respectively. With some of the really light pellets that are available (10 to 11 grains), there is no doubt that a velocity of 685 fps could be reached.

Third, the Daisy PowerLine 22X gives velocities that are also somewhat below the advertised maximum of 550 fps. However, this little gun simply cannot drive heavy pellets that fast. With the lighter Gamo Match and Ruko Match, it managed to give 511 and 514 fps, respectively. With a really light pellet, a velocity of 535 fps was obtained. Keep in mind that the manufacturer has an acceptability window for velocity that is rather large. Temperature, lubrication, pumping routine, and other factors influence velocity. Within reason, the maximum velocity achieved is less important than velocity uniformity and accuracy. The testing shows that all of the guns gave highly reproducible velocities.

With a really heavy pellet like the Beeman Kodiak (21.41 grains), the maximum velocities are quite low. The average .22 caliber pellet weighs around 14.3 grains and some of the

match pellets are even lighter. These are the pellets that are normally used in velocity testing to get high values.

Finally, examination of the maximum velocities shown in the table suggests that the velocity is inversely related to pellet weight. With each gun, the highest velocity obtained was with the Ruko Match pellet, which at 13.86 grains was the lightest pellet tested. The velocities with the Beeman Kodiak were quite low, but it is an enormous pellet.

While the maximum velocities obtained generally decrease with increasing pellet weight, it is worth doing a little more detailed analysis of the data. The first thing to try when looking for a trend in data is to prepare a graph, in this case a graph of maximum velocity vs. pellet weight. In fact, we need such a graph for each of the three .22 caliber rifles tested as was done in Chapter 5 for the .177 caliber rifles. Therefore, a graph was prepared showing pellet velocity vs. pellet weight for each rifle.

Each of the graphs clearly indicates a good inverse relationship between the maximum velocity obtained and the pellet weight. Note that for the Benjamin 392 and the Daisy 22X, one point lies quite far below the line in each case. That point corresponds to the Eley Wasp pellet for which the velocities were low considering that the pellet weighs 14.43 grains. This pellet was difficult to chamber in both the Benjamin 392 and Daisy 22X. In fact, one of these pellets would not chamber in my wife's Daisy and it had to be forced out of the muzzle with a rod.

The skirt of the Eley Wasp measures .230 inch and it is quite thick. In the Benjamin 392 and Daisy 22X rifles, it is simply hard to squeeze the skirt down to about 0.224 inch to chamber the pellet and that results in a low velocity. While the Eley Wasp weighs only 14.43 grains, it gave velocities from the Daisy 22X that are lower than those with the Gamo Master Point that weighs 16.32 grains. Despite the considerable weight difference, the velocities produced by these two pellets were virtually identical in the Benjamin. The Eley Wasp chambered easily in the Crosman 2200 and gave a velocity that is in line with its weight. It should be mentioned that in .177 caliber, the Eley Wasp behaved normally with all of the rifles.

In view of the fact that the pellets have different diameters, skirt thicknesses, weight distributions, etc., it is remarkable that the relationship between velocity and pellet weight is so uniform. With these relationships, the owner of one of these guns can determine the weight of the pellet being used and estimate the maximum velocity attainable rather closely. The fact that the relationships are so uniform also is a tribute to the excellence of these fine air rifles.

Conclusions

This chapter and Chapter 5 contain a large amount of data that resulted from a great deal of experimentation and experience with American multi-pump air rifles. There is no way to describe the performance of a large number of air rifles without showing the data that forms the basis for the analysis. However, the results show, quite possibly for the first time, what you should realistically be able to get out of your multi-pump pneumatic air rifles. It has been declared in some circles that this type of air rifle is of marginal accuracy because the pumping procedure is not very reproducible. For most of the rifle/pellet combinations, the accuracy is anything but mediocre. The data obtained by determining velocities using a chronograph should help to dispel that myth. All of the multi-pump guns gave very reproducible velocities that were at least as good as those obtained from the break-action rifles tested.

Note that air rifles having velocities of more than 500 fps have severe restrictions for export to Canada. Several of the air rifles tested in this work are available in a lower powered "export" version. These should not show up in the United States, but it can happen. It has happened to me twice, so read the box to determine the maximum velocity specification, not just the model number. Uniform velocity is only one factor in determining accuracy. The groups obtained show that these guns, while not match rifles, are certainly capable of fine sporting accuracy even if they are not suitable for competitive target shooting, not that a multi-pump pneumatic would be chosen for competition anyway. If only the smallest group obtained was given as the "accuracy" of each gun, as is done for some of the imports, they would appear quite accurate!

While on the subject of accuracy, another factor must be considered. When a spring-piston rifle is fired, a large, heavy piston and spring lurch forward when the sear is released. This happens before the pellet leaves the barrel. This much mass changing position causes motion of the rifle, which makes it difficult to control the gun as the shot is being taken. The shooter of this type of air rifle must learn to hold it in precisely the same way for each shot if accurate and reproducible shooting is to be achieved. When a multi-pump pneumatic rifle is fired, only air rushes forward and the rifle remains essentially stationary. You may have to pump a spring piston rifle only once, but there is no free lunch. They are not easier to shoot accurately.

We have already mentioned that the imported air rifles are tested with the lightest pellets available in order to achieve the high advertised velocities (this is known as marketing). The results obtained in this work show that there is a good correlation between pellet weight and the maximum velocity for a given rifle. We can now estimate the velocity that would result if a .177 caliber rifle were tested with a 6.7-grain pellet to that produced with a 7.9 grain pellet. For example, if a Benjamin 397 gives a velocity of 725 fps with a 7.9 grain pellet, it would give approximately (7.9/6.7) x 725 = 855 fps with a 6.7 grain pellet. That means that a Benjamin 397 is comparable in power to many of the spring-piston rifles.

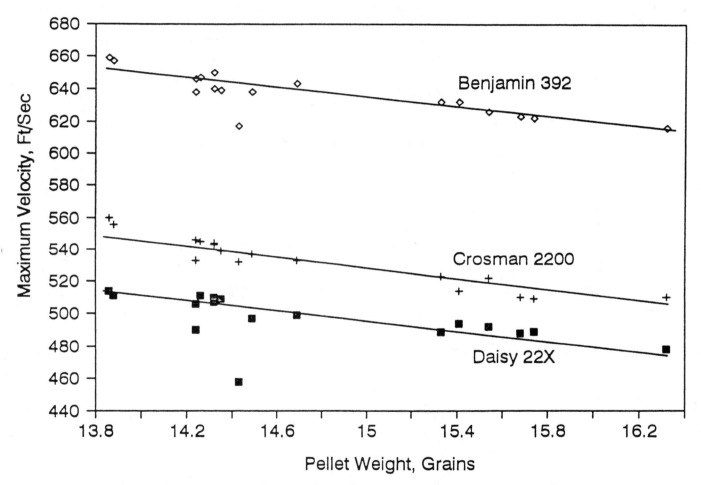

Relationship between pellet weight and velocity in three pneumatic pellet guns.

In .20 caliber, a light pellet used to test spring-piston rifles weighs 9.2 grains. If a Sheridan gives a velocity of 600 fps with a 14.3-grain pellet, it would give approximately 750 to 775 fps with a pellet weighing 9.7 grains. Even the 10.32-grain Beeman H&N Match pellet gave well more than 700 fps in the Sheridans.

Some spring-piston rifles in .22 caliber are tested with a pellet weighing 11.9 grains. If a Benjamin 392 gives a 14.3-grain pellet a velocity of 640 fps, this would be equivalent to a velocity of perhaps 750 fps with the light pellet.

One of my spring-piston rifles gives a velocity that is more than 200 fps lower than that advertised. The reason is that I normally shoot a pellet weighing about 35 percent more than that used to give the "maximum" velocity of the rifle.

Of course the calculated velocities above are approximations, but they show that the more powerful American multi-pump pneumatics are not too far behind the spring-piston arms in power. Given the fact that the pneumatics are smaller, lighter, and less expensive, they certainly provide an attractive alternative as serious airguns. Let me state once again that the spring-piston rifles are beautiful, capable instruments that give outstanding performance. I own some and I enjoy using them. The results obtained by testing three of them were presented in the previous chapter. However, they are not the only competent airguns available.

Other aspects of the performance of the American air rifles discussed in this chapter and Chapter 5 will be examined in Chapters 7, 8, and 10. The results obtained certainly demonstrate that these fine guns give excellent performance for their cost, and one or more of them should meet most of your airgun needs.

CHAPTER 7

THE PELLET'S PUNCH

We are in an energy crisis in this country. Energy is required to heat and cool buildings, provide lighting, transport people and goods, and is used for numerous other activities. Energy is almost the basis for our way of life. All types of firearms operate because of energy changes, and so do airguns.

This is a book about *airguns*. Consequently, in order to understand how airguns operate, we need to understand a few basic concepts about energy from physics. Don't get worried. You used the same principles when you picked up this book. Guns that use gases other than air for propulsion, whether the gas is carbon dioxide (CO_2) or some other compressed gas, will not be discussed specifically. However, much of what is presented in terms of the basic principles of propulsion is equally applicable to all types of air and gas rifles. Unless you are already knowledgeable about how airguns work, this chapter will give you the information you need to understand what goes on inside your air rifle.

Energy stored in stretched bands of a slingshot or compressed air in an airgun can be used to launch projectiles.

A compressed gas, such as the CO_2 in these cylinders, makes an effective propellant.

What is Ballistics?

The science of *ballistics* deals with the launching of projectiles and their flight characteristics. *Internal* ballistics deals with the forces acting on a projectile and the motion of the projectile inside the launching device. *External* ballistics deals with the motion of a projectile after it leaves the muzzle, which is the bullet's flight. At an advanced level, both areas of ballistics involve some very complicated physics, and they involve problems that are too sophisticated to be dealt with in a book such as this. However, as this is a user's guide to airguns, some of the practical considerations related to the propulsion and flight of a pellet need to be described. You need not be a rocket scientist to comprehend the basic principles. Most of them are directly observable in daily experiences.

It may seem that since air rifles are short-range guns, there would be no reason to study the flight of pellets. Perhaps in toppling pop cans this is true, but for serious work, either target or hunting, such knowledge is valuable. A crow at 40 yards is an entirely different proposition than a paper target at 10 meters. Therefore, the more you know about the flight of pellets, the better. Moreover, it is valuable to understand the behavior of different types of pellets, especially if you are somewhat unsure of the distance to the target. In this chapter, some of the basic principles of internal ballistics of airguns will be explained in an elementary fashion. Chapter 8 will present a simplified view of pellet flight for the air gunner. Together, these chapters provide a basis for further study and experimentation.

Air Power

Air is available everywhere and it is one of a very small number of things still free of charge. The ammunition for an air rifle consists only of the projectiles or pellets. This makes an air rifle enormously efficient in terms of weight and volume required for carrying and storing ammunition. It also means that air rifles are quite economical to shoot.

Sir Isaac Newton's First Law of Motion says (among other things) that an object at rest remains at rest unless it is acted upon by a net force. In order to move a projectile, there must be some net force acting on the projectile. In the case of a slingshot, that force is supplied by the stretched bands. In the case of an arrow, the force is supplied by the flexed

This .177 caliber Crosman Copperhead domed pellet fired from a Daisy 880 has just shown its power by penetrating a 5/8-inch board.

limbs of the bow. To explain how airguns work, we will first give an elementary description of what happens when a firearm is fired.

In the case of guns, the force on the bullet is supplied by the rapid expansion of gas under high pressure. Firearms use propellant powders that burn to generate a large volume of gas in a very short time. That gas, expanding as it does, forces the projectile down the bore with increasing velocity until it leaves the barrel. In a general way, increasing the amount of powder (within limits!) increases the velocity of the projectile. Likewise, increasing the length of the barrel gives the expanding gases a longer distance to push on the base of the bullet, which also results in the bullet achieving higher velocity. The burning powder generates gas that produces a high pressure inside the arm.

Pressure is defined as the amount of force per unit of area, and one familiar set of units is *pounds per square inch*, lb./in.² (sometimes written as psi). Thus, we can write the expression for pressure (*P*) as:

$$P = \frac{F}{A}$$ (1)

where *F* is the force and *A* is the area. Modern firearms have pressures as high as 50,000 psi generated when firing occurs, while the average pressure inside an automobile tire is about 30 psi.

The area of a circle (the circular base of the bullet) is given by the square of the radius times 3.142 (pi). A .30-caliber bullet, which has a diameter of 0.308 inch or a radius of 0.154 inch, has an area of its base that is

Area = πr² = 3.142 (0.154 in.)² = 0.0745 in² (2)

Therefore, if the chamber pressure is 50,000 psi, the force on the base of the bullet is obtained by solving Equation (1) for *F* and substituting the known quantities.

F = *P* x *A* = 50,000 psi x 0.0745 in.² = 3,726 lbs. (3)

A force of this magnitude accelerates the bullet down the bore at an enormous rate.

So what does this have to do with the velocity of the projectile? First, a very small amount of physics that deals with the motion of objects needs to be reviewed. The *velocity* of a moving object is the distance it travels per unit of time. It may be expressed as miles per hour (mph), feet per second (fps), or meters per second (mps). For bullets and pellets, the usual units are feet per second (fps) or meters per second (mps). One meter is equivalent to 3.267 feet.

Acceleration is the rate of change in velocity over time. For example, when an object is dropped from a great height, it increases its velocity by 32.16 fps for each second of fall. In other words, the acceleration due to gravity is 32.16 fps per second or 32.16 fps². This acceleration is equivalent to 9.80 mps².

A projectile (either a bullet or pellet) originally has a velocity of zero while it is resting in the chamber. When the gun is fired, the projectile increases in velocity as it moves down the bore. In other words, the projectile is accelerated. What is the connection between the acceleration of the projectile and the force acting on its base?

The relationship between force and acceleration is given by Newton's Second Law of Motion, which can be written as:

$$\text{Force} = \text{Mass} \times \text{Acceleration} \qquad (4)$$
$$F = M \times A$$

As was mentioned earlier, the force acting on projectiles from the various types of guns is supplied by the expansion of gas. In a firearm, the gas is generated by the combustion of the powder, which is a solid before it burns. In gas-propellant guns (regardless of whether the gas is air or carbon dioxide), a compressed gas is allowed to expand at the time the gun is discharged. The gas is allowed to occupy a much larger volume, but at a lower pressure (the pressure of the atmosphere). Thus, a gas initially at some high pressure (P_1) occupies a small volume (V_1) and it expands to a larger volume (V_2) at the ambient atmospheric pressure (P_2). The physical law that relates changes in pressure and volume for a given amount of gas is known as Boyle's Law and it can be written as:

$$P_1 \times V_1 = P_2 \times V_2 \qquad (5)$$

This equation says that the pressure of the gas multiplied by the volume of the gas is the same before and after the gas expands.

When an air rifle is discharged, the compressed air expands, which pushes the pellet down the bore. Not much can be done about the atmospheric pressure (normally about 14.7 psi), which will be the final pressure of the expanded air. How much the gas expands (to its final volume, V_2) will be determined by the initial volume of the gas (V_1) and the pressure to which it is compressed (P_1). The internal volume of the gas reservoir in an air rifle is small, but it is the same from shot to shot. Its volume is determined by the design of the rifle. What does change is the pressure to which the gun is pumped. Modern multi-pump air rifles achieve pressures of 800 to

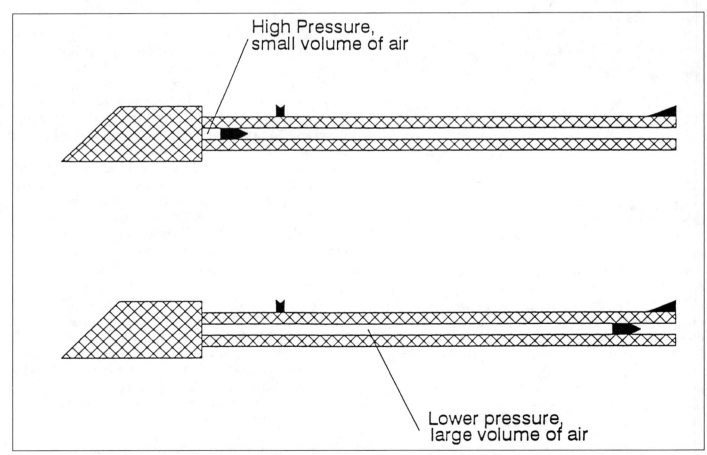

High Pressure,
small volume of air

Lower pressure,
large volume of air

As the pellet moves down the bore, the air pressure decreases because the volume of air behind the pellet gets larger. Therefore, the force on the base of the pellet decreases continuously as the pellet moves.

Even though power is important, accuracy is more important, and only extensive testing will show what type of pellet your rifle shoots best.

1,200 psi in the compressed air reservoir. This is sufficient to accelerate pellets to velocities of several hundred fps as the pellet moves down the barrel.

Acceleration of the pellet as it passes down the barrel is not uniform. It is much more rapid in the first few inches of travel. In other words, a barrel 24 inches long will not give a velocity twice that produced in a barrel 12 inches long. The reason is that the pressure in the air rifle is highest at the time of discharge and it decreases as the pellet starts to move, which allows the gas to expand to a larger volume and thus lowers the pressure. This results in a smaller net force acting on the pellet the farther down the barrel it moves. Also, as the pellet moves down the barrel, it encounters resistance from the air inside the barrel. The faster the pellet is moving, the greater this air resistance will be. The pellet will be moving faster the farther down the barrel it is, but its rate of velocity increase will be lower.

Pellet Power

For many years, the debate has raged as to what constitutes bullet effectiveness on game. One school of thought teaches that the major factor is bullet velocity, while the other teaches that bullet weight is the most important quantity. To substantiate these points of view, a variety of numerical indices have been developed. The equations involved are usually developed so that the point of view of the developer is supported by some calculated "index of lethality" or stopping power. This debate is alive and well in connection with the use of air rifles on living targets. One group feels that a 7.9-grain, .177 caliber pellet traveling at 1,000 fps is more devastating to animate objects than is a 14.3-grain, .22 caliber pellet traveling at 650 fps. The other group feels the opposite. Who is correct? What other factors are involved? How can you decide what gun/pellet combination to use for hunting and pest control? We will now attempt to throw some light on this subject.

One of the considerations that is relevant to any discussion of pellet effectiveness is kinetic energy, the energy it possesses because of its motion. If you ever have been hit by a thrown baseball, you know what kinetic energy is. I once experienced it when I was hit in the back of the head by a rock from my brother's slingshot. This is a simple equation from elementary physics for kinetic

$$KE = \frac{1}{2}mv^2 \tag{6}$$

energy, where m is the mass of the moving object and v is its velocity.

Weight and *mass* are not the same, and we need to know the mass of the moving object to use the equation. The *weight* of an object is a measure of the force that gravity exerts on the object. A barbell that weighs 180 pounds on earth would weigh about 30 pounds on the moon because the force of gravity on the moon is about one-sixth of that on earth. However, *mass* is the amount of matter (how much stuff) present and that is the same on earth as it is on the moon. A 180-pound barbell contains the same amount of iron regardless of where it is. Thus, the weight of an object depends on where the object is, but its mass does not. A

baseball moving at 90 mph would hit you with the same energy on the earth or on the moon because its mass is the same. In order to use the equation above, we must know the *mass* of the pellet, not its *weight*.

We saw in an earlier section that Newton's Second Law of Motion is

$$\text{Force} = \text{Mass} \times \text{Acceleration} \tag{7}$$
$$F = M \times A$$

For falling objects, the force is the gravitational force and the acceleration is that due to gravity, which on earth is 32.16 feet per second per second (32.16 ft/sec^2 and it is usually labeled g). The force in the earth's gravitational field is usually given in *pounds* but bullet weights are given in grains. We need to know the relationship between *grains* and *pounds*, which is 1 pound = 7,000 grains. Because one pound is 7,000 grains, dividing the bullet weight in grains by 7,000 converts it to pounds. Since $F = MA$, solving for M when we use g instead of the acceleration, A, gives

$$M = \frac{F}{g} = \frac{\text{Bullet weight (grains)}}{7,000 \times 32.16} \tag{8}$$

Substituting this expression for mass in the equation for kinetic energy and noting that 7,000 x 32.16 = 225,120, we obtain

$$KE = \frac{1}{2}mv^2 = \frac{1}{2} \times \frac{\text{Bullet weight (grains)}}{225,120} \times v^2 \tag{9}$$

This equation can be simplified to give

$$KE = \frac{\text{Bullet weight (grains)}}{450,240} \times v^2 \tag{10}$$

The use of this equation will now be illustrated. It may look messy, but it is very simple.

Suppose a .177 caliber pellet weighing 7.9 grains is moving at 900 fps. What is its kinetic energy?

$$KE = \frac{7.9}{450,240} \times 900^2 = 14.2 \text{ ft lbs} \tag{11}$$

For comparison, a .22 long rifle has about 140 foot-pounds at the muzzle, so it is immediately obvious that even a powerful air rifle is feeble compared to a .22 rimfire *firearm*. Sup-

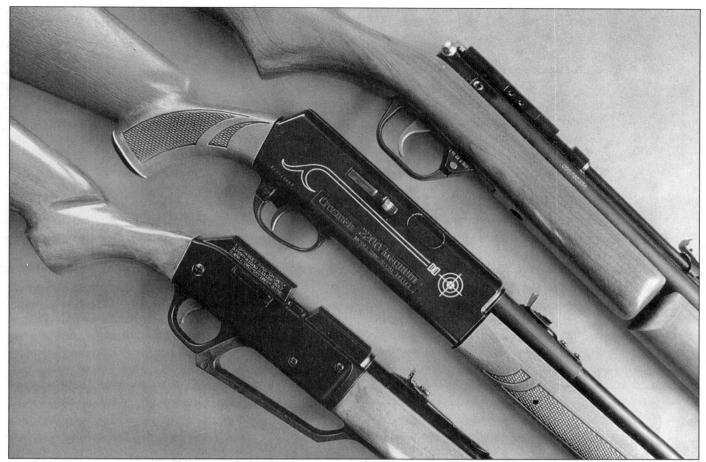

These three .22 caliber rifles deliver magnum or near-magnum performance. They are, from top, the Benjamin 392, the Crosman 2200B, and the Daisy 22X.

pose a 14.3-grain, .22 caliber pellet is moving at 650 fps. What is its kinetic energy?

$$KE = \frac{14.3}{450,240} \times 650^2 = 13.4 \text{ ft lbs} \quad (12)$$

Many countries use the metric system with the kinetic energy expressed in joules. The conversion factor is 1 foot-pound = 1.356 *joules.*

A kinetic energy of 13.4 foot-pounds is equivalent to 18.2 joules as is shown in this simple calculation:

13.4 ft. lbs. x 1.356 joules/ft. lb. = 18.2 joules

The term "magnum" is sometimes applied to air rifles that produce more than about 12 foot-pounds of energy. Such guns are considered to be "high-powered" weapons that are suitable for pest control and small-game hunting. Many .177 caliber pellets weigh 7.9 grains while .20 and .22 caliber pellets weigh 14.3 grains. This means that an average .177 pellet must be driven about 825 fps to constitute a "magnum" by providing 12 foot-pounds of kinetic energy while a .20 or .22 pellet traveling at 615 fps may be considered a "magnum." In fact, air rifles producing energies greater than 12 foot-pounds are considered firearms in Britain, and they are subject to severe restrictions. A similar situation exists in Germany.

It is interesting that the two countries that produce most of the high-powered spring-piston guns are among the most restrictive on their possession! Clearly, the powerful air rifles are produced for export, primarily to the United States, since Canada and other countries have restrictions on air rifles that have muzzle velocities greater than 500 fps. We are indeed fortunate in the United States that airguns are not yet so regulated, but some localities and states do have restrictions on ordering airguns by mail and their use.

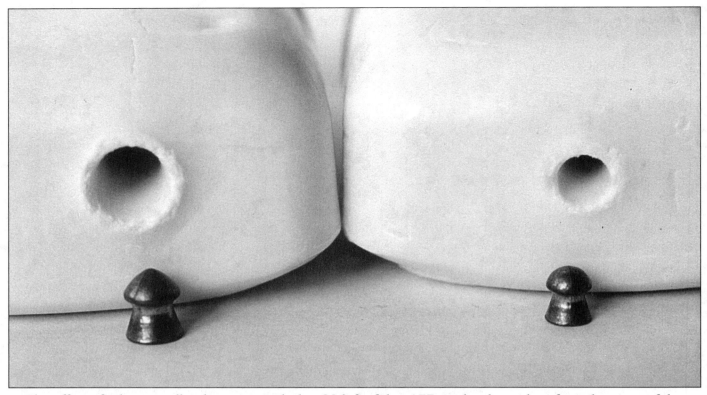

The effect of a larger pellet diameter, with the .22 left of the .177, is clearly evident from the sizes of the entrance holes in bars of soap.

From the foregoing discussion and the data presented in earlier chapters, it is clear that the Benjamin and Sheridan .20 and .22 caliber rifles meet the criterion of 12 foot-pounds for magnum status, since they have muzzle velocities that are above 615 fps. However, a few other American air rifles come very close. For example, the Benjamin Model 397 (.177 caliber, 800 fps, 11.2 foot-pounds), the Crosman 2200 (.22 caliber, 595 fps, 11.2 foot-pounds), the Daisy 22X (.22 caliber, 550 fps, 9.6 foot-pounds) and the Crosman 2100 (.177 caliber, 725 fps, 9.2 foot-pounds) come very close to fitting in the magnum category. Moreover, game is not usually shot an inch from the muzzle, so muzzle energy is not the only consideration. As we will discuss later, pellet design and downrange performance vary considerably, so the models listed above can be very effective with the right ammunition and good shot placement.

Internal Forces

When a pneumatic air rifle is pumped, air is compressed in a reservoir. At the time of discharge, the compressed air is released, forcing the pellet down the barrel. Let us now show how this translates into the kinetic energy of the pellet.

Suppose the internal pressure in a .177 caliber pneumatic is 800 psi before discharge. The *radius* of the .177 pellet is one-half the diameter or 0.0885 inches so the *area* of the base of the pellet is

$$A = \pi r^2 = 3.1416 \times (0.0885 \text{ in.})^2 = 0.0246 \text{ in.}^2 \quad (13)$$

Therefore, if a pressure of 800 psi operates on the base of the pellet, the force generated is

force = pressure x area

$$F = P \times A = 800 \text{ lb/in.}^2 \times 0.0246 \text{ in.}^2 = 19.7 \text{ lbs.} \quad (14)$$

Thus, a force of 19.7 pounds is generated on the pellet to force it down the bore. However, a great deal of this force is required to overcome friction and move the pellet. If you force a pellet through the bore of an air rifle with a cleaning rod, you will be convinced of this fact. Furthermore, as the pellet moves faster and faster down the bore, it meets with greater resistance from the air inside the bore. Therefore, the *effective* or *net* force on the pellet that results in its acceleration is considerably *less* than that generated by the compressed air.

Let us use these basic principles to determine the kinetic energy an air rifle should produce. Suppose that the force generated on the base of a .177 caliber pellet by the compressed air is 15 pounds at the time of firing and that it drops to 5 pounds by the time the pellet exits the muzzle. The pressure drop does not actually decrease in a linear way as the pellet passes down the bore, but let us assume that it does in order to simplify the problem. In that case, the average force on the base of the bullet is midway between the initial 15 pounds and final 5 pounds (which is calculated as $(15 + 5)/2 = 10$ pounds). Further, let us *estimate* the force necessary to push the pellet against the force of friction and air in the bore as 5 pounds. That leaves a net force of only 5 pounds pushing on the pellet to accelerate it as it moves down the bore. If the rifle has a 24-inch (2-foot) barrel, a force of 5 pounds operating over a distance of 2 feet imparts an energy to the pellet that is the force times the distance:

$$5 \text{ lbs.} \times 2 \text{ ft.} = 10 \text{ ft. lbs.}$$

This is approximately the kinetic energy of a 7.9-grain, .177 pellet moving at 755 fps.

We see from the foregoing discussion that to achieve higher velocity, we could increase the pressure of the compressed air, reduce the weight and/or friction of the pellet, or use a longer barrel. There is a practical upper limit to the pressure, but increasing the number of pumps certainly does increase the velocity of the pellet. The use of longer barrels is not practical after about 16 to 20 inches, because by the time the pellet reaches a point near the muzzle, the air has expanded so much and the pressure is so low that the friction of the pellet in the bore is as great as the force of the air on the base of the pellet. Thus, there is no gain in velocity and, in fact, the velocity may actually be less in a longer barrel. This is exactly the case in the .22 rimfire, where the small powder charge burns quickly and maximum velocity is achieved in about 16 to 18 inches of barrel length.

It is well-known that some of the very high velocities (for airguns) reported for imported spring-piston air rifles are achieved using the lightest weight pellets available. However, as we shall see, these projectiles lose their velocity very quickly. Pellet designs that reduce fric-tion are another matter entirely. The "waist" of a pellet allows only the skirt (base) and the head to make contact with the walls of the barrel. This reduces friction and results in higher velocities than would result if the pellet were cylindrical and contacted the bore over the entire length of the pellet.

The same type of analysis can be performed by considering a .22 caliber air rifle. The area of the base of a pellet of .22 caliber (a diameter of 0.224 inches, radius 0.112 inches) is:

$$A = \pi r^2 = 3.1416 \times (0.112 \text{ in.})^2 = 0.0394 \text{ in.}^2 \quad (15)$$

If the pressure of the compressed air is 800 psi at the time of the shot, the force on the base of the bullet is:

$$F = P \times A = 0.0394 \text{ in.}^2 \times 800 \text{ lb./in.}^2 = 31.5 \text{ lbs.}$$

It looks as if the larger pellet should gain a much greater kinetic energy than the .177 pellet. However, there are a couple of tradeoffs here. First, the larger pellet has more bearing surface on the bore, so friction is greater for a .22 caliber pellet than for one of .177 caliber. Second, the volume of the bore is much greater in a .22 caliber gun than it is in a .177 caliber. Therefore, the compressed air is expanding into a larger volume and the pressure drops more quickly. As a result, the force on the base of the bullet decreases more rapidly than it does in a smaller bore. In actual practice, a .22 caliber pellet will acquire a greater kinetic energy than will a .177 caliber pellet if the guns operate at the same initial pressure, but the difference is not nearly as great as would be indicated by the difference in bore diameter. Thus, an initial pressure of 800 psi might give 8 to 10 foot-pounds of kinetic energy to a .177 pellet, but 12 to 14 foot-pounds to a .22 caliber pellet. While the .177 pellet will achieve a higher velocity than one in .22 caliber, the .22 pellet will attain a greater kinetic energy.

We have simplified the consideration of internal ballistics greatly. First, the actual internal pressure in the compressed air chamber is not known, but it is in the 800 to 1,200 psi range. The best the author could get was "it has never been measured but that sounds about right" from some technicians at the factories. Second, the drop in air pressure as the pellet moves down the bore is not *linear*, as was assumed, but we have not used an actual mathematical function to describe it. To do so would involve mathematics beyond the level of this book. Third, the friction and air resistance retarding the motion of the pellet is undoubtedly not the same all along the bore. Friction should be greatest at the beginning of pellet travel when the rifling first cuts grooves in the pellet. Air resistance would be highest near the muzzle, where the pellet velocity is the highest. These forces must vary in some complex way with the velocity of the pellet, which is changing as it moves out the barrel. An exact analysis of an air rifle's internal ballistics is complex. However, the basic ideas presented in this section are sound and they give reasonable estimates to the behavior of a pellet.

We set out initially to provide an elementary analysis of the operation of guns powered by compressed gas. The analysis given in this chapter is only an introduction, but it illustrates how these wonderful devices work.

Effect of Altitude

On our trips to the Big Horn Mountains of Wyoming, my wife and I take along a couple of air rifles. There is a lot of space to roam around in, and our air rifles provide plenty of fun. Where we spend much of our time is at an altitude of 8,400 feet. As I became more involved with research on air rifle performance, it became apparent that I should take a chronograph to the mountains. Things just might not be what they seem.

At sea level, atmospheric pressure will support a column of mercury 76 centimeters or 29.92 inches high. This pressure, equivalent to 14.70 psi, is one atmosphere. At high altitude, atmospheric pressure is lower because part of the atmosphere lies below you. There are fewer gas molecules (oxygen and nitrogen) in a given volume of air as one goes higher in altitude.

When fired at high altitude, both multi-pump and break-action rifles give lower velocity.

The Daisy 880 is easy to pump, but each stroke gives a smaller velocity increase at high altitude.

When you give a multi-pump rifle a pump stroke, a chamber fills with air. Completing the stroke forces the air into a reservoir under pressure. The next stroke adds more air and further increases the pressure inside the reservoir. Completing eight or 10 pump strokes (depending on the maximum number for that particular rifle) gives maximum pressure.

If each pump stroke is filling a chamber with air that gets forced into the reservoir, the amount of air must depend on the number of molecules of gas contained in the chamber. At high elevation, the air is "thinner," so 10 pump strokes would not give the same pressure in the reservoir as they would near sea level. I had thought this through in the abstract and figured that it probably would not make much difference. On the moon, where there is no atmosphere, you could

pump as many times as you want, but there would be no compressed air in the reservoir. However, it did seem to me that my air rifles did not shoot quite the same in the mountains as they did at home, where the elevation is 820 feet.

Now I found myself at an elevation of 8,400 feet with airguns and a chronograph! The rifles were a Daisy 856, Daisy 880, and a Sheridan Silver Streak. The Daisy 880 is about 10 years old and is one of the metal-receiver versions. The behavior of all three rifles had been well-studied at an elevation of 820 feet, and their performance is absolutely predictable. After getting the chronograph set up, the Daisy 856 was given 10 pumps and loaded with a Dynamit Nobel RWS Meisterkugeln pellet. Upon firing, the chronograph showed 559 fps from a rifle that averages 622 fps at an elevation of 820 feet! This test was repeated with several other pellets with similar results. Next, the old Daisy 880 was tested. With each type of pellet, the velocity was 10 to 12 percent lower than that rifle normally gives.

These results were so intriguing that another series of tests was conducted at the Buffalo, Wyo., rifle range, where the altitude is 5,500 feet. At this altitude, the velocities were intermediate between those obtained at 820 feet and 8,400 feet, exactly as expected. The results obtained with the Daisy rifles at all three altitudes are summarized in the table (page 119).

When fired at an elevation of 5,500 feet, both the Daisy 856 and Daisy 880 lose about 4 to 5 percent in velocity, depending on the pellet. There is a similar loss as the elevation changes from 5,500 feet to 8,400 feet. Overall, the two Daisy rifles gave velocities at 8,400 feet that are 88 to 92 percent of what they shoot at 820 feet. The Sheridan Silver Streak showed a similar velocity loss. A 10 percent reduction in velocity corresponds to a 19 per-

cent reduction in kinetic energy. For plinking, this is of no consequence, but it has more serious implications if you are using an air rifle at high altitude for hunting and pest control. You may wish to select a more powerful rifle than you initially thought was necessary after reviewing the data (see Chapter 10).

These results show that the two Daisy rifles lose 8 to 12 percent of their velocity when fired at an altitude of 8,400 feet, compared to when they are fired at 820 feet above sea level. I wish I could have tested all of my multi-pump pneumatics in the mountains, but there is a limit to how many airguns can be crowded into the truck when traveling for several weeks. I have no doubt that other models would give similar results.

The other multi-pump pneumatic in my summer airgun arsenal was a Sheridan Silver Streak. This rifle was tested at 5,500 and 8,400 feet, using four types of pellets. The table (top of next page) shows the results obtained when eight pumps were used.

Velocity measurements made at an elevation of 5,500 feet gave the data shown in the tables.

A Comparison of Velocity Obtained at Three Elevations (10 pumps)

	Daisy 856 Velocity Altitude, ft.			Daisy 880 Velocity Altitude, ft.		
Pellet	820	5,500	8,400	820	5,500	8,400
Beeman Crow Magnum	619	589	536	674	631	600
Beeman Silver Sting	633	590	556	665	621	604
Crosman domed	622	589	558	677	637	621
Crosman pointed	626	596	573	682	633	620
Crosman Premier (L)	615	594	571	682	632	619
Crosman Premier (H)	568	535	507	607	569	552
Crosman Wadcutter	628	600	573	679	638	623
Daisy pointed	656	625	589	700	657	644
Daisy Power Pellet	582	551	520	645	607	585
Daisy Wadcutter	637	615	583	684	653	634
RWS Meisterkugeln.	622	591	559	666	633	608
Gamo Hunter	643	610	582	694	653	632
Gamo Master Point	621	605	578	673	641	625

The results given by all the multi-pump rifles are simple to interpret. Each opening of the pumping chamber by swinging the pump lever admits a fixed volume of air, but there are fewer molecules in the same volume of the thinner air at high elevation. Therefore, less air is stored in the reservoir and the pellet is given lower velocity when the gun is fired.

But the break-action rifles are immune to this effect, aren't they? To answer this question, look at how they operate. Cocking the rifle moves a piston to the rear, against the tension of a strong spring. When the rifle is fired, the spring pushes the piston forward, compressing the air in a chamber. That chamber has a fixed volume and in the thinner air at high elevation, the chamber contains fewer molecules of gas (oxygen and nitrogen). As the piston moves forward, there is less air to be compressed and the pellet will not be given a velocity as high as it would get at lower altitude. In other words, the break-action rifles will shoot at lower velocity in higher elevations, exactly as the multi-pump rifles do.

To test this, the Gamo 500, Beeman S1, and the Gamo Hunter were fired at 5,500 and 8,400 feet above sea level with a variety of pellets. The results obtained are shown in a table that is given in Chapter 5. The velocities shown in that table indicate that there is a 5 to 7 percent loss in velocity when the altitude changes from 5,500 feet to 8,400 feet. In general, the velocity loss is at least as great as that for the multi-pump rifles, and possibly slightly greater.

Pre-charged pneumatic (PCP) rifles have a relatively large reservoir that is filled with air under high pressure (2,000 to 3,000 psi). If a PCP rifle is pumped up to a given pressure, the altitude will not make any difference because the pressure inside the reservoir is the same regardless of the altitude. However, you now need a source of compressed air or an external pump that can be used to charge the reservoir. If you are pumping up the reservoir at high altitude, you will have to pump a lot longer than you would at sea level. But because they are pre-charged to a given pressure, they will perform the same as long as that pressure is met initially.

Also, rifles powered by carbon dioxide (CO_2) will perform the same at any altitude because the pressure inside the gas cylinder is the same anywhere. It is determined by the nature of carbon dioxide and its tendency to vaporize.

Velocities From a Sheridan Silver Streak at Different Elevations

	Velocity, feet per second		
Pellet	820 ft.	5,500 ft.	8,400 ft.
Beeman Crow Magnum	623	606	584
Benjamin/Sheridan Cyl.	627	581	563
Benjamin/Sheridan Diabolo	630	586	562
Beeman H & N Match	716	663	622

However, the CO_2 rifles are highly dependent on temperature. The pressure generated by the CO_2 decreases rapidly as the temperature is decreased. In fact, the pressure, and therefore the velocity, is much lower at 50 degrees F than it is at 70 degrees F. The vapor pressure of carbon dioxide is 653 psi at 50 degrees F and 852 psi at 70 degrees F. Thus, a CO_2-powered rifle gives considerably lower velocity when fired at a temperature of 50 degrees F than it does at 70 degrees F.

While the reduction in velocity by multi-pump and break-action rifles is bad enough, the energy of a pellet depends on the square of the velocity. This means that if an air rifle gives 90 percent of its normal velocity at some high elevation, the pellet has only 81 percent of the energy it does at low elevation. For knocking pine cones off trees in the mountains, this does not make much difference. It does make a big difference if you are hunting marmots in the mountains with an air rifle.

A Misconception About Multi-Pump Rifles

When air is compressed, it undergoes a rise in temperature. There is a popular misconception that pumping up a pneumatic air rifle causes the air in the reservoir to be heated to a temperature that is considerably higher than that of the surrounding atmosphere. Then, as the gun is kept pumped up, the heat is slowly lost and as the temperature drops, the pressure in the reservoir drops. In this case, the velocity should be lower if the rifle remains pumped up for some time.

To test this, a Daisy 856 was given eight pumps and loaded with a Daisy pointed pellet. When fired immediately, the velocity was 609 fps. After pumping and loading again, the rifle was allowed to stand for 30 minutes and then fired. The velocity measured 606 fps. The two-shot test was repeated with identical results.

When a multi-pump rifle is pumped up, the pumping takes place over a time interval. Also,

The Daisy 22X is the least powerful .22 caliber rifle tested, but the larger pellets make it effective for pest control.

the amount of air compressed during each stroke is quite small. As a result, almost all of the heat generated by compressing the air is dissipated during the pumping. Allowing the pumped rifle to stand awhile does not cause the temperature to drop enough to produce any noticeable effect on pellet velocity.

Those who state that the velocity produced by multi-pump rifles is reduced because of heat loss from the compressed air probably have never tried it. As I said earlier, this is a popular misconception. Of course, a leaking valve will cause air loss, and this will show up if the gun is allowed to stand after pumping.

When a break-action rifle is cocked, a piston is moved to the rear against a strong spring and a chamber fills with air. When the rifle is fired, the piston is driven forward and all of the air in the chamber is compressed in a very short time interval. As a result, the air is heated to a very high temperature, and there is no opportunity for the heat to dissipate. The temperature is so high that combustible oils and solvents can be ignited. This behavior is known as "dieseling" and the rifle will emit smoke, either upon firing or when the gun is cocked for the next shot. Because of this, only oils designed specifically for airguns should be used to lubricate break-action rifles.

While some understanding of the internal forces at work in an air rifle is desirable, it is what happens after the pellet leaves the muzzle that counts most. What are the factors affecting the flight of pellets? How do pellets differ in their flight characteristics? How can my gun be sighted to maximize effectiveness at different ranges? The answers to some of these questions have not been readily available. There has been much less research on the paths of pellets than there has been on the flight of bullets. In the next chapter, some of my research and observations on the external ballistics of pellets will be summarized.

CHAPTER 8

THE PELLET'S PATH

When an outfielder throws a ball toward home plate, he does not throw it horizontally from shoulder height. If he did, the baseball would hit the ground before traveling very far. Instead, he throws the baseball somewhat upward so it will reach home plate as it comes down. In effect, he has "sighted in" on home plate. Precisely the same procedure is used in adjusting the sights on a rifle.

I once witnessed a remarkable display of shooting ability. In the top of a tree almost 100 yards away, two starlings were swaying back and forth in the breeze. A friend with a .22 rimfire declared that he would shoot the pair. At his first shot, nothing happened. At his second shot, the first starling fell from the tree to the ground, and the third shot took out the second bird. At that distance, there had to be

Before you can make use of ballistic calculations, the velocity must be known. A chronograph is essential, and you can buy a good one for around $100.

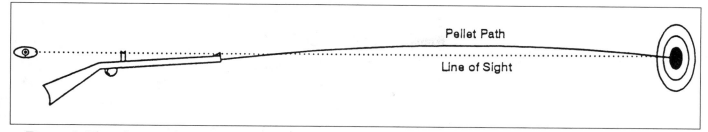

Figure 1: *This depicts the trajectory of a pellet when the rear sight is raised so that the gun is tipped slightly upward. The pellet strikes the point of aim at the target, but crosses the line of sight at a shorter distance.*

allowance made for the drop of the bullet and its deflection by the wind. My shooting buddy was successful only because he thoroughly understood the flight of the bullet and how distance and wind affected it.

Such knowledge is acquired through practice, but in this chapter, the basic principles will be described. Understanding these principles can make you a more effective shooter under field conditions.

Trajectory

The term trajectory applies to the path of a moving object. From the time a projectile leaves the muzzle, there are forces acting on it that prevent it from following a straight-line path. First, gravity acts on the projectile so that if it is fired horizontally, it begins its downward fall to earth. There is no such thing as a bullet that travels straight for a while, then starts to drop. Bullet drop begins immediately. If the projectile is fired vertically, the pull of gravity back toward the earth causes the projectile to lose velocity, eventually stopping and falling back to earth.

A second force acting on the projectile is that of air resistance. As a projectile moves through the air, it encounters a resistance caused by its having to "push" molecules of the air out of its path. The amount of air present at sea level under normal conditions is sufficient to cause a pressure of about 14.70 psi, which supports a column of mercury 29.92 inches or 76 centimeters in height. On top of Pike's Peak (elevation 14,002 feet), there is less air and the normal atmospheric pressure there is much less than it is at sea level. Therefore, a bullet fired on top of Pike's Peak will encounter less resistance from the air and it will lose velocity less rapidly than if it was

fired at sea level. Thus, we see that air resistance will vary with altitude.

For bullets moving slower than the speed of sound (about 1,100 fps, as in the case of almost all air rifles), the air resistance increases as the velocity of the bullet increases. A projectile moving at 800 fps will have much more air resistance acting on it than will the same projectile moving at 600 fps. Therefore, the faster projectile will lose its velocity more rapidly, but, of course, it will always be moving faster than if it had started with a lower initial velocity.

It also stands to reason that the larger the diameter of the projectile, the more air resistance it will encounter. There are actually other factors to consider because the projectile of larger diameter will usually have a larger mass (it "weighs" more), which causes the effect of air resistance to be less. This will be dealt with in greater detail later, but the greater the mass of the object, the greater the force required to alter its path.

Finally, if there is a wind blowing across the path of the bullet, it will be blown off course to some extent. Because pellets are much less efficient ballistically than bullets fired from firearms, they are affected even more by crosswinds. Thus, the effects of gravity, air resistance, and crosswinds complicate describing the motion of any projectile. In fact, these effects make a mathematical approach to ballistics a formidable problem. Fortunately, we can understand a lot without getting very mathematical.

The sights on an air rifle are attached above the bore. When the arm is sighted in, the sights are adjusted so that the projectile hits at the point of aim at a given distance. Figure 1 shows the usual relationship of the pellet's path to the line of sight.

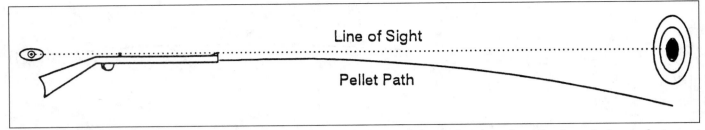

Figure 2: This depicts the relationship of the pellet path to the line of sight when the bore is in perfect alignment with the line of sight.

By changing the position of the rear sight (the front sight is usually fixed in position and height), the barrel is aligned so that it points slightly upward. This allows the pellet to rise and meet or cross the line of sight. Otherwise, if the line of sight and the bore were exactly parallel, the pellet would always be below the line of sight as shown in Figure 2.

The process of sighting in relates to adjusting the sights so that when they are aligned on the target, the bore points slightly upward in order for the pellet to rise in its flight to strike the point of aim on the target.

There are two possible cases in which the pellet path can meet or cross the line of sight. These are shown in Figure 1 and Figure 3.

In the case shown in Figure 3, the path of the pellet is such that it rises to the line of sight exactly at the target distance and is below the line of sight at all shorter distances. This would not be the usual situation. With the curved path of a pellet fired from an air rifle, the situation shown in Figure 1 is usual. If an outfielder throws a baseball from shoulder height slightly upward toward home plate, the baseball will come back to shoulder height at some distance along its path. In the same way, the pellet will cross the line of sight at two distances. This is no different from the behavior of any rifle. The longer distance is considered to be the range for which the piece is sighted.

The height of the bullet path above the line of sight at the midpoint of the distance for which it is sighted is called the mid-range trajectory. It is not uncommon for a centerfire rifle to be sighted for hunting large game so that the mid-range trajectory is as much as 3 inches because this height difference would not cause a miss on the large target. Likewise, the bullet falling as much as 3 inches below the line of sight at distances longer than the range for which the piece is sighted will not cause a missed shot on a large animal.

Suppose it is determined that some maximum deviation (for example, 3 inches) of the projectile from the line of sight can be tolerated without causing a miss. The longest distance at which the deviation is within this tolerance is called the point-blank range, which is illustrated in Figure 4. If the allowed maximum deviation from the line of sight is only 2 inches, the point-blank range will be shorter than that for the 3-inch example, because less deviation from the line of sight is allowed.

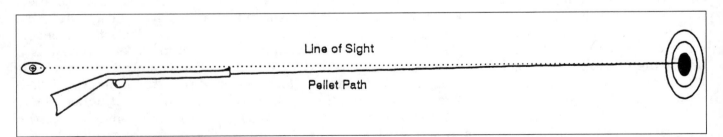

Figure 3: This shows the relationship of the pellet path and the line of sight when the target is close enough so that the pellet rises to exactly the point of aim at the target distance. Because of the curved path of a pellet, this could happen only at very short distance and the bullet does not cross the line of sight, but meets it at the target.

Adam learned valuable lessons about trajectory by shooting at targets placed at different distances.

All of these concepts apply to air rifles and their projectiles. The major difference between pellets and bullets is that because the pellets have lower initial velocities and lose their velocity much more quickly than bullets, the trajectories are much more curved. Also, air rifles are by their nature intended for small targets, so the acceptable deviation of the pellet's path from the line of sight is much smaller than 3 inches. Consequently, the air rifle is a short-range arm. While air rifles have limited range, it is no

less important to understand the paths of their projectiles.

How should your air rifle be sighted? Obviously, for target shooting, the sights should be adjusted so that the pellet strikes the point of aim at the desired distance. For other types of shooting, including pest control and hunting, targets may be encountered at varying distances. In this case, first decide how much above or below the line of sight the pellet may strike and still have the shot hit the intended target. For example, there is very little margin

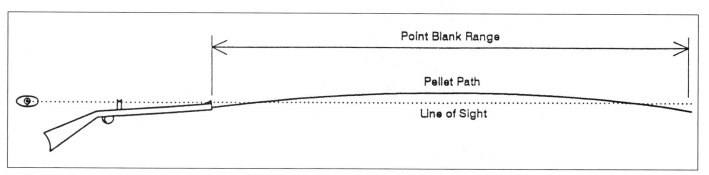

Figure 4: The point-blank range is the longest distance at which the path of the pellet does not rise above or fall below the line of sight by more than some acceptable amount.

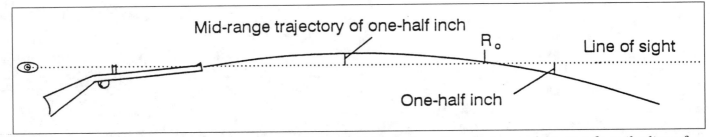

Figure 5: This shows the trajectory for the flight of a pellet when the maximum deviation from the line of sight is 1/2 inch. R_o is the distance for which the gun is sighted in.

for error in shooting at sparrows. Suppose you determine that the maximum amount you want the pellet's path to deviate from the line of sight is 1/2 inch. Then the gun should be sighted so that the trajectory is represented as shown in Figure 5.

In this case, R_o is the distance at which the gun is sighted in. Unfortunately, there is no exact way to determine what R_o should be without doing some shooting. The trajectory of the pellet will depend on its initial velocity, its shape (ability to penetrate air), and other vari-

A .20 caliber Sheridan shooting the Crosman Premier pellet with a ballistic coefficient of 0.040 makes a superb combination for varmint hunting.

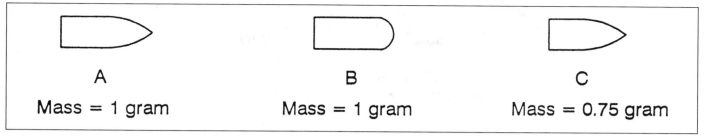

Figure 6: Projectiles A and B have the same mass but different point shapes. Projectiles A and C have the same point shape but different weights.

ables. We will give some basic principles later, but we need to know a little more about projectile flight.

Ballistic Coefficient

The concept of the ballistic coefficient is very simple. Suppose a tennis ball and a golf ball have the same weight. If both are thrown with the same velocity at the same angle, the golf ball will carry farther. It does so because it penetrates air better. It has a higher ballistic coefficient.

Consider three projectiles all having the same diameter as shown in Figure 6. Suppose that they all leave the muzzle with the same velocity. Projectiles A and B have the same weight, but projectile A has a much more streamlined shape and will pass through air more efficiently. Projectiles A and C have the same point profile, but projectile A is heavier because it has a longer base section. Therefore, projectile A will pass through air with a lower rate of velocity loss because it takes a greater force to reduce the velocity of a heavier object. The brakes on a large truck must be able to exert a greater stopping force than those on a compact car. It is harder to stop the truck.

One practical consequence of these ideas about air resistance is that if two pellets having different weights are fired from the same air rifle, the lighter one will almost always have the higher initial velocity. However, it will also lose its velocity much more quickly so that at a range of 25 to 30 yards, the heavier pellet may actually be traveling faster than the lighter one. The heavier pellet would, of course, have greater energy than the lighter one at that range. All this assumes that the profiles of the pellets are not greatly different.

So, what we want is the heaviest, sharpest pointed pellet available? Well, not necessarily. First, heavy pellets cannot be driven as fast as lighter ones. Therefore, the overall trajectory of a heavy pellet may not be as flat as that of a light one. The flatter trajectory of a light pellet might make it easier to hit small targets because the path of the pellet would deviate less from the line of sight. Second, a sharp-pointed pellet gives greater penetration, but it does not give a "punched out" hole in a paper target (known as the "signature" on the target), which is desirable for scoring purposes. Moreover, the fact that the pointed pellet penetrates better may not be an advantage. For pest shooting, it may be preferable for the pellet to deliver more of its energy on the target rather than to pass through the target and travel a great distance farther. These ideas will be developed more fully in Chapter 10. For now, we will return to the discussion of the ballistic coefficient.

The ballistic coefficient (C) of a projectile is simply a number. It gives a measure of the ability of the projectile to resist velocity loss as it passes through air. We have already explained that the ability of a projectile to pass through air is related to the weight, shape, and diameter of the projectile. For very efficient projectiles that pass through air well, the ballistic coefficient may be in the 0.3 to 0.5 range, while for very inefficient projectiles it may be as low as 0.01 to 0.10. Long, pointed bullets used in centerfire rifles are in the former class, while round balls used in muzzle-loading rifles and blunt pistol bullets are in the latter. Unfortunately, so are airgun pellets.

This small book on airguns is not the place for an extensive discussion of the theory of ballistics, drag models, space functions, and so on. Fortunately, as in many other branches of science, it is possible to make use of the results without having to understand all of the underlying theory. You don't have to know how an automatic transmission works to be able to use one. The basis for discussing projectile motion involves comparing the loss of velocity for the projectile under discussion to that for some "standard" projectile. Then, a set of tables can be constructed to compare flight characteristics of other test projectiles to those of the standard projectile. Different models of standard projectiles have been described in terms of the diameter, weight, and radius of the point relative to the diameter (known as the "ogive"). None of these projectiles resembles an airgun pellet, but the calculations work surprisingly well anyway.

One of the most successful approaches to ballistics calculations is that of Col. James M. Ingalls, which resulted in what is commonly referred to as Ingalls' Tables. These tables give values for the so-called space function for different values of velocity. The space function is the distance in feet that the standard projectile would have travelled while its velocity dropped from one specified velocity to a lower one.

Ingalls' Tables give as one entry the velocity starting at 3,600 fps, with decreasing values to 100 fps. Below 1,000 fps, the useful range of velocities for airgun pellets, the velocity is tabulated at intervals of 1 fps. In the table, the space function value (S) is tabulated beside the corresponding velocity (v). Thus, a value of v can be chosen and the value of S can be read from the table. The ballistic coefficient for the projectile can be calculated from the values of

S corresponding to the two known velocities at different distances.

In Chapter 7, we described how altitude affects the velocity of pellets. Strictly speaking, the ability of a pellet to pass through air also varies with altitude. Dealing with this problem is certainly beyond the scope of this book. The discussion below will clarify and illustrate the application of ballistic coefficients to problems in airgun external ballistics.

Ballistic Calculations

Modern ballistic science and the computer have given shooters the tools to perform numerical experimentation on their ammunition. Bullets used in handloading ammunition are made by companies that have done an enormous amount of experimentation. As a result, accurate ballistic coefficients are available for almost any bullet. Sophisticated ballistics programs are now available from all of the major bullet manufacturers. The computations give excellent results with the calculated values for velocity, energy, trajectory, and wind deflection, generally agreeing well with experimental values obtained from actual firing.

While this is true for the rifle shooter, what is the status of the airgunner with regard to ballistics? The answer to the question is that while much is available for the rifle shooter, things are a little less certain for the airgunner. First of all, ballistic coefficients for pellets are much lower than for bullets (0.01 to 0.05 vs. 0.10 to 0.50). Second, velocities of pellets are much lower than those of bullets, except perhaps those fired from handguns. Third,

Pellets having different profiles pass through air with different ease, so they have different ballistic coefficients.

Although the .177 caliber Daisy 880 gives higher velocity than some of the .22 caliber rifles, the larger pellets are more effective on pests.

there has been much less experimentation by airgunners. Not only have fewer airgunners calculated anything, even fewer have conducted experimental work using a chronograph and determining drop tables. For shooting at a distance of 10 meters, not a great deal matters except accuracy. All of that is changing as more air gunners are using high-powered air rifles at longer ranges for hunting and field shooting.

One practical application of ballistic calculations is that the results give a good approximation to the velocity and trajectory of a particular pellet when the initial velocity is known. There is no need to give specifics on the ballistics programs, since each comes with a manual and is largely menu driven after it is installed. However, in order to achieve an understanding of what type of information we can gain from the calculations, we will illustrate their use.

Appendix C shows a set of ballistics tables that were calculated for the conditions that are appropriate for air rifles. The range is limited to 50 yards and the ballistic coefficients vary from 0.01 to 0.04 in increments of 0.0025. A standard sight-in distance of 30 yards and a line of sight 1.5 inches above the bore were assumed. What is calculated is the remaining velocity and the point of impact in relation to the line of sight as a function of distance.

In order to illustrate how to use a ballistics table, the table for a pellet having a ballistic coefficient of 0.02 is reproduced here. This table and the others shown in Appendix C were calculated by assuming that the line of sight is 1.5 inches above the bore. Therefore, the point of impact is at -1.50 inches from the line of sight at the muzzle. The table shows where the point of impact will be relative to the line of sight at distances of 10, 20, 30, 40, and 50 yards when the gun is sighted in at 30 yards. The data is shown in the form 446/-2.33, which indicates a velocity of 446 fps and a point of impact of 2.33 inches below the line of sight.

Suppose your Daisy 856 gives a muzzle velocity of 575 fps when using a pellet that has a ballistic coefficient of 0.02 and you want to know the trajectory and velocity out to 50 yards when sighted in at 30 yards. Read down the left-hand column to find the muzzle velocity of 575 fps. Then read horizontally to find that at 10 yards, the corresponding entry is 540/+0.25, which indicates a velocity of 540 fps, with the pellet striking 0.25 inch above the line of sight. For a distance of 30 yards, the entry 476/0.00 indicates a remaining velocity of 476 fps, with the point of impact at the line of sight. At 40 yards, the remaining velocity is 446 fps and the point of impact is 2.33 inches below the line of sight. At 40 yards, this deviation would cause you to miss a sparrow if your gun was sighted in for 30 yards and you did not aim high.

The ballistic tables shown in Appendix C were calculated using ballistic coefficients ranging from 0.01 to 0.04 in increments of 0.0025. Does this mean that if you use a pellet with a ballistic coefficient of 0.0210 that the tables are of no use? To answer that question, consider the example above and look at the table in the appendix for a ballistic coefficient of 0.0225, since the value for your pellet

A fast-shooting, break-action rifle such as the Beeman S1 being used here makes a good choice for smaller game and pests, but it is still a .177 caliber.

Ballistic Coefficient = 0.02

M. V., ft./sec.	Range, yds				
	10 yd.	20 yd.	30 yd.	40 yd.	50 yd.
400	374/+1.63	350/+2.22	327/0.00	305/-5.52	285/-14.71
425	398/+1.35	375/+1.95	348/0.00	325/-4.75	304/-12.82
450	422/+1.04	395/+1.68	370/0.00	345/-4.27	323/-11.35
475	445/+0.82	417/+1.38	391/0.00	366/-3.75	342/-10.15
500	469/+0.65	440/+1.23	412/0.00	386/-3.22	361/-8.93
525	493/+0.49	462/+1.05	434/0.00	406/-2.90	380/-7.87
550	517/+0.36	485/+0.92	455/0.00	426/-2.59	399/-6.95
575	540/+0.25	507/+0.80	476/0.00	446/-2.33	418/-6.40
600	564/+0.15	529/+0.69	497/0.00	466/-2.10	437/-5.76
625	587/+0.05	552/+0.60	518/0.00	486/-1.89	456/-5.24
650	611/-0.03	574/+0.51	539/0.00	506/-1.71	475/-4.76
675	634/-0.10	596/+0.42	560/0.00	526/-1.57	494/-4.73
700	658/-0.15	618/+0.38	581/0.00	545/-1.40	512/-3.96
725	681/-0.21	640/+0.32	601/0.00	565/-1.25	530/-3.62
750	704/-0.26	661/+0.27	621/0.00	584/-1.17	548/-3.33
775	726/-0.31	682/+0.22	641/0.00	602/-1.08	566/-3.07
800	749/-0.36	703/+0.17	660/0.00	620/-0.98	583/-2.86
825	771/-0.39	723/+0.13	679/0.00	638/-0.89	599/-2.64
850	793/-0.42	743/+0.10	697/0.00	655/-0.81	615/-2.44
875	815/-0.45	762/+0.07	714/0.00	671/-0.74	630/-2.26
900	836/-0.48	781/+0.05	731/0.00	687/-0.67	645/-2.09
925	856/-0.51	798/+0.02	747/0.00	701/-0.62	659/-1.94

(0.0210) is between 0.0200 and 0.0225. If your Daisy 856 sends the pellet out of the muzzle with a velocity of 575 fps, the table at the top of the next page shows the data for the two ballistic coefficients.

At 30 yards, the difference amounts to only 10 fps and at 40 yards, the difference is only 13 fps. The point of impact differs by only 0.10 inch. At ranges shorter than 30 yards, there is no more than 0.03 inch difference in the calculated trajectories (compared to a pellet diameter of 0.177 inch!) and no more than 7 fps difference between the calculated velocities. The pellet under consideration was assumed to have a ballistic coefficient of 0.0210, so the calculated values would be very close to those tabulated using a ballistic coefficient of 0.02. Clearly, there is no great error in using a table calculated for a ballistic coefficient of 0.02 with a pellet having an actual ballistic coefficient of 0.0210.

Using a table calculated for a ballistic coefficient of 0.04 with a pellet that actually has a ballistic coefficient of 0.02 introduces more serious errors as shown on the next page.

These lines of data are taken from the appropriate tables in Appendix C.

Even in this case, the trajectories out to 40 yards probably are not different enough to detect with your Daisy 856. However, the calculated velocities differ considerably.

The illustrations should convince you that if your favorite pellet has a ballistic coefficient of 0.029 you can use the table corresponding to a ballistic coefficient of 0.030 and get answers that are as accurate as you will ever need. The calculated velocity and trajectory will be within the shot-to-shot variation and accuracy of most air rifles.

In summary, the tables shown in Appendix C are of sufficient scope to cover all practical situations. Examining the tables for examples with high muzzle velocity, especially for pellets with relatively high ballistic coefficients, shows that in these flat-shooting situations, the gun could easily be sighted in for 40 yards. It would still have a trajectory that does not deviate more than 1 inch above the line of sight. Such a sighting makes it easier to hit targets at 50 yards or farther if the gun is sufficiently

	M.V.	10 yd.	20 yd.	30 yd.	40 yd.
C = 0.0200	575	540/+0.25	507/+0.80	476/0.00	446/-2.33
C = 0.0225	575	544/+0.22	514/+0.77	486/0.00	459/-2.23

accurate. Keep in mind that a 1-inch group at 50 yards is very good for an airgun. A calculated point of impact as exact as -2.41 inches at a range of 50 yards is meaningless for a gun that shoots 2-inch groups and can logically be expected to hit 1 inch above or below the sighting point at that distance.

The ballistic tables shown in Appendix C do not include kinetic energies because the energy depends on the weight of the pellet. The equation presented in Chapter 7, KE = $(1/2)mv^2$, can be used to calculate the kinetic energy at various distances after the velocity is determined. We can also tabulate the kinetic energy per grain of pellet weight at different velocities. Multiplying the pellet weight in grains by the value shown in the table will give the kinetic energy.

Suppose your Crosman 2200 shoots a 14.3-grain Crosman Premier pellet with a ballistic coefficient of 0.035 at a muzzle velocity of 550 fps. What will be the trajectory for the pellet and its velocity and energy at distances up to 50 yards? You must specify some distance that the gun is sighted for, and we will assume that the distance is 30 yards. Also, your brother-in-law says that his Benjamin 392, shooting the same pellet with a muzzle velocity of 650 fps, will hit closer to the point of aim at 50 yards than your Crosman will at 40 yards when both guns are sighted in at a distance of 30 yards. Is he correct? Would it be totally ridiculous for you to take a shot at a crow 40 yards away with your Crosman 2200?

Ballistic calculations can give answers to such questions, but you need to know the muzzle velocity and the ballistic coefficient of the pellet. It is also necessary to specify how far the line of sight is above the bore. For scoped rifles, this is usually about 1.5 inches. The table on page 134 shows the results calculated for a pellet having a ballistic coefficient of 0.035 with muzzle velocities of 550 (for your Crosman 2200) and 650 fps (for your brother-in-law's Benjamin 392).

Let us use this information to answer the questions above. First, the results show that in order to be sighted in at 30 yards, your Crosman will need to be shooting 0.79 inch high at 20 yards. That should cause no problem with hitting most targets at ranges shorter than 30 yards. The point of impact will be 2.22 inches low at 40 yards when the gun is sighted in at 30 yards. So, over a range of 40 yards, the pellet does not deviate more than 2.22 inches from the line of sight. What this means is that a 40-yard shot at a crow with your Crosman is certainly not out of the question. Have no fear. With a strongly constructed pellet and a remaining kinetic energy of 7.2 foot-pounds, it will be a dead crow. You must still check the accuracy at that range.

As usual, your brother-in-law is wrong. When sighted in at 30 yards, the pellet from his Benjamin will hit almost 4 inches low at 50 yards while pellets from your Crosman would strike 2.22 inches low at 40 yards. Because of that, I believe that he should limit his shots to about 45 yards, where the point of impact will be 2.6 inches low. However, since the pellet from his gun never rises more than 0.43 inch above the line of sight when sighted in for 30 yards, he could sight in at 35 yards. This would give a maximum height of 0.76 inches at 20 yards, making the point of impact only 1.8 inches low at 45 yards and 3.13 inches low at 50 yards. He could even sight in at 40 yards by being 1.21 inches high at 25 yards. His pellets then would be 2.2 inches low at 50 yards. That sighting actually turns his Benjamin into a pretty fair 50-yard pest gun if he can keep his pellets on a 2-inch circle at that distance. A remaining energy of 9.4 foot-pounds would take care of most pests at that distance if the pellet is placed accurately.

	M.V.	10 yd.	20 yd.	30 yd.	40 yd.
C = 0.02	575	540/+0.25	507/+0.80	476/0.00	446/-2.33
C = 0.04	575	557/+0.14	540/+0.67	523/0.00	507/-1.94

Kinetic Energy per Grain of Weight at Different Velocities

Velocity, ft./sec.	Energy per grain, ft. lbs.	Velocity, ft./sec.	Energy per grain, ft. lbs.
400	0.355	650	0.938
425	0.401	675	1.012
450	0.450	700	1.088
475	0.501	725	1.167
500	0.555	750	1.249
525	0.612	775	1.334
550	0.672	800	1.421
575	0.734	825	1.512
600	0.800	850	1.605
625	0.868	875	1.700

Let us consider one additional use of the ballistic tables. Suppose your air rifle shoots a pellet with a ballistic coefficient of 0.015 at 600 fps. How much different will the trajectory be over a distance of 40 yards if you switch to a pellet having a ballistic coefficient of 0.0225? Examination of the ballistic tables shown in Appendix C yields the data shown on the next page.

The difference amounts to only 0.36 inch at 40 yards. With most air rifles, a 1 inch group at 40 yards is quite acceptable, so you would never be able to detect a difference of 0.36 inch. This means that unless you have a super-accurate rifle or compare pellets having greatly different ballistic coefficients, the differences will be negligible.

A Crosman with a good scope makes an effective rifle for small game and pests out to about 40 yards.

Data Calculated for a .22 Caliber Crosman Premier Pellet ($C=0.035$)

Range, (yd)	Crosman 2200			Benjamin 392		
	Velocity (ft./sec.)	Energy (ft./lb.)	Height (in.)	Velocity (ft./sec.)	Energy (ft. lb.)	Height (in.)
0	550	9.61	-1.50	650	13.42	-1.50
10	531	8.96	+0.26	627	12.49	-0.09
20	512	8.33	+0.79	605	11.69	+0.43
30	494	7.75	0.00	584	10.83	0.00
40	476	7.20	-2.22	564	10.10	-1.40
50	459	6.69	-5.97	544	9.40	-3.95

In this chapter, we have presented an elementary study of exterior ballistics. Details on how to calculate ballistic coefficients are shown in Appendix E. The attempt is not to make the reader an expert on ballistics, but rather to provide enough of the principles of the science to allow the air rifle shooter to understand the flight of a pellet. These are fascinating subjects for airgunners and firearm users alike, but we have barely scratched the surface. For readers who wish to learn more about ballistics, the standard book dealing with the subject is *Hatcher's Notebook*, 3rd Edition, by Julian S. Hatcher, and published in 1962 by Stackpole Books, Harrisburg, Pa. Many illustrations of ballistic calculations as well as theory are provided in this book. Those interested in further ballistics calculations should see Appendix E: Ballistics Equations for more information.

We will turn our attention in Chapter 10 to the use of air rifles in the area of hunting, where the subject of external ballistics is of greater practical importance.

	M.V.	10 yd.	20 yd.	30 yd.	40 yd.
$C = 0.0150$	600	552/+0.21	508/+0.78	466/0.00	428/-2.36
$C = 0.0225$	600	568/+0.12	537/+0.67	508/0.00	480/-2.00

Shown here are, from left, the Daisy pointed, Beeman Silver Sting, Beeman Silver Jet, Beeman Kodiak, and Crosman Copperhead pointed pellets. The terminal performance of these pellets will be quite different because of their different construction.

CHAPTER 9

FUN AND GAMES

Starting Right

A couple of years ago in the Big Horn Mountains of Wyoming, 12-year-old Elizabeth and 9-year-old Steven had their first "shooting practice," as Steven called it. They quickly learned sight picture, breath control, and trigger squeeze. After pop cans at 10 yards were turned into sieves, it was time for more fun and games. Pop cans placed on the stubs of lodgepole pines became large jungle cats that wanted to eat Uncle Jim. Careful shooting with the air rifle would be required to save the uncle. Each time the little Crosman 760 spoke, a pop can rattled to the ground to yells of "This is so cool!" Later, pine cones were the targets of opportunity. Elizabeth and Steven got their start with an airgun, and Aunt Kathy got some wonderful photos. Kids have enjoyed shooting this way since the late 1800s.

Elizabeth and Steven had never been around when airguns were fired. When I demonstrated how the Crosman 760 functions, both of them put their hands over their ears, expecting a loud boom. Both expected to be jolted by recoil when firing the air rifle. They simply did not know what to expect because of seeing guns fired on TV and in movies. Eliza-

This photo shows why the Beeman S1 is not a good choice for some women and kids. It is too much gun.

This pellet fired at approximately 600 fps from a Daisy 880 almost exited from this 5/8-inch board. Air rifles are not toys.

Twelve-year-old Elizabeth can easily pump, load, and shoot a Daisy 856.

When preparing for a family airgun session, Keith shows Victoria and Olivia that the gun is unloaded and reviews its operation and safety procedures.

A pellet trap is one answer to stopping pellets safely.

beth and Steven were greatly relieved to find out that there was very little noise and no recoil in shooting a multi-pump air rifle. Shooting the airgun was fun and that allowed them to become good shots in a couple of sessions. Therein lies the advantage of using airguns to teach shooting skills to beginners.

Airguns are serious shooting tools. Only very recently, an employee in a sporting goods store told me that the store did not stock inexpensive airguns. "They are just toys," was the comment. I hope that the evaluations described in Chapters 5, 6, and 10 will dispel that myth! Even a Daisy 856 or 880 or a Crosman 66 can send a pellet through a 5/8-inch board. Never treat an air rifle as a toy. To do so is to invite disaster.

When youthful shooters are just getting started, select a suitable air rifle. If you are about half or two-thirds grown, it is impossible to concentrate on sight picture and trigger squeeze when a 7-pound, 44-inch airgun is waving around. My wife is an experienced shooter with considerable strength, but she will not shoot my Beeman S1 or Gamo Hunter break-action rifles. She shoots for fun and shooting those rifles involves work. The cocking

Paper targets, pop cans, an air rifle and a lot of empty space allow Adam to enjoy shooting.

Daisy offers many paper targets of conventional and game types.

These targets show the different approaches of Daisy and Crosman to making interesting paper targets.

Although valuable as collectibles now, targets such as these were popular many years ago.

action requires a force of 30 to 40 pounds and the rifles are too heavy for general plinking fun.

Of course, pumping a multi-pump air rifle is work, too, and some would argue that repeatedly shooting a break-action rifle is less work in the long run. This is true, provided that you have the strength to cock the latter.

My wife's favorite air rifle is the Daisy 856, which regularly sells for $30 to $35. She has carried and enjoyed shooting this rifle in the Midwest and the mountains of Wyoming because it is light and of easily portable size. It is unbelievably easy to pump, remarkably accurate, and weighs only about 3 pounds. It has an excellent trigger pull, good sights, and is powerful enough for pest control. The Crosman 66 is also a good choice, but it is slightly harder to pump and the trigger action is not as crisp. Even though I shoot anything that launches bullets, I frequently use a Daisy 856, 880, or 22X when shooting for fun. However, I face game and pests armed with a Crosman 2200, a Benjamin, or a Sheridan.

Match the airgun to the shooter. Don't expect a 10- or 12-year old to master shooting skills with a Benjamin, Sheridan, or a long,

Targets showing squirrels and other animals are currently available and afford valuable practice for hunters.

A board with a groove makes a handy target stand for snack crackers.

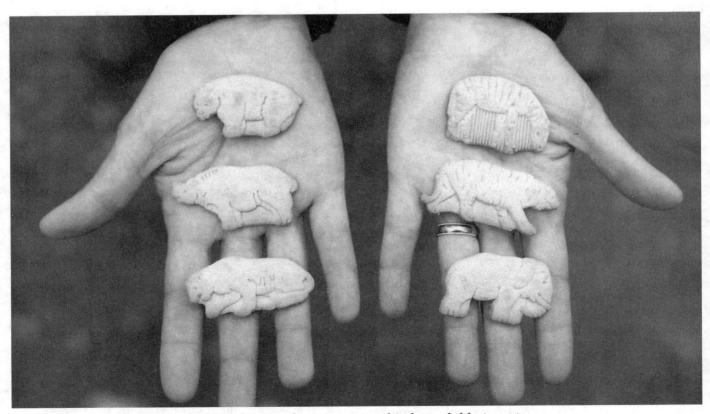

Frangible targets like animal crackers make interesting, biodegradable targets.

Walking and shooting in the wide-open spaces make an enjoyable afternoon for Kathy and me.

heavy break-action air rifle. Airguns are inexpensive enough that a beginning shooter can start with a rifle that costs less than $50 and move up to a heavier, more powerful gun as skills and maturity advance.

Setting up an Airgun Range

Airguns are relatively quiet and the multi-pump rifles are essentially recoilless. With the multi-pump rifles, you can shoot with low power indoors and with more power outdoors by varying the number of pumps. Most break-action rifles are cocked once and give "full power" only. The multi-pump rifles are perfectly adapted to shooting indoors in a basement or hallway. Since many municipalities forbid shooting airguns outdoors, this may be the only way available to shoot without going to a range. Make absolutely certain that it is impossible for anyone to walk into the line of fire! You can gain valuable practice and improve your shooting by setting up a range as short as 5 yards, although 10 yards or 10 meters (33 feet) would be better. What you must have is a backstop that will stop pellets safely.

While on the subject of safety, always practice safe gun handling when shooting an airgun. They are not toys and most of them state so right on the gun. The warning is: They can cause serious injury or death if handled improperly and an accident occurs. Refer to the appropriate section of Chapter 3, and be sure to instruct any inexperienced shooters with you regarding proper gun etiquette.

Metal pellet traps are available at low cost. For the reasons discussed in Chapter 3, never shoot steel BBs at a steel trap! The metal traps consist of an open-front metal box with a

Metal silhouettes can be lined up and shot at different distances or they can be set up in a walk-and-shoot course.

The Daisy 856 is an ideal "cracker" rifle.

Any discussion of air rifles between the author and his brother, Larry, usually ends up like this.

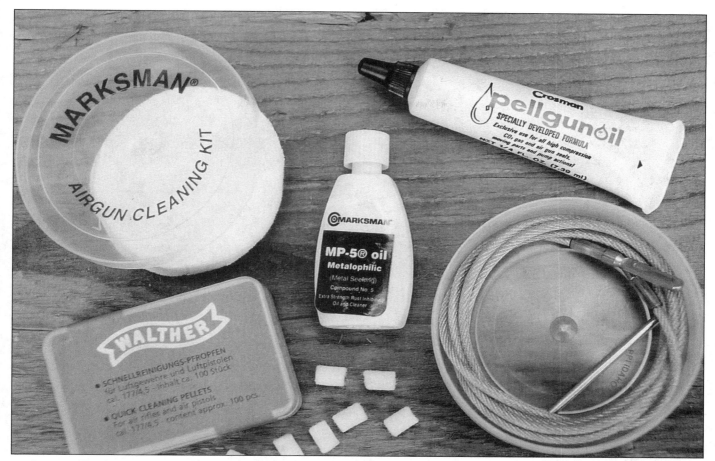

An air rifle deserves to be properly maintained. Follow the instructions in the owner's manual when using products such as these.

slanted back that deflects lead pellets down into a trough. On impact, lead pellets are flattened and their energy is spent. Metal pellet traps should be used at a minimum distance of 10 yards or so because of the possibility of some lead back splash.

Metal pellet traps are available in different thicknesses to stop projectiles of different energy. Do not buy a trap that is designed to stop .177 pellets traveling at 600 fps and shoot it with a high-powered air rifle that shoots pellets at 1,000 fps. The back of the trap will be badly dented in short order.

For home use, a perfectly suitable pellet or BB trap can be made from a cardboard box containing old newspapers or magazines. Targets are taped to one side of the box. Fill this side of the box with loosely crumpled newspapers. The back of the box (away from the target) is then filled with more tightly packed newspapers or magazines. With this arrangement, the pellets penetrate the front of the box and the loose papers.

Then they are stopped by the more sturdy packing in the back of the box. The pellets are slowed by the loose paper and do not bounce off of the tighter packing in the back of the box.

Do not attach targets to the box with metal clips or wooden clothespins, since they may cause ricochets if they are accidentally hit. Hang an old blanket, carpet, or heavy cloth behind the box. Any stray pellet hitting this backdrop has its energy safely absorbed.

If you are fortunate enough to live where you can shoot in wide open spaces, pellet traps are not much of a problem. Just remember to have lots of open space behind your intended target. Fired at an optimum angle (about 30 degrees), many pellet rifles will shoot up to 300 yards. Fired at a target 25 yards away on the ground, pellet travel will be much less. However, do not overlook the necessity of having a suitable clear area in which to shoot. Pellets will almost always ricochet from the ground behind the target.

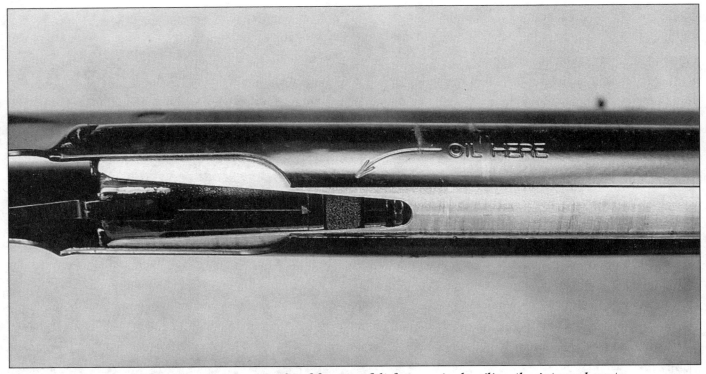

Most multi-pump rifles have a wiper made of foam or felt for sparingly oiling the internal parts.

Targets

Air rifle competition has been part of the Olympic Games since 1984. In the 2000 Olympic Games, the first gold medal was awarded to Nancy Johnson in women's air rifle competition. This formal target shooting requires highly specialized rifles (costing a few thousand dollars) that are fired from the three standard positions (standing, kneeling, and prone). The paper targets (with incredibly small 10-rings) are shot from a distance of 10 meters.

The equipment requirements are not as stringent for competition at a lower level, but it is still a specialized sport. This book is not about target air rifles. It is concerned with the performance characteristics of multi-pump pneumatic rifles suitable for general sport and recreational uses. Incidentally, some break-action rifles are not very suitable for target competition either. When the gun is discharged, a heavy piston and spring lurch forward, before the pellet starts its travel down the bore. For reasons discussed in Chapter 5, this is not conducive to great accuracy. However, some spring-piston guns, particularly the recoilless models that utilize a counter-spring system, are extremely accurate and designed for competition.

Punching paper targets is still a good way to enjoy using an air rifle. In fact, until you establish good shooting form, it is probably the best way. Shooting at a pop can involves sort of lining up the sights, squeezing the trigger, and hearing a plink when the pellets hit the can. When shooting paper targets, the sights are lined up in a particular way and the shot is taken. However, when the pellet hits the paper, you can tell if it is the 7, 9, or 10 ring that is hit. A shot receives the score of the highest value ring touched. In other words, by shooting paper, targets and keeping score, you can tell if your shooting is improving. That may be a little more difficult when you shoot pop cans.

Paper targets are always suitable for airgun shooting. If you do not aspire to air rifle competition, there are several types of novelty targets available. Daisy markets paper targets arranged for playing ticktacktoe, baseball, and other games. Crosman markets targets made of foam that create a highly visible hole. Various animal targets are available in the form of squirrels, rabbits, groundhogs, and crows, with a bullseye on the animal. Life-size targets of this type can provide valuable practice for hunting small game and pests with an air rifle. However, one older squirrel target I have has the bullseye in a place where no squirrel should be shot!

I suppose the target most often shot with airguns is the ubiquitous tin can. However, this is not a good target for several reasons. Pellets not hitting a can dead-on may ricochet and do so at a variety of angles. Because they are made of soft aluminum, beverage cans are more appropriate targets for airguns. You must have a lot of open space behind and around the target because of the uncertainty in where the shot (hit or miss) may go. Also, metal cans should be recycled. Still, it is fun to

make a can go rolling and to hear that ping of a pellet as it hits the can.

Variations on the "shoot the can" theme provide additional challenges. Assuming you have a wide-open place to shoot, see how many shots it takes competitors to move a pop can a certain distance, say 5 feet. Another variation is to have competitors start with pop cans 10 yards away and see which shooter can move his or her pop can farther with a specified number of shots (say five shots).

For fun and games, any number of items can make interesting targets. Snack crackers, mints, lollipops, etc., all disintegrate when they are hit and they are biodegradable. We once bought a package of "fine" imported mints that were

Shooting is more fun as a group activity.

about the diameter of a quarter. They were so fine that they wouldn't melt and couldn't be chewed! They certainly went to pieces when hit with pellets, however, and that is how we finally got rid of the things. Nieces and nephews took great pleasure in popping them, up close at first and then at gradually increasing distances.

While spending time in the Big Horn Mountains of Wyoming, my wife and I have had loads of fun removing pine cones (which are 1 to 1 1/2 inches in diameter) from trees. We like to start on a branch and work our way along it. We can do this because there is nothing for miles around. Some of the pine cones are really attached and we have observed that .22 caliber pellets remove them much more readily than do pellets of .177 caliber.

In open spaces, it is also possible to set up a walk-and-shoot course. Targets at different distances are shot from specified stations. This is very similar to the animal targets that are shot in a 3-D target archery match.

Silhouettes

I was carrying my favorite rifle and crawling around the boulder trying to get a look at a hog that was anything but your usual farm animal. The heat was oppressive. The buzzing mosquitoes and gnats were all I could hear. Just another couple of feet and I would be able to see him. After several seconds of almost imperceptible motion, I could see the whole animal. It was only 30 yards away! Slowly, I raised my rifle and centered the top of the post in the peep sight. I moved the top of the post to the center of his shoulder and slowly squeezed the trigger. That was it. The sound of the pellet striking metal. The hog was down and not moving. It was a successful hunt.

Such is a silhouette safari with an airgun. It can be only for fun, but field target matches involve shooting metallic targets in the shape of animals under competitive rules. The rules govern the type of air rifle used with the categories involving different weight classes, etc.

In this type shooting, metal silhouettes of animals are shot and knocked over at distances up to 50 yards. One organization that sponsors and regulates competition of this type is the American Airgun Field Target Association, AAFTA. As in formal target competition, the rifles used are specialized for that sport.

Use your imagination to devise targets and games for airgun fun. Always follow the rules for safe shooting. If anything is questionable, don't do it!

For most shooters, airguns are used for wholesome fun and family recreation. Elizabeth and Steven experienced exactly that type of fun in the Big Horn Mountains. I hope that many years from now, Elizabeth and Steven pick up an old Crosman 760 at a flea market or antique mall and relive a snapshot of their past as they look at that great American icon, the airgun. Better yet, I hope that they are still able to buy a new Crosman 760 and spend some time with their nieces and nephews. That air rifle has been around for 35 years and more than 8 million have been sold. It may still be around for many years! I am sure that Elizabeth and Steven will remember that day in the Big Horn Mountains with the lodgepole pines glowing against a cloudless Wyoming sky and how they saved Uncle Jim with the good shooting of a Crosman 760.

CHAPTER 10

HUNTING AND PEST CONTROL

The use of the 30-30 Winchester on elk is widely and vocally proclaimed in some circles to be unsporting and inhumane. However, this author remembers well an article written by an elk hunter describing his success. He was using a rifle chambered for a very flat-shooting, modern caliber. He went on to describe taking a shot at an elk at very long range and managing to hit it. He then described how he was unable to come close on his next two or three shots and how fortunate he was that the elk had lain down, enabling him to get close enough to finally kill it. His first shot was not a well-placed one. Is this type of hunting more humane or sporting than that of a woodsman who stalks to within 100 yards and gets in a killing first shot with a 30-30? I think not. It is not the caliber of the rifle used that makes hunting some species humane.

In the hands of the legendary Howard Hill, a longbow was a wonderfully effective tool. In the hands of a novice archer, it is not. A squirrel shot between the eyes with an accurately placed pellet from an air rifle is harvested more humanely than one shot in the ham with a .22 rimfire hollow point. The essence of this discussion is that an air rifle of moderate to high power, shooting an appropriate pellet, can be an effective means of harvesting small game or dispatching pests.

Only a few types are shown here, but the pellet chosen goes a long way in determining air rifle performance.

From the outset, it should be made clear that we are talking about game generally no larger than rabbit or squirrel. Typical pests that may be handled by pellet guns include sparrows, pigeons, starlings, crows, and rats. An antiques mall in Billings, Mont., is located in a large old building, and it had a problem with pigeons roosting in the attic. When I took an old, collectible airgun from a display to buy it, the woman working there asked where it came from. She was surprised to find that it had been there for some time. She exclaimed, "I brought my pellet gun from home to get rid of the pigeons upstairs. I could have used that one!" This is pest control by an airgun where a firearm would have been out of the question. There are numerous instances of this type.

The relatively low power and low noise of an air rifle make it perfect for such pest control inside buildings or near populated areas.

For more than 50 years, the .20 caliber Sheridan has been a popular rifle for small-game hunting.

An Airgun Hunter's Code

In all cases where game animals or pests are hunted, the user of a pellet gun must impose a code of ethics that encompasses these points:

1. All laws regarding the use of airguns for the taking of game or destruction of pests must be strictly obeyed. First check state and local laws carefully.

2. The shooter must use an air rifle of considerable power. This is not work for BB guns or other low-powered airguns. An airgun that is adequate for sparrows or starlings may not be suitable for squirrels.

3. Select the ammunition to be used very carefully and do considerable testing. Performance characteristics of pellets must be evaluated before a live target is shot, not while it is escaping after being wounded.

4. Shots must be taken at short range only. Pellets lose their velocity rapidly and a pellet

Many types of pellets are available including, from left, the Daisy Pointed, Gamo Hunter, Crosman Copperhead Wadcutter, and Beeman Crow Magnum pellets.

may have adequate power for the job at 15 to 20 yards, but not at 40 yards.

5. Your gun/sight/pellet combination must allow you to place your shot with extreme accuracy. The lethal zone for some types of targets hunted with airguns may be no larger than 1 inch in diameter. To be able to hit a 2-inch circle is simply not good enough in such cases.

6. Practice, practice, practice until you can meet the objectives in No. 5.

7. If your situation does not comply with all of these points, DO NOT SHOOT AT ANY LIVE TARGET.

If all the guidelines given above are met, an airgun may provide interest, variety, and skill development for hunting and pest control where it is legal to do so. In a check with several state game or conservation departments, I found that in most cases, an airgun is simply another gun as far as the taking of small game is concerned. However, in any aspect or type of hunting today, groups that have an agenda to outlaw the whole sport are watching the hunters. Having the skill and ethics to be effective in the activity helps to establish credibility and legitimacy. In other words, it does a great deal of harm to our cause when hunters misuse their legal rights.

Pellet Performance

Several factors influence the effectiveness of a pellet on a live target. The velocity, caliber, weight, and point shape are all important. The most important factor is bullet placement.

Accuracy is paramount in hunting with an air rifle. Test several types of pellets in your rifle to see what works best.

Obviously, it is better to place a .177 caliber pellet in the head of a rat, than one of .22 caliber in its rear end. For our purposes here, we will assume that the pellet can be delivered accurately to the desired location on the target. Having taken that as a necessary first step, we now want to look at the other factors that determine pellet performance.

A sparrow or a mouse is a very fragile target, so a pellet does not meet with much resistance. Any pellet traveling at a reasonable velocity from an air rifle will transfer enough energy to the target to get the job done. However, the impact of a flat or hollow point pellet will transfer more energy to the target than will a pointed pellet that passes through the target without losing as much velocity.

Except for the fact that larger species like pigeons or crows require the use of an airgun of higher power, the same approach is useful for these pests. The best choice would be an air rifle of considerable power firing one of the pellets designed for rapid energy deposit. The typical wadcutter design is good and the hollow points like the Beeman Crow Magnum

(knowing that there is such a pellet makes me want to go hunting!) or the Dynamit Nobel Super-H-Point are even better. The body structure of smaller birds is not difficult to penetrate, which is why shotguns using shot size as small as No. 8 (about 0.10 inch diameter) are effective on small game birds. Of course, the shot are spherical and travel at higher velocity than do pellets fired from airguns. Also, multiple (but random) hits are assumed with a shotgun. However, air rifles can be extremely effective on pigeons and crows with good shot placement from a gun of relatively high power.

Evaluating Pellet Performance

The airgun enthusiast who wishes to give hunting (either small game or pests) a try, may not initially buy a new air rifle for this activity. After trying it and becoming addicted to the sport, he/she may want a new air rifle. Even though a new gun may not be obtained for the first few hunts, some new ammunition might, and perhaps should, be obtained. With the enormous number of pellet types available, how does one decide what to use? Of course, the first requisite is accuracy, because if the pellet cannot be delivered to the desired spot on the target, all other factors are of little importance. If the only use of the airgun is shooting paper targets, accuracy and cutting nice round holes in the paper are the only considerations.

The truth is that many airgun shooters go to one of the "marts" and buy a box of whatever type of pellet is available and use them in their airguns for everything. It may well be that these shooters are not realizing optimum performance from their air rifles. A person who hunts game or pests with an air rifle owes it to the sport to use the most effective ammunition available regardless of the type of gun used. The attitude that "I have only this inexpensive air rifle and it doesn't make any difference what I use in it" simply does not do justice to the sport or the game. The air rifle may be

Before making a choice on a rifle/pellet combination, I always test velocity, accuracy, and penetration.

Any pellet used for hunting and pest control should give excellent accuracy. The hollow-pointed Beeman Crow Magnum and the Crosman Copperhead Pointed pellets are outstanding for hunting different types of game.

inexpensive but by now we have shown conclusively that some inexpensive guns have a lot to offer in terms of performance. You certainly ought to maximize that performance by selecting the most effective ammunition.

What characteristics are considered when pellet performance is being evaluated? While there may be other criteria that are useful, the three that will be considered in this chapter are accuracy, penetration, and energy transfer (the last of these loosely means "smash"). While these components of pellet performance may easily be identified, the problem is how to evaluate them. We will assume that you intend to hunt game where all three factors come into play. Obviously, if you are shooting sparrows, accuracy is about the only requisite, since not much penetration or energy transfer is required.

Accuracy

Accuracy is the easiest of the performance components to be evaluated. Assuming that the

airgun hunter already has the gun, pellet accuracy can be determined by shooting some groups at perhaps 30 yards with different types of pellets. To do this, mount a scope on

Accurate shooting under hunting conditions requires a lot of practice.

A bench rest is seldom available when hunting, so Randy assumes a kneeling position, which is steadier than standing.

the gun and use a bench rest. There is no point in trying to determine accuracy of a particular gun/pellet combination by shooting offhand using open sights. The accuracy of the pellet will not be determined, but the ability of the shooter will be. The purpose of the scope is to reduce sighting errors to an absolute minimum and the purpose of the bench rest is to remove the effects of about 5 feet of swaying, shaking bone and muscle. Having said that, and assuming that you are ready to evaluate pellet accuracy, here are some suggestions.

There is probably no need for shooting 10-shot groups. Hunting accuracy, either with a firearm or airgun, is different from target accuracy, where many shots are the norm. My personal bias is for five-shot groups, but many shooters prefer to shoot three-shot groups. However, it is important that several groups be obtained and that the average group size be compared for each pellet being tested. Measure the groups! It is not good enough to "eyeball" the targets and arrive at an "I think this is better" conclusion. Make measurements and keep records of the data you obtain.

Some specifications for the accuracy of air rifles give group sizes that are incredibly small, perhaps 0.15 inch at 10 meters. First of all, 10 meters is not a practical hunting distance. Second, the fine print goes on to explain that the group size given is the smallest three-shot group obtained and that out of an unspecified number! The smallest group is an accident just as the largest group is. Such figures are as meaningless as the batting average for a baseball player with one time at bat. What has meaning is the average for a large number of trials. Any scientist or engineer knows that about his/her data.

Suppose you have an air rifle that has a maximum of eight pumps. Accuracy may be somewhat different with six or seven pumps than it is with eight. However, since the evaluation is being conducted with hunting in mind, do not reduce the power level to four pumps even if accuracy is better, because the power level (as indicated by penetration and energy transfer) may be inadequate to humanely kill the target.

Unfortunately, live targets are not always encountered at 10 meters (33 feet), the usual distance for airgun competition and testing. If you hunt with an airgun, you may encounter the game at distances from a few feet to perhaps 40 or 50 yards. There is some practical limit to the range at which you may be justified in shooting at a live target. Pellets (even the most efficient ones) lose velocity rapidly, so they do not deliver enough power to the target to be effective at ranges of much more than 40 to 50 yards. Of course, this depends on the gun and pellet and on how large and tough the quarry is.

When taking shots in the field, using a tree as a rest gives the author's brother, Curt, an advantage in accuracy.

Try sighting the air rifle at 25 yards and then shooting groups at 20, 30, and 40 yards to see how the point of impact differs at these distances. You may be amazed at how much the point of impact changes as the range changes. An airgun sighted to hit the point of aim at 25 yards may shoot as much as 2 to 3 inches low at 40 yards. It now becomes apparent that your ability to judge distance is important. It is also extremely important to know where the point of impact will be at intermediate ranges. Moreover, the remaining energy of the pellet is so much lower at longer ranges that precise bullet placement is even more important. Therefore, you should shoot groups to determine accuracy not only at the distance for which the

Shown here are some of the American air rifles that are suitable for hunting and pest control. They are, from top, the Benjamin 392, Crosman 2200B, Daisy 22X, Crosman 2100B, and Sheridan Silver Streak.

gun is sighted, but also at shorter distances and at the longest distance that your gun may be realistically used.

None of the multi-pump pneumatic air rifles is as powerful as some of the European "magnum" spring-piston guns. Even those guns have only 6 to 9 foot-pounds of kinetic energy remaining at 50 yards. A practical upper-range limit for any American airgun is probably around 40 to 50 yards, and then only if it will print groups of about 1 to 1.5 inches. Try shooting groups at say 30 yards and see what you get. You may find out that your gun will not consistently hit a tennis ball-sized target (about the size of the body of a crow) at this distance and you may find out just how much a gentle breeze will cause a pellet to drift off course. In that case, your longest practical range is shortened to a distance at which you can call your shots on a target of appropriate size.

In Chapter 7, the reduction of velocity at high altitude was discussed. If you plan to hunt small game and varmints at high altitude, you should do so with an air rifle of considerable power. My tests show that the reduction in velocity amounts to about 10 to 12 percent when air rifles are fired at an elevation of 8,400 feet. That corresponds to a reduction in kinetic energy of about 20 percent. For hunting with an airgun in the mountains, I recommend that you take your most powerful air rifle for the job.

After a considerable amount of experimentation, you should identify a few types of pellets that give acceptable accuracy in your particular gun. These pellets should now be evaluated in terms of penetration and energy transfer.

This book is about American multi-pump pneumatics and their performance. The results of determining accuracy at 10 yards were presented in Chapters 5 and 6, and they show that the rifles are quite accurate. In view of the fact that hunting game or pests would

Although not the most powerful .22 caliber rifle, the Daisy 22X gives fine accuracy and it is suitable for hunting at close distances.

involve shots at longer ranges, I have conducted tests to see how the rifles might perform. Because of the number of guns involved and the large number of pellet types available, selected testing was conducted at 30 and 50 yards to show what can be expected.

The first rifle tested was the Crosman 2100, which was fired using the 10.5-grain Crosman Premier pellet. A 4X scope (not an airgun scope, so it has a considerable amount of parallax) was mounted. For each shot, the eye was positioned as carefully as possible. At 30 yards, firing with six pumps gave three-shot groups of 0.43, 0.57, 0.19, 0.61, 0.44, and 0.53 inch. This rifle clearly has the accuracy for effective use at 30 yards and beyond.

A Benjamin 397 also was tested at 30 yards, using the 10.5-grain Crosman Premier pellet and six pumps. In this case, two scopes were used on different occasions. The first was a 3-9X Bushnell that was intended for use on centerfire rifles (it had a lot of parallax at 30 yards). Even so, three-shot groups measured 0.59, 0.65, 0.59, 0.71, 0.82, and 0.26 inch, for an average of 0.60 inch. On the other occasion, the 3-12X BSA airgun scope was mounted. Three-shot groups measuring 0.35, 0.56, 0.70, and 0.47 inch were obtained, for an average of 0.52 inch.

Testing the Benjamin 397 at 50 yards was conducted with the 3-12X BSA scope and the 10.5 grain-Crosman Premier pellet. Three-shot groups measured 1.20, 1.57, 1.46, 0.96, and 1.52 inches for an average of 1.34 inches. Unfortunately, there was a slight breeze and it caused the groups to be spread out horizontally. I believe that under ideal conditions, the .177 caliber Benjamin is capable of doing even better. This level of accuracy rivals that of the best spring-piston rifles.

Testing of a .20 caliber Sheridan also was conducted at 30 yards with a peep sight. With six pumps, the Crosman Premier pellets gave an average group size of 0.74 inch, which is as good as I can see. At 50 yards, a few groups averaged 1.93 inches and this with the ordinary Sheridan cylindrical pellet, which is not a match-grade pellet. I have no doubt that this rifle is capable of even better accuracy with a scope and some judicious selection of ammunition.

My .22 caliber Benjamin 392 was fired at 30 yards with a 12X airgun scope using six pumps

and the Crosman Premier pellet. Ten three-shot groups averaged 0.63 inch center-to-center. This is outstanding accuracy, and when coupled with the power of the Benjamin .22, it means that it is an effective hunting rifle.

The last rifle tested at long range was the Daisy 22X. The 3-12X airgun scope was mounted and shooting was conducted at 30 yards, using several pellets that showed good accuracy in the testing at 10 yards. In each case, three-shot groups were obtained with the rifle given eight pumps. The groups obtained with the Daisy pointed pellet measured 0.53, 0.75, 0.72, 0.44, and 0.88 inch for an average of 0.66 inch. With the Dynamit Nobel Meisterkugeln pellet, the groups obtained were 0.45, 1.16, 0.75, 1.00, and 1.11 inches for an average of 0.89 inch. The Gamo Master Point gave an average group size of 0.92 inch with the groups being 1.19, 1.03, 0.38, 1.13, and 0.88 inches. The Gamo Magnum gave groups measuring 1.25, 0.41, 0.73, 0.81, and 0.61 inch for an average of 0.76 inch. The overall average of all groups at 30 yards is only 0.81 inch. Clearly, the Daisy 22X has the accuracy required to be an effective hunting arm at 30 to 35 yards.

To really stretch the point, the Daisy 22X was fired at 50 yards using the Daisy pointed pellet with eight pumps. The three-shot groups measured 1.38, 2.17, 1.64, 1.70, and 2.00 inches for an average of 1.78 inches. With the BSA airgun scope, it was possible to observe the pellet clearly throughout most of its flight. The muzzle velocity of the 15.68 grain Daisy pellet is only about 460 fps when eight pumps are used, so the trajectory is quite curved. In fact, a mid-range trajectory of approximately 7.5 inches was necessary to have the pellet hit the point of aim at 50 yards. Also, there was a slight breeze and it was possible to observe the drift of the pellet on its way to the target. These factors limit accuracy, but the results show that the Daisy 22X is an accurate rifle. It is not a 50-yard varmint rifle because of its low velocity, which gives a very curved trajectory. But it would be very suitable for shots at 30 to 35 yards, and that makes it a good choice for smaller pests and game. For longer ranges and larger targets, a more powerful rifle should be chosen.

There is no doubt that some of the other rifles that performed well at 10 yards are suitable for use at 30 to 35 yards. These tests should be ample evidence that American multi-pump pneumatic air rifles are viable choices for serious uses. I never feel under-gunned when using them in situations where an airgun is appropriate. It must be emphasized that the choice of ammunition is extremely important. You must have a pellet that gives the required on-target performance, but it must also be accurate. With any air rifle, you should experiment to find a pellet that has these characteristics in your rifle.

Penetration

Assuming that the required accuracy criterion has been met, the effectiveness of airgun pellets on game depends on the amount of material that is displaced by the pellet. In other words, the volume of the wound channel produced determines how much tissue destruction has occurred. Of course, any wound in the brain of a small living target converts it into a dead target. But in general, the amount of material moved out of its normal position determines the destructive power of the shot on the target. As one noted gun writer said, "Big bullets let in a lot of cold air." While this is certainly true, it is still necessary for the bullet to puncture the hide and give some penetration.

The two factors that determine the volume of the wound channel are its length (how deeply the projectile penetrates) and the diameter of the hole. A penny striking flat on a live target would create a large-diameter wound, but it would not penetrate deeply. A needle stuck into the live target would give depth of penetration, but almost no matter is displaced because the wound is of extremely small diameter. The pointed and domed pellets give

deeper penetration, while hollow or flat points give wider wound channels. The most effective bullet would penetrate the entire critter, but not exit and waste energy, while making the largest possible hole.

A case has just been made for considering penetration as one factor related to bullet performance. But how can penetration be measured? The bodies of small game and pests could be shot and autopsies performed to determine the measurements of wound channels. I did not take biology classes and have a real aversion to dissecting carcasses. Apparently, most other scribes that deal with the use of air rifles for hunting do too, since such information is lacking. As an alternative, some medium or material is sought that can easily be used to study the penetration of various pellets. We will describe the penetration tests after discussing the closely related topic of energy transfer.

Energy Transfer

When a projectile traveling at high velocity passes through a fluid medium, cavitation occurs. This means that the particles of the fluid are forced outward by the penetrating projectile and as they rush outward, they form a cavity that is larger in diameter than the diameter of the projectile. A demonstration of this phenomenon can be seen when a piece of fruit or a can of juice is struck with a high-velocity rifle bullet. Flesh consists partially of water and other biological fluids. Therefore, when a bullet strikes flesh, a cavity can be formed such that the wound channel is somewhat larger in diameter than the bullet itself. The formation of a large wound channel results in a rapid rate of transfer of its energy to the target.

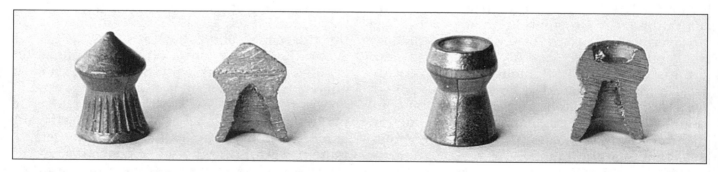

Two excellent pellets for hunting are the Beeman Silver Sting, left, and the Beeman Crow Magnum. The Silver Sting gives deeper penetration while the Crow Magnum gives greater smash.

The design of a pellet greatly affects its penetration and the diameter of the wound channel.

If a bullet has a sharp point and does not expand, such as a full metal-jacketed bullet, it can force its way smoothly through the target without disrupting much tissue. Such a full metal-jacketed bullet would penetrate very deeply because it would lose its energy slowly rather than transferring it to the medium by forming a large wound channel. If a bullet expands in a target, the wound channel widens as the energy of the bullet is spent by causing a widening cavity.

Air rifle pellets move at relatively low velocities compared to those of rifle bullets, especially those from most centerfire rifles. Consequently, the extent of cavitation is much smaller than when the target is struck with a bullet from a rifle. All other things being equal and assuming no expansion, a sharp-pointed pellet will penetrate more deeply than a flat-pointed one. Thus, the pointed pellet gives a longer wound channel, but not necessarily a wider one. Both length and diameter of the wound channel are factors in determining the overall wound extent. A flat-pointed pellet forces the material in the target outward at a large angle to the path of the pellet and thus gives some cavitation. As a result, the wound channel will be shorter but larger in diameter than that of a pointed pellet.

What type of pellet is most effective? There is no one answer to that question because it depends on the game. There is no reason to use a pellet that will penetrate five inches of crow body since a crow body is only about three inches thick. A pellet that penetrates more than that is going to waste part of its energy on the landscape. On the other hand, there is no justification for using a pellet that penetrates only 1/2 inch in flesh if one is shooting crows. The most effective pellet is one that gives a large wound channel and enough penetration to pass at least halfway (preferably more) through the intended game.

Testing pellet penetration is sometimes done by shooting them into some semi-solid

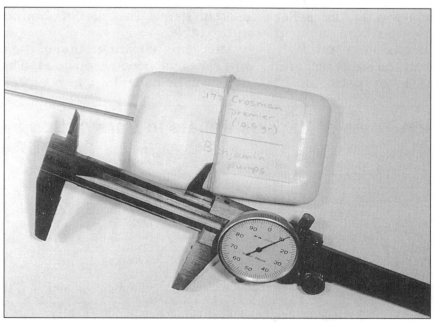

I used a brass rod and dial caliper to measure the depth of pellet penetration in bars of soap.

The greater effect produced by a pellet of larger diameter is clearly visible from these bars of soap shot with .177, left, and .22 caliber pellets.

degrees F; they were unwrapped as they were used. The bars were as uniform as modern "soap science" could produce.

The tests were conducted to obtain some experimental data that would provide a basis for comparing the performance of different types of pellets in a given caliber and the same type of pellet in different calibers. In order to keep some things nearly constant, the three guns used were a Benjamin 397 in .177 caliber, a Sheridan Silver Streak in .20 caliber, and a Benjamin 392 in .22 caliber. The information given in Chapters 5 and 6 shows that these guns are of very similar power, and in all cases the guns were given six pumps.

material. However, it must be borne in mind that any such material (putty, dough, wet cement, starch paste, etc.) has a consistency that is highly temperature dependent. Changing the temperature of the material only a few degrees can change the resistance to cavitation enormously. Therefore, all such experiments are subject to considerable variability.

With these principles in mind, several types of pellets were tested by shooting them into bars of soap. Soap is a uniform material that is harder than most living targets, and it allows the dimensions and shapes of the cavities produced by the pellets to be examined. The cavities do not close up after the pellet penetrates. In these tests, the bars of soap used were all taken from one large multiple pack. Therefore, they were of the same age and they were stored in the large pack at 72

Penetration of the pellets was measured by firing them into bars of soap from a distance of 5 feet. In order to keep the pellets from exiting the bar, shots were directed into the ends of the bars, which were placed against a board as a backstop. Pellet velocity was either measured or estimated from the tables given in Appendices A and B. The depth of penetration was measured by using a brass rod of small diameter inserted into the bullet channel to the back of the pellet. Pellets selected for testing included pointed, hollow point, wadcutter and domed types in order to show what might be expected when these popular types are used on game. The results obtained are shown in the table.

After careful examination of the bars of soap, several facts became obvious. These observations will be listed here in no special order.

Penetration Tests of Various Pellets in Bars of Soap

Cal.	Pellet	Wt., gr.	Approx. velocity	Penetration inches
.22	Beeman Crow Magnum	18.47	550	1.83
.22	Beeman Kodiak	21.41	520	2.90
.22	Crosman Pointed	14.35	600	2.52
.22	Crosman Premier	14.34	600	2.47
.22	Crosman Wadcutter	14.32	600	1.97
.20	Beeman Crow Magnum	12.99	590	1.38
.20	Benjamin Cylindrical	14.28	570	2.43
.177	Beeman Crow Magnum	8.28	650	1.36
.177	Crosman Pointed	7.97	670	2.38
.177	Crosman Premier	10.50	600	2.61

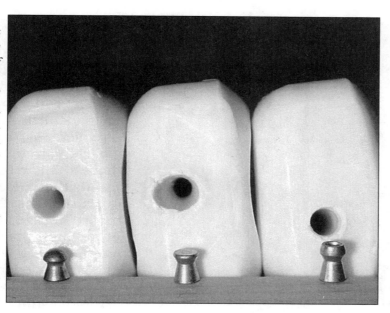

These three bars of soap display the effects of being shot with, from left, the .22 caliber Crosman Premier, Crosman wadcutter, and Beeman Crow Magnum pellets. Note the gaping hole produced by the wadcutter and how the hole produced by the Crow Magnum opens up after pellet entry.

8. The Beeman Kodiak .22 caliber pellet gave the deepest penetration recorded. Even with its low velocity, the heavy pellet (21.41 grains) penetrates extremely well.

9. The diameter of the bullet channel in the soap is obviously much larger for the .22 and .20 caliber pellets than for .177 pellets. Only the channel of the .177 caliber Beeman Crow Magnum came close to the diameter of those of the larger calibers and its penetration was only 1.36 inches.

1. The .22 Crosman Wadcutter gave the largest entrance hole, but penetration was somewhat less than that of either the domed or pointed pellets.

2. The Beeman Crow Magnum in all three calibers gave bullet channels that widen out noticeably after penetrating about 1/4 inch.

3. The Beeman Crow Magnum gave the smallest depth of penetration.

4. Except in .177 caliber, the pointed pellets gave deepest penetration.

5. The 10.5-grain Crosman Premier in .177 caliber penetrated extremely well. At 10.5 grains, it is a heavy pellet for the caliber and it has a very heavy, rounded nose.

6. The Crosman .22 Wadcutter imparted a real "smack" to the bar of soap and caused some bulging of the sides.

7. There was a pronounced difference in how hard the bar of soap was knocked against the backstop when the .20 and .22 caliber pellets hit it compared to the impact of .177 pellets, because of the greater momentum of the heavier pellets in these calibers.

No one is going to claim that these experiments answer all the questions about pellet penetration and energy transfer. Although a rather limited number of pellet types was used, the results do give some clear indications of what the pellets can do. The argument could be made that other brands of pellets of the same general type (pointed, domed, hollow point, etc.) might have given different results. There probably would be slight differences, but I did not want to shoot all the soap in the closet to find out. The results obtained are

The Beeman Kodiak is a huge pellet weighing 21.4 grains in .22 caliber. In spite of having the lowest velocity, it gave the deepest penetration in soap of any caliber or pellet type tested.

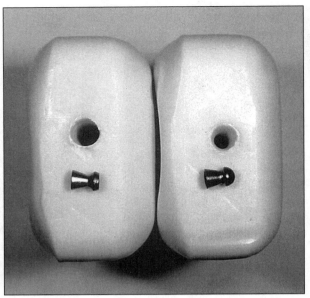

Two outstanding pellets for hunting are the Beeman Crow Magnum and the Crosman Premier. Note the difference produced by these pellets in .177 caliber when they are fired into bars of soap.

very likely indicative of what you would get with most other pellets of the same types.

After having done a considerable amount of experimental work with virtually all of the multi-pump American air rifles available and a great number of brands and types of pellets, I have come to some conclusions. For general plinking and small pests, I will use any pellet available. For larger pests and small game, I want to choose my ammunition more carefully. While I am going to give some of my preferences here, other choices might work equally well.

I am impressed with the performance of the Beeman Crow Magnum pellet in all calibers. It expands well, and it gives a wide bullet channel. While in .22 caliber it is a relatively heavy pellet (18.47 grains), the Crow Magnum is a relatively light pellet (12.99 grains) in .20 caliber and only about average weight (8.28 grains) in .177 caliber. The much greater relative weight in .22 caliber gives it quite a bit more penetration in that caliber than in the .20 and .177, even though the smaller calibers have higher velocity. I would select this pellet for pests like crows, starlings, and pigeons over any other because it is devastating. The Beeman Crow Magnum gives good accuracy in almost all air rifles, but it did not give the best accuracy in any of my rifles.

For game like rabbits and particularly squirrels, I want a pellet that gives greater penetration. For hunting, I do not care for any of the pellets that are essentially hollow

lead shells. The tests described here and years of use suggest to me that the Crosman Copperhead pointed pellet will penetrate as deeply as anything. Almost equal to it are the Crosman domed and the Crosman Premier. All of the Crosman pellets (even the wadcutter) have shallow base cavities and heads that are essentially solid, which makes them very hard-nosed pellets. They are accurate, and their high ballistic coefficients give them excellent downrange energy.

In .20 caliber, the Beeman Crow Magnum and any one of the domed pellets (Crosman Premier, Crosman domed, or Benjamin cylindrical) will give enough versatility for all targets.

In .177 caliber, the Beeman Crow Magnum is an excellent choice for the smaller species, and for the larger critters, the 10.5-grain Crosman Premier will give deep penetration.

Finally, one other .22 caliber pellet that I have tried deserves mention. That pellet is the Beeman Kodiak, which at 21.41 grains causes velocities to be unimpressive. What is impressive is the effect when the big bullet hits. For short-range shooting at larger game and pests, it is a good choice.

There are dozens of excellent pellets available. I am in no way suggesting that those discussed above are better than others that could be chosen for the same types of shooting. Obviously, I shoot many other types of ammunition in my air rifles. The choices described above constitute my "minimum ammo dump" and I could get by with those alone. It is quite certain that other choices are equally good or better for particular airguns. If you like the Beeman Silver Jet, Daisy pointed, Dynamit Nobel RWS Superpoint, Gamo Hunter, or some other pellet and it gives good accuracy in your gun, by all means use it. Some experimentation would still be valuable. The tests show clearly that not all pellets give equal accuracy in a particular rifle, and some rifles are more picky than others.

In most cases, a pointed or rounded pellet still seems preferable for general hunting.

Because pellets lose velocity rapidly, it is essential that the remaining velocity be as high as possible when the pellet reaches the target. Also, this assures the flattest trajectory possible, which makes hitting distant targets easier. Given the fact that pellets traveling at low velocity do not cause much cavitation, penetration is probably more important than the slightly more efficient energy transfer of flat and hollow-pointed pellets. This is the reason that pointed pellets are almost always dubbed "field" ammunition.

A new pellet from Daisy is the Power Pellet, which has a 1/8-inch steel ball in the head. It easily penetrated this board.

The data in Chapter 8 shows that the pointed and domed pellets—particularly the Crosman Premier and pointed, Benjamin Diabolo, and Crosman Domed pellets—retain velocity well and have high ballistic coefficients. Also, we have described how these pellets have smaller base cavities than most other pellets. Accordingly, such sturdy pellets hold their shape on impact and penetrate well. It is hard to fault such pellets for pest and game hunting if they are suitably accurate in your gun. That is not to say that many other types of pellets are not effective on game, because they certainly are.

Caliber Considerations

In view of the foregoing discussion, it is now possible to reach some conclusions regarding the effectiveness of air rifles of different calibers. However, the analysis of the effect of pellet caliber is clouded by a different issue. First, several American air rifles can be considered essentially as pairs having comparable power. The Daisy 880 and 22X are similar guns in .177 and .22 caliber, respectively. The Crosman 2100 and 2200 constitute such a pair as do the Benjamin 397 and 392. What one must keep in mind is that in each of these pairs, the .177

model gives about 100 to 125 fps higher velocity than the .22 caliber. Thus, the comparison is between a .177 caliber pellet at higher velocity with the larger .22 caliber pellet at a somewhat lower velocity. If both are traveling at the same velocity, the .22 caliber is considerably more potent than the .177 caliber.

Suppose the comparison to be made is between a .177 caliber pellet at 800 fps and a .22 caliber pellet at 685 fps, the top velocities listed by the manufacturer for the Benjamin 397 and 392 Models, respectively. First of all, let's assume that the .177 caliber pellet weighs 7.9 grains and the .22 pellet weighs 14.3 grains, because these are approximately the average pellet weights in those calibers. At the velocities given above, the kinetic energies are 11.2 foot-pounds for the .177 and 14.9 foot-pounds for the .22 caliber. This means that the .22 pellet has 32 percent more energy than the .177 caliber pellet.

Moreover, the frontal area of the pellets are 0.0246 square inch for the .177 and 0.0394 square inch for the .22 caliber. That is a 60 percent larger cross sectional area for the .22 caliber. Thus, the .22 caliber has 32 percent more energy and it also gives a much wider wound channel.

The holes in bars of soap show that the larger calibers displace much more material. Shown here are, from left, the effects of .177, .20, and .22 caliber pellets of similar construction.

.22 caliber (14.3 grains). The older Sheridan cylindrical pellets weighed 15 to 16 grains. Even for the 14.3 grain pellet, the .20 has about the same energy as a .22 caliber Benjamin Model 392, but the .20 caliber pellet is more efficient ballistically because it is smaller in cross sectional area. In fact, the Crosman Premier domed .20 caliber pellet has a ballistic coefficient of 0.040, while the .22 caliber Premier pellet has a ballistic coefficient of 0.035. Thus, it is not uncommon to find that a .20 caliber pellet may have higher remaining velocity at a practical range of say 25 to 35 yards than a .22 caliber one of the same weight if they have the same muzzle velocity.

Sometimes penetration of the .20 caliber pellet may be slightly greater than that of the .22 caliber, but the smaller cross sectional area of the .20 caliber (0.0314 square inch, compared to the .22's 0.396 square inch) works against it in creating a large wound channel. In the final analysis, there is little difference between the

This logic, while not necessarily perfect and complete, gives an indication of what is commonly known among airgunners. The larger calibers are more effective on game, especially as the game considered gets larger. That is why the imported .25 caliber spring piston rifles are the choice of knowledgeable hunters who plan to tackle larger species like groundhog and prairie dog. These big airguns still have the problem of rapid loss of pellet velocity, so even with such a gun, the practical range is no more than about 50 yards. Still, it would be very interesting if some American airgun maker would offer a multi-pump pneumatic in .25 caliber that could give a velocity of approximately 550-575 fps with a pellet of average weight with that caliber.

We have not mentioned the .20 caliber to this point. The various Sheridan models in .20 caliber drive pellets at up to 675 fps. Some .20 caliber pellets weigh about the same as those in

Although not a scientific test, this board shows the effect of being hit with a cylindrical .20 caliber Sheridan pellet.

If you want your wife or a youngster to enjoy airgun hunting, an airgun should be chosen that is relatively light and easy to pump like the Daisy 22X that Kathy is using here.

.20 and .22 calibers as long as pellets of the same weight and type are considered.

While the analysis above has dealt with the Benjamin and Sheridan guns so that specific velocities of comparable models in different calibers could be compared, the same conclusions are reached if you consider the Daisy 880 and 22X or the Crosman 2100 and 2200 pairs. In each case, the .177 caliber gun gives muzzle velocities about 125 fps higher than those of the .22 caliber. The bottom line is that if you plan to include much hunting with your airgun, get one of the larger calibers. However, an imported, super-accurate .177 caliber spring-piston airgun might have a muzzle velocity as high as 1,000 to 1,100 fps. Guns of this type raise the performance of the .177 caliber to a different

Although pellets do not drill holes, this old .177 caliber Daisy 880 is accurate and effective.

Sometimes you find yourself out there where an air rifle simply may not handle anything you encounter. The author goes prepared.

ity of 700 fps reaches the target traveling at 600 fps. Although the pellet has lost some velocity (about 14 percent), this should not affect the rotational velocity even that much. Suppose the pellet travels 2 inches into the target and stops. A pellet that spins one turn in travelling 14 inches will spin only a fraction of a turn in traveling two inches. Two inches is 1/7 of the 14 inches required for one turn, so the projectile will turn only 1/7 of a revolution while penetrating 2 inches into the body of a critter. This can hardly be called drilling! In fact, as the pellet pushes its way through tissue, the wound channel is slightly expanded and may not even touch the sides of the pellet where the very, very shallow rifling grooves are. Those grooves would have absolutely no effect on the wound channel.

Suppose that the penetration is 3 inches instead of two inches. The pellet would rotate 3/14 or 0.21 of a revolution. That hardly makes it a drill. No, the "drill effect" is a "say it fast and don't think about it" piece of nonsense, not science. If there was a drill effect, it would be greater for a .20 caliber than it is for .177 or .22 because the .20 has a rate of twist that is one turn in 12 inches of barrel length. Incidentally, some .177 caliber rifles have a rate of twist of one turn in 16 inches, which makes the spin analysis even less favorable!

Until relatively recent times, the vast majority of the imported spring-piston guns were sold in .177 caliber. In recent years, the number of models being offered in .20 and .22 calibers has increased greatly, and several are made in .25 caliber. They are, justifiably, receiving high acclaim. As a consequence, most of the articles dealing with the use of airguns for hunting over the years were based on experience with the .177 caliber because it was so much more widely used then. It may be that some of the "analysis" claiming that the .177 caliber is more effective than the .22 was based on experience with a high-velocity .177 with no .22 of comparable power being avail-

level and they may be more effective than a larger-caliber gun that has a much lower velocity. A comparison of one of these high-velocity .177 air rifles with an identical model in .20 or .22 caliber, which would have a velocity of around 850 to 900 fps would still favor the larger caliber for pests and game of larger size.

It is important to remember that most .177 caliber pellets lose velocity faster than those in .20 or .22 caliber. Thus, much of the superiority of the .177 caliber because of its higher velocity disappears at ranges beyond 30 yards. The flatter trajectory of the .177 is an advantage in shot placement at the longer ranges, but a .177 does not equal a .20 or .22 in displacing material when forming a wound channel.

Certain writings describing airgun performance on game refer to the "drill effect" of the pellet in the animal and ascribe some greater effectiveness to the .177 caliber because of it. Let us take a look at the facts. First, both .177 and .22 caliber airguns have barrel-twist rates of about one turn in 14 inches, while the Sheridan .20 caliber has a twist rate of one turn in 12 inches. For simplicity, let us assume that a pellet fired with a muzzle veloc-

An air rifle equipped with good sighting equipment that is properly sighted in is essential in hunting.

able for comparison. The rapid increase in the number of .20 and .22 caliber guns sold of the spring-piston type is not based on their superior accuracy. It is based largely on the fact that bigger pellets do more damage to tissue or "big bullets let in a lot of cold air!"

Recommendations

Realistically, what capabilities do air rifles possess for hunting and pest control? Assuming that the accuracy criteria are met, how far should you consider shooting at what? In order to answer that question, we will need to establish some criteria for energy requirements for the taking of different species. Unfortunately, there is no scientific way to do this. It certainly depends on where the target is hit and with what. In general, the criteria that I would suggest as minimum requirements are shown in the table.

Suggested Minimum Energy and Velocity Requirements

Species Category	Typical species*	Minimum Energy (ft lb)	Velocity, .177 Cal. 7.9 grains (ft/sec)	Velocity .20 or .22 Cal. 14.3 grains (ft/sec)
I	Sparrows, mice	2	325	250
II	Starlings, rats	3	400	300
III	Crows, pigeons	5	550	425
IV	Rabbits, squirrels	7	650	500

* Also for other species of similar size in each category

Suggested Maximum Range Of Airguns For Each Species Category*

Gun	Caliber	I	II	III	IV
				Maximum Range, yards	
Crosman 760B	.177	70	45	10	Not Recommended
Crosman 66BX	.177	75	60	20	Not Recommended
Daisy 856	.177	75	60	20	Not Recommended
Daisy 880	.177	75	65	25	Not Recommended
Crosman 2100B	.177	75	75	35	15
Crosman 2200B	.22	75	75	60	35
Daisy 22X	.22	75	75	45	20
Benjamin 392	.22	75	75	75	60
Benjamin 397	.177	75	75	45	30
Sheridan CB9, C9	.20	75	75	75	60

*Category I, sparrows, mice; Category II, starlings, rats; Category III, crows, pigeons; Category IV, rabbits, squirrels. Also for species of similar size in each category.

While pellets having less energy can certainly kill any of these species, it seems to me that these minimum values are reasonable and give some indication of what is required to be humane in hunting these species. It is better to err on the side of using more power than necessary, rather than less.

The remaining velocity of any pellet depends on the initial velocity and the ballistic coefficient of the pellet. Selecting a pellet with a high ballistic coefficient results in more retained energy at the target. For example, if a 7.9 grain .177 pellet starts out at 700 fps, it will arrive at a target 40 yards away with a velocity of 502 fps if the ballistic coefficient of the pellet is 0.015. It will arrive with a velocity of 545 fps if the ballistic coefficient of the pellet is 0.020. The higher ballistic coefficient helps, but it does not make an air rifle that is suitable for starlings into a squirrel rifle. For longer shots at game, a pellet should be selected that has a high ballistic coefficient.

The American multi-pump pneumatics were listed in Chapter 2, along with the maximum pellet velocities advertised for them. Given the energy and velocity requirements shown previously for various species, we could now give an estimation of the maximum range that each gun might be used on each species. We do that by determining the range at which pellets from each gun at its maximum power still delivers the energy requirement for taking various species suggested in the table, assuming a suitable ballistic coefficient for the pellet. For .177, .20, and .22 calibers we will use pellet ballistic coefficients of 0.016, 0.030, and 0.025, respectively, in the calculations. These values are approximately correct for some of the available field pellets in these calibers. When the calculations are performed, we find that the suggested minimum energies can be achieved out to the ranges shown in the table above.

Having the power to dispatch a species at more than 75 yards in no way indicates that

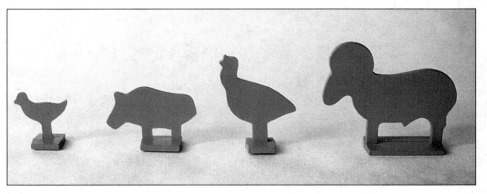

Silhouettes can provide valuable practice for the hunter using an air rifle.

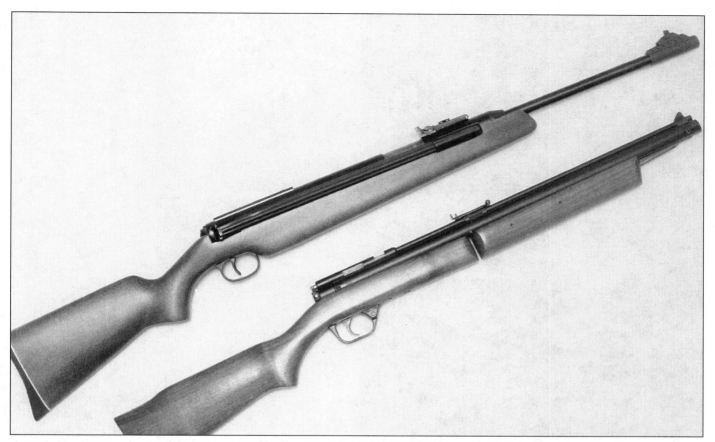

The size difference between the RWS Diana Model 48 in .25 caliber and a .22 caliber Benjamin is great. The difference in performance is much less than the size difference would suggest.

shots should be taken at such ranges. Even though a .177 caliber pellet fired at 600 fps arrives at 75 yards with about 2 foot-pounds of energy, it also arrives about 2 1/2 feet low when sighted for 25 yards! A .30-06 has enough energy to kill sparrows at two miles, but the trick is to hit one. A .22 Benjamin or a .20 Sheridan has sufficient energy to kill squirrels at 60 yards, but it would be unthinkable to attempt it. A practical limit for shooting live targets is perhaps 35 to 40 yards, because the chance of a wounded critter is too high at greater distances. Pellet placement is just too uncertain at longer distances.

Do not rely too much on caliber. I will illustrate this statement by telling of my own experience. It seemed to me to be essential that I own at least one very powerful air rifle, so I bought a .25 caliber that was advertised to deliver 750 fps. When I chronographed it with the Beeman Crow Magnum pellet, which weighs about 26.4 grains, I was astonished to read 537 fps on the instru-

ment! I called the importer and related my story only to hear: "That's about right for that pellet."

It seems that the manufacturer tests the .25 caliber with pellets of about 17 grains, which is very light for the caliber. My comment to the representative was, "You mean I bought an 8 1/2-pound gun of that size only to find that it is not that much more powerful than my American-made Benjamin .22?" After a moment of silence, the representative indicated that was in fact the case. You see, the Benjamin will shoot a rather heavy .22 caliber pellet at more than 600 fps. That doesn't make it a .25, but the difference is not as much as the size, weight, and cost difference would suggest. Of course, the .25 would still be more effective on game for the reasons discussed above. However, do not be misled. A well-placed pellet of the right construction from an American air rifle is still adequate. Incidentally, I don't plan to buy any more expensive, imported spring-piston air rifles.

With this rifle/scope combination, I can get groups of less than 1 inch at 25 yards.

In all fairness, the major factor in the effectiveness of any air rifle on game is pellet placement. The same principle applies to big-game hunting with centerfire rifles. A deer shot in the heart or spine with a 30-30 Winchester is going to be dead more quickly than one shot in the stomach with a .375 H & H Magnum. The effectiveness of an air rifle for hunting depends much more on the hunter than on the caliber of the airgun. An acquaintance has successfully hunted squirrels and rabbits over the years with a Daisy PowerLine 880, which I rate as unsuitable for that purpose. I have deliberately been conservative in the recommendations, but it does show what a good hunter can do with a rifle of moderate power.

It all boils down to choosing appropriate pellets, practicing diligently, getting close, and placing the shot precisely while obeying all applicable laws. Hopefully, we have in this chapter set forth some of the basic ideas and principles that should help you be a better hunter with your air rifle.

Interest in hunting with airguns is on the rise. There are an increasing number of places where hunting may be possible, but the close proximity of civilization makes the use of a firearm unwise or inconsiderate. In such situations, an airgun may be a logical choice of arm, and the selection of equipment and ammunition is extensive. Although many municipalities do not permit shooting airguns, there are a lot more places where an airgun can be used than where a firearm can be fired. No doubt the challenge of hunting with an airgun appeals to a large number of outdoors enthusiasts. But a significant factor in the use of air rifles is that for many people (including me), it is going afield with an old friend. The old friend seems more personal in a world that is growing more and more impersonal. My being out there with an airgun lets me know that some things have not changed and I can still be in touch with the past — the way it was when I started and perhaps the way it was when you started.

There really are too many starlings. They provide Jason and me with practice for squirrel hunting.

The future of hunting depends on the next generation of hunters. Training future hunters is an important task for those of us who love the sporting life. American air rifles are appropriate tools for that task.

Where to Get Information

If you plan to use an air rifle for taking game or pest control, it is necessary to determine the current rules and regulations for your area. Ignorance may be bliss, but you may get a citation for illegal use of an airgun if you are not fully compliant with the rules. In some states, you may also have your equipment confiscated. Listed in Appendix D is a state-by-state guide on where to obtain hunting regulations and related information.

Appendix A:

VELOCITY/ACCURACY DATA FOR .177 RIFLES

Velocities Obtained From the Crosman 760B at 8 Pumps
(Velocity in feet per second)

Shot	Beeman Hollow Point	Crosman Domed	Crosman Pointed	RWS Meisterkugeln	Gamo Match
1	508	462	462	481	484
2	508	472	446	469	498
3	502	470	448	476	484
4	506	476	460	470	485
5	506	471	462	473	499
Ave.	506	470	456	474	490
Std. Dev.	2	5	8	5	8

Accuracy of the Crosman 760B at 10 Yards With 8 Pumps

Pellet	(Group Size in Inches)		
	Largest	Smallest	Ave. of Five 3-shot Groups
Crosman Premier (7.9 gr)	0.30	0.23	0.26
Crosman Pointed	0.62	0.23	0.43
Daisy Pointed	0.46	0.22	0.33
RWS Meisterkugeln	0.39	0.23	0.30
RWS Super-H-Point	0.46	0.19	0.37

Velocities Obtained From the Daisy 856F With 8 Pumps

Shot	Beeman Flat Head	Daisy Pointed	Daisy Wadcut.	RWS Meisterkugeln	Gamo Match
	(Velocity in feet per second)				
1	581	613	596	582	601
2	576	611	592	583	607
3	576	615	599	588	600
4	578	613	596	577	602
5	576	615	596	578	601
Ave.	577	613	596	582	602
Std. Dev.	2	2	2	4	3

Accuracy of the Daisy 856F at 10 Yards With 8 Pumps

Pellet	Largest	Smallest	Ave. of Five 3-Shot Groups
	(Group Size in Inches)		
Beeman Crow Magnum	0.31	0.18	0.26
Daisy Pointed	0.35	0.18	0.26
Crosman Premier (7.9)	0.36	0.16	0.21
RWS Meisterkugeln	0.34	0.14	0.26
Gamo Master Point	0.27	0.19	0.23

Velocities Obtained From the Crosman 66BX at 8 Pumps

Shot	Beeman Flat Head	Crosman Domed	Crosman Pointed	RWS Meisterkugeln	Gamo Match
	(Velocity in feet per second)				
1	568	578	576	558	590
2	573	580	579	567	587
3	566	580	577	563	596
4	551	571	583	545	589
5	553	569	577	547	596
Ave.	562	576	578	556	592
Std. Dev.	10	5	3	10	4

Accuracy of the Crosman 66BX at 10 Yards With 8 Pumps*

Pellet	(Group Size in Inches)		
	Largest	Smallest	Ave. of Five 3-Shot Groups
Beeman Crow Magnum	0.50	0.22	0.35
Crosman Premier (7.9)	0.36	0.25	0.29
Crosman Pointed	0.45	0.22	0.33
RWS Meisterkugeln	0.19	0.36	0.27
RWS Superdome	0.50	0.17	0.36

* (Using a Weaver V22 scope set at 6 power)

Velocities Obtained From the Daisy 880 at 8 Pumps

Shot	(Velocity in feet per second)				
	Beeman Crow Magnum	Crosman Domed	Daisy Pointed	RWS Meisterkugeln	RWS Superdome
1	563	574	596	571	567
2	568	573	594	561	561
3	563	571	589	561	571
4	565	577	593	558	563
5	565	574	592	558	568
Ave.	565	574	593	562	566
Std. Dev.	2	2	3	5	4

Accuracy of the Daisy 880 at 10 Yards With 8 Pumps

Pellet	(Group Size in Inches)		
	Largest	Smallest	Ave. of Five 3-Shot Groups
Crosman Premier (7.9)	0.87	0.36	0.68
Daisy Pointed	0.54	0.28	0.39
Daisy Wadcutter	0.88	0.28	0.54
RWS Meisterkugeln	0.58	0.29	0.45
Gamo Magnum	0.47	0.19	0.35

Velocities Obtained From the Crosman 2100B at 8 Pumps

Shot	Beeman Hollow Point	Crosman Domed	Crosman Pointed	RWS Meisterkugeln	Gamo Magnum
	(Velocity in feet per second)				
1	753	723	737	709	707
2	757	727	732	704	710
3	754	722	727	704	712
4	753	730	732	709	707
5	756	733	733	711	709
Ave.	755	727	732	707	709
Std. Dev.	2	5	4	3	2

Accuracy of the Crosman 2100B at 10 Yards With 8 Pumps

Pellet	Largest	Smallest	Ave. of Five 3-Shot Groups
	(Group Size in Inches)		
Crosman Premier (7.9)	0.33	0.13	0.19
Beeman Crow Magnum	0.34	0.24	0.30
RWS Meisterkugeln	0.27	0.18	0.21
RWS Superdome	0.24	0.14	0.18
Gamo Master Point	0.27	0.08	0.16

Velocities Obtained From the Benjamin 397 at 6 Pumps

Shot	Beeman Silver Sting	Crosman Pointed	RWS Meisterkugeln	RWS Supermag	Gamo Match
	(Velocity in feet per second)				
1	655	668	665	640	687
2	661	666	672	643	692
3	661	665	666	640	694
4	665	671	670	638	689
5	658	672	665	640	693
Ave.	660	668	668	640	691
Std. Dev.	4	3	3	2	3

Accuracy of the Benjamin 397 at 10 Yards With 6 Pumps

Pellet	(Group Size in Inches)		
	Largest	Smallest	Ave. of Five 3-Shot Groups
Beeman Crow Magnum	0.35	0.16	0.26
Crosman Pointed	0.29	0.19	0.26
Crosman Premier	0.18	0.05	0.13
RWS Meisterkugeln	0.23	0.18	0.20
RWS Supermag	0.26	0.17	0.22

Velocities Obtained for the Gamo Sporter 500 at 5,500 feet

Shot	Crosman Pointed	Daisy Pointed	Gamo Master Pt.	Gamo Hunter	RWS Meisterkugeln
1	700	745	695	728	680
2	708	739	691	722	687
3	698	740	698	724	684
4	702	736	703	725	694
5	704	736	705	726	681
Ave.	702	739	698	725	685
Std. Dev.	4	4	6	2	6

Velocities Obtained for the Gamo Sporter 500 at 8,400 feet

Shot	Crosman Pointed	Daisy Pointed	Gamo Master Pt.	Gamo Hunter	RWS Meisterkugeln
1	645	680	649	660	636
2	650	693	649	661	631
3	655	689	650	661	631
4	650	689	646	660	635
5	651	684	645	660	639
Ave.	650	687	648	660	634
Std. Dev.	4	5	2	1	3

Velocities Obtained for the Gamo Hunter at 5,500 feet

Shot	Crosman Wadcutter	Gamo Hunter	Daisy Pointed	Gamo Master pt.	RWS Meisterkugeln
1	817	863	903	842	839
2	809	871	898	844	839
3	820	862	896	847	835
4	808	863	908	846	841
5	819	867	898	842	835
Ave.	815	865	901	844	838
Std. Dev.	6	4	5	2	3

Velocities Obtained for the Gamo Hunter at 8,400 feet

Shot	Crosman Wadcutter	Gamo Hunter	Daisy Pointed	Gamo Master pt.	RWS Meisterkugeln
1	751	807	839	787	773
2	748	789	833	786	774
3	750	796	831	785	772
4	774	796	831	791	765
5	747	794	834	781	769
Ave.	748	796	834	786	771
Std. Dev.	3	7	3	4	4

Velocities Obtained for the Beeman S1 at 5,500 feet

Shot	Crosman Pointed	Gamo Hunter	Beeman Silver St.	RWS Hobby	Beeman Crow Mag.
1	762	808	754	834	751
2	754	814	725	831	741
3	756	799	733	811	750
4	762	797	726	808	739
5	770	807	722	811	744
Ave.	761	805	734	819	745
Std. Dev.	6	7	13	12	5

Velocities Obtained for the Beeman S1 at 8,400 feet

Shot	Crosman Pointed	Gamo Hunter	Beeman Silver St.	RWS Hobby	Beeman Crow Mag.
1	703	733	721	795	719
2	701	738	718	758	720
3	701	739	718	777	718
4	698	764	715	763	715
5	707	772	719	766	722
6	700	765	—	787	—
7	685	721	—	—	—
8	698	751	—	—	—
9	713	—	—	—	—
10	705	—	—	—	—
Ave.	701	749	718	770	719
Std. Dev.	7	18	2	12	3

APPENDIX B:

VELOCITY/ACCURACY DATA FOR .20 AND .22 RIFLES

Velocities Given by the Sheridan CB9 Blue Streak at 6 Pumps
(Velocity in feet per second)

Shot	Ben./Sheridan Cyl. (new)	Crosman Domed	Beeman Crow Magnum	Beeman H & N Match	Sheridan Diabolo
1	557	566	596	641	569
2	558	561	597	644	567
3	560	565	600	641	566
4	553	565	603	647	570
5	554	563	602	647	570
Ave.	556	564	600	643	568
Std. Dev.	3	2	3	3	2

Velocities Given by the Sheridan C9 Silver Streak at 6 Pumps
(Velocity in feet per second)

Shot	Ben./Sheridan Cyl. (new)	Crosman Domed	Beeman Crow Magnum	Beeman H & N Match	Sheridan Diabolo
1	569	577	587	660	576
2	567	572	586	659	579
3	566	578	590	658	580
4	567	577	588	660	582
5	571	576	584	655	578
Ave.	568	576	587	658	579
Std. Dev.	2	2	2	2	2

Velocities Given by the Sheridan C9PB at 6 Pumps
(Velocity in feet per second)

Shot	Ben./Sheridan Cyl. (new)	Crosman Domed	Beeman Crow Magnum	Beeman H & N Match	Sheridan Diabolo
1	574	576	599	663	581
2	573	576	598	666	582
3	569	577	599	662	584
4	571	579	597	664	580
5	572	580	604	664	584
Ave.	572	578	599	664	582
Std. Dev.	2	2	3	1	2

Velocity Obtained Using Max. No. of Pumps for Each Sheridan Rifle
(Velocity in feet per second)

Pellet	CB9	C9	C9PB
Beeman H&N Match	695	702	714
Beeman Crow Magnum	632	643	659
Sheridan Diabolo	612	617	631
Crosman Domed	608	623	640
Crosman Premier	607	615	627
Sheridan cylindrical (new)[1]	597	612	625
Sheridan cylindrical (old)[2]	586	571	602

[1] (ave. wt. 14.306 gr.)
[2] (ave. wt. 15.209 gr.)

Velocities Obtained From the Daisy PowerLine 22X at 8 Pumps
(Velocity in feet per second)

Shot	Daisy Pointed	Dynamit Nobel (RWS) Meisterkugeln	Crosman Pointed	Gamo Match	Gamo Master Point
1	463	486	482	490	455
2	463	474	479	489	457
3	456	485	478	492	456
4	453	481	487	489	457
5	464	483	480	489	456
Ave.	460	482	481	490	456
Std. Dev.	5	5	4	1	1

Accuracy of the Daisy PowerLine 22X at 10 Yards With 8 Pumps
(Group Size in Inches)

Pellet	Largest	Smallest	Ave. of Five 3-Shot Groups
Daisy Pointed	0.35	0.05	0.23
RWS Meisterkugeln	0.45	0.18	0.28
Beeman Crow Magnum	0.42	0.22	0.32
RWS Superdome	0.37	0.06	0.27
Gamo Master Point	0.30	0.12	0.24

Velocities Obtained From the Crosman 2200B at 8 Pumps
(Velocity in feet per second)

Shot	Crosman Pointed	Dynamit Nobel (RWS) Meisterkugeln	Daisy Pointed	Gamo Hunter	Beeman Silver Jet
1	544	546	505	522	545
2	537	544	506	521	537
3	543	545	509	522	542
4	549	554	510	524	546
5	549	552	511	523	545
Ave.	544	548	508	522	543
Std. Dev.	5	4	3	1	4

Accuracy of the Crosman 2200B at 10 Yards With 8 Pumps
(Group Size in Inches)

Pellet	Largest	Smallest	Ave. of Five 3-Shot Groups
Crosman Pointed	0.35	0.17	0.26
Crosman Premier	0.97	0.25	0.71
Crosman Wadcutter	0.61	0.28	0.46
RWS Meisterkugeln	0.31	0.18	0.26
Gamo Magnum	0.81	0.41	0.57

Velocities Obtained From Benjamin 392 at 6 Pumps

(Velocity in feet per second)

Shot	Crosman Pointed	Dynamit Nobel (RWS) Meisterkugeln	Beeman Silver Jet	Benjamin Diabolo	RWS Super H-Point
1	601	605	596	596	590
2	599	601	600	599	590
3	600	602	599	601	591
4	600	600	595	596	589
5	595	603	598	595	590
Ave.	599	602	598	597	590
Std. Dev.	2	2	2	3	1

Accuracy of the Benjamin 392 at 10 Yards With 6 Pumps

(Group Size in Inches)

Pellet	Largest	Smallest	Ave. of Five 3-Shot Groups
Crosman Premier	0.35	0.22	0.31
RWS Meisterkugeln	0.40	0.04	0.24
Beeman Crow Magnum	0.52	0.17	0.36
Crosman Pointed	0.31	0.15	0.23
Daisy Pointed	0.31	0.14	0.23

APPENDIX C:

BALLISTICS TABLES

The ballistics tables presented in this appendix are adequate for most airgun and pellet combinations. The range of muzzle velocities (abbreviated M.V. in the tables) from 400 to 950 fps is appropriate for American airguns with the lower part of the range being applicable to rifles using a small number of pumps or to multi-pump pistols. A range of ballistic coefficients from 0.010 to 0.040 in increments of 0.0025 is included because this range encompasses the vast majority of values for airgun pellets. Thus, this set of tables is adequate for almost any calculation required for American multi-pump air rifles.

In the computations, a line of sight 1 1/2 inches above the bore was assumed. All of the entries are given in the form of velocity (feet per second)/deviation from the line of sight (inches). Thus, 587/+0.34 indicates a velocity of 587 fps with the pellet striking 0.34 inches above the line of sight. An entry of 537/-1.32 indicates a velocity of 537 fps and a point of impact that is 1.32 inches below the line of sight. At the muzzle, the velocity is the muzzle velocity and the point of impact is at -1.50 inches below the line of sight.

For high velocity air rifles, having the rifle sighted in at 30 yards does not necessarily indicate the most effective sighting. In those cases, it may be preferable to sight in at 40 yards so that the pellet does not strike so far below the line of sight at longer ranges, especially when pellets having higher ballistic coefficients are used.

Ballistic Coefficient = 0.01					
	Range (yards)				
M.V. (fps)	10 yds.	20 yds.	30 yds.	40 yds.	50 yds.
400	350/+2.13	305/+2.90	266/0.00	230/-7.76	199/-21.86
425	373/+1.79	325/+2.54	283/0.00	246/-6.77	213/-19.07
450	395/+1.48	345/+2.18	301/0.00	262/-5.94	227/-16.83
475	417/+1.21	366/+1.92	319/0.00	278/-5.31	241/-14.91
500	440/+0.99	386/+1.69	337/0.00	294/-4.67	256/-13.31
525	462/+0.80	406/+1.47	355/0.00	310/-4.23	270/-11.90
550	485/+0.62	426/+1.26	374/0.00	326/-3.78	284/-10.78
575	507/+0.48	446/+1.10	392/0.00	342/-3.43	299/-9.71
600	529/+0.36	466/+0.97	410/0.00	359/-3.06	313/-8.80
625	552/+0.25	486/+0.86	428/0.00	375/-2.73	328/-7.96
650	574/+0.16	506/+0.75	446/0.00	391/-2.47	342/-7.27
675	596/+0.07	526/+0.66	463/0.00	407/-2.26	356/-6.63

Ballistic Coefficient = 0.01

700	618/+0.00	545/+0.58	481/0.00	422/-2.07	370/-6.04
725	640/-0.07	565/+0.51	498/0.00	438/-1.89	384/-5.54
750	661/-0.13	584/+0.44	515/0.00	453/-1.74	398/-5.08
775	682/-0.18	602/+0.38	531/0.00	468/-1.60	411/-4.74
800	703/-0.23	620/+0.33	548/0.00	483/-1.47	424/-4.41
825	723/-0.28	638/+0.28	563/0.00	497/-1.37	437/-4.10
850	743/-0.31	655/+0.25	578/0.00	510/-1.26	449/-3.83
875	762/-0.35	671/+0.21	592/0.00	523/-1.17	460/-3.57
900	781/-0.38	687/+0.18	606/0.00	535/-1.09	471/-3.26
925	798/-0.41	701/+0.15	619/0.00	546/-1.02	482/-3.16
950	815/-0.43	715/+0.12	631/0.00	557/-0.96	491/-2.99

Ballistic Coefficient = 0.0125

M.V. (fps)	Range (yards)				
	10 yds.	20 yds.	30 yds.	40 yds.	50 yds.
400	359/+1.91	323/+2.63	289/0.00	258/-6.73	230/-18.52
425	383/+1.60	343/+2.27	308/0.00	276/-5.87	246/-16.24
450	406/+1.30	365/+1.96	327/0.00	293/-5.18	262/-14.30
475	428/+1.06	386/+1.73	346/0.00	310/-4.62	278/-12.75
500	451/+0.84	407/+1.48	366/0.00	328/-4.08	294/-11.33
525	474/+0.66	428/+1.27	385/0.00	346/-3.69	310/-10.26
550	497/+0.51	449/+1.11	405/0.00	364/-3.26	326/-9.12
575	520/+0.38	470/+0.98	424/0.00	381/-2.87	342/-8.32
600	543/+0.27	491/+0.85	443/0.00	399/-2.55	359/-7.43
625	566/+0.17	512/+0.74	462/0.00	417/-2.37	375/-6.68
650	589/+0.08	533/+0.65	481/0.00	434/-2.13	391/-6.07
675	611/+0.00	553/+0.57	500/0.00	451/-1.95	407/-5.57
700	633/-0.07	573/+0.49	519/0.00	469/-1.78	422/-5.12
725	656/-0.13	594/+0.42	537/0.00	485/-1.62	438/-4.69
750	678/-0.19	613/+0.36	555/0.00	502/-1.48	453/-4.33
775	699/-0.24	633/+0.31	573/0.00	518/-1.36	468/-4.00
800	721/-0.28	652/+0.27	590/0.00	534/-1.24	483/-3.69
825	742/-0.32	670/+0.23	607/0.00	549/-1.15	497/-3.43
850	762/-0.36	688/+0.19	623/0.00	564/-1.06	510/-3.20
875	782/-0.39	705/+0.15	638/0.00	578/-0.98	523/-2.99
900	802/-0.42	722/+0.12	653/0.00	591/-0.93	535/-2.80

Ballistic Coefficient = 0.0125

925	820/-0.45	738/+0.09	667/0.00	604/-0.87	546/-2.64
950	838/-0.47	753/+0.06	680/0.00	616/-0.81	557/-2.48

Ballistic Coefficient = 0.0150

M.V., (fps)	Range (yards)				
	10 yds.	20 yds.	30 yds.	40 yds.	50 yds.
400	366/+1.79	335/+2.45	305/0.00	278/-6.18	253/-16.73
425	389/+1.47	356/+2.09	325/0.00	297/-5.36	271/-14.60
450	413/+1.19	378/+1.85	345/0.00	316/-4.72	288/-12.87
475	436/+0.95	400/+1.61	366/0.00	334/-4.20	305/-11.48
500	459/+0.74	421/+1.33	386/0.00	353/-3.76	322/-10.24
525	482/+0.58	443/+1.18	406/0.00	372/-3.27	340/-9.17
550	506/+0.44	465/+1.02	426/0.00	390/-2.90	357/-8.18
575	529/+0.32	486/+0.89	446/0.00	409/-2.62	375/-7.29
600	552/+0.21	508/+0.78	466/0.00	428/-2.36	392/-6.56
625	575/+0.11	529/+0.68	486/0.00	447/-2.14	410/-5.99
650	598/+0.03	551/+0.59	506/0.00	465/-1.94	427/-5.46
675	621/-0.04	572/+0.51	526/0.00	483/-1.76	444/-4.98
700	644/-0.11	593/+0.43	545/0.00	502/-1.60	461/-4.57
725	667/-0.17	614/+0.37	565/0.00	519/-1.46	477/-4.20
750	689/-0.22	634/+0.32	584/0.00	537/-1.32	494/-3.85
775	711/-0.27	654/+0.28	602/0.00	554/-1.21	510/-3.55
800	733/-0.31	675/+0.23	620/0.00	571/-1.12	525/-3.29
825	755/-0.35	693/+0.19	638/0.00	587/-1.04	540/-3.05
850	776/-0.39	712/+0.14	655/0.00	603/-0.96	555/-2.84
875	796/-0.42	730/+0.11	671/0.00	618/-0.88	568/-2.65
900	816/-0.45	747/+0.08	687/0.00	632/-0.82	582/-2.48
925	836/-0.48	764/+0.06	701/0.00	645/-0.75	594/-2.33
950	855/-0.50	780/+0.03	715/0.00	658/-0.69	606/-2.18

Ballistic Coefficient = 0.0175

M.V. (fps)	Range (yards)				
	10 yds.	20 yds.	30 yds.	40 yds.	50 yds.
400	371/+1.70	343/+2.31	317/0.00	294/-5.72	271/-15.44
425	394/+1.40	365/+2.02	338/0.00	313/-5.03	289/-13.51

Ballistic Coefficient = 0.0175

	10 yds.	20 yds.	30 yds.	40 yds.	50 yds.
450	418/+1.11	388/+1.76	359/0.00	332/-4.40	307/-11.99
475	441/+0.87	410/+1.46	380/0.00	352/-3.97	326/-10.66
500	465/+0.69	432/+1.28	401/0.00	371/-3.43	344/-9.49
525	488/+0.54	454/+1.11	421/0.00	391/-3.00	362/-8.41
550	512/+0.39	476/+0.96	442/0.00	411/-2.73	381/-7.47
575	535/+0.28	498/+0.84	463/0.00	430/-2.44	399/-6.65
600	559/+0.17	520/+0.73	484/0.00	449/-2.22	417/-6.13
625	582/+0.08	542/+0.63	504/0.00	469/-2.00	436/-5.54
650	606/-0.01	564/+0.55	525/0.00	488/-1.80	454/-5.05
675	629/-0.08	586/+0.40	545/0.00	507/-1.64	472/-4.61
700	652/-0.14	607/+0.39	565/0.00	526/-1.49	490/-4.23
725	675/-0.19	628/+0.34	585/0.00	545/-1.34	507/-3.85
750	697/-0.24	649/+0.29	605/0.00	563/-1.21	524/-3.54
775	720/-0.29	670/+0.24	624/0.00	581/-1.13	541/-3.27
800	742/-0.34	690/+0.20	643/0.00	599/-1.04	557/-3.02
825	764/-0.38	710/+0.15	661/0.00	615/-0.96	573/-2.81
850	786/-0.41	729/+0.11	678/0.00	632/-0.88	589/-2.62
875	807/-0.44	748/+0.09	695/0.00	647/-0.80	603/-2.43
900	827/-0.47	766/+0.06	712/0.00	662/-0.73	617/-2.26
925	847/-0.49	783/+0.04	727/0.00	677/-0.67	630/-2.11
950	867/-0.52	800/+0.01	742/0.00	690/-0.63	642/-1.97

Ballistic Coefficient = 0.0200

M.V. (fps)	Range (yards)				
	10 yds.	20 yds.	30 yds.	40 yds.	50 yds.
400	374/+1.63	350/+2.22	327/0.00	305/-5.52	285/-14.71
425	398/+1.35	375/+1.95	348/0.00	325/-4.75	304/-12.82
450	422/+1.04	395/+1.68	370/0.00	345/-4.27	323/-11.35
475	445/+0.82	417/+1.38	391/0.00	366/-3.75	342/-10.15
500	469/+0.65	440/+1.23	412/0.00	386/-3.22	361/-8.93
525	493/+0.49	462/+1.05	434/0.00	406/-2.90	380/-7.87
550	517/+0.36	485/+0.92	455/0.00	426/-2.59	399/-6.95
575	540/+0.25	507/+0.80	476/0.00	446/-2.33	418/-6.40
600	564/+0.15	529/+0.69	497/0.00	466/-2.10	437/-5.76
625	587/+0.05	552/+0.60	518/0.00	486/-1.89	456/-5.24
650	611/-0.03	574/+0.51	539/0.00	506/-1.71	475/-4.76

Ballistic Coefficient = 0.0200

675	634/-0.10	596/+0.42	560/0.00	526/-1.57	494/-4.73
700	658/-0.15	618/+0.38	581/0.00	545/-1.40	512/-3.96
725	681/-0.21	640/+0.32	601/0.00	565/-1.25	530/-3.62
750	704/-0.26	661/+0.27	621/0.00	584/-1.17	548/-3.33
775	726/-0.31	682/+0.22	641/0.00	602/-1.08	566/-3.07
800	749/-0.36	703/+0.17	660/0.00	620/-0.98	583/-2.86
825	771/-0.39	723/+0.13	679/0.00	638/-0.89	599/-2.64
850	793/-0.42	743/+0.10	697/0.00	655/-0.81	615/-2.44
875	815/-0.45	762/+0.07	714/0.00	671/-0.74	630/-2.26
900	836/-0.48	781/+0.05	731/0.00	687/-0.67	645/-2.09
925	856/-0.51	798/+0.02	747/0.00	701/-0.62	659/-1.94
950	876/-0.53	815/-0.01	763/0.00	715/-0.59	672/-1.82

Ballistic Coefficient = 0.0225

M.V. (fps)	Range (yards)				
	10 yds.	20 yds.	30 yds.	40 yds.	50 yds.
400	377/+1.59	355/+2.17	335/0.00	315/-5.29	296/-13.96
425	401/+1.27	378/+1.91	356/0.00	335/-4.61	316/-12.30
450	425/+0.99	401/+1.56	378/0.00	356/-4.14	335/-10.95
475	449/+0.76	423/+1.29	400/0.00	377/-3.63	355/-9.78
500	472/+0.62	446/+1.19	421/0.00	397/-3.00	375/-8.39
525	494/+0.47	469/+1.02	443/0.00	418/-2.81	394/-7.46
550	520/+0.34	492/+0.88	465/0.00	439/-2.48	414/-6.78
575	544/+0.22	514/+0.77	486/0.00	459/-2.23	434/-6.09
600	568/+0.12	537/+0.67	508/0.00	480/-2.00	453/-5.52
625	591/+0.03	560/+0.58	529/0.00	500/-1.80	473/-5.00
650	615/-0.05	582/+0.49	551/0.00	521/-1.63	492/-4.54
675	639/-0.11	604/+0.41	572/0.00	541/-1.47	511/-4.14
700	662/-0.17	626/+0.36	593/0.00	561/-1.30	530/-3.77
725	685/-0.22	648/+0.31	614/0.00	581/-1.22	549/-3.45
750	709/-0.28	670/+0.25	634/0.00	600/-1.12	568/-3.17
775	732/-0.33	691/+0.20	654/0.00	619/-1.02	586/-2.95
800	754/-0.37	713/+0.15	674/0.00	638/-0.93	603/-2.72
825	777/-0.40	733/+0.12	693/0.00	656/-0.84	620/-2.50
850	799/-0.43	753/+0.09	712/0.00	673/-0.76	637/-2.29
875	821/-0.46	773/+0.06	730/0.00	690/-0.69	653/-2.12

Ballistic Coefficient = 0.0225

900	842/-0.49	792/+0.03	747/0.00	706/-0.64	668/-1.97
925	863/-0.52	810/+0.00	764/0.00	721/-0.60	682/-1.83
950	883/-0.54	828/-0.02	780/0.00	736/-0.55	695/-1.71

Ballistic Coefficient = 0.0250

M.V. (fps)	Range (yards)				
	10 yds.	20 yds.	30 yds.	40 yds.	50 yds.
400	379/+1.57	359/+2.13	340/0.00	323/-5.02	305/-13.50
425	403/+1.24	383/+1.86	363/0.00	343/-4.50	325/-11.83
450	427/+0.96	406/+1.52	385/0.00	365/-3.98	345/-10.60
475	451/+0.76	428/+1.33	407/0.00	386/-3.38	366/-9.23
500	475/+0.59	451/+1.14	429/0.00	407/-3.03	386/-8.10
525	499/+0.45	474/+1.00	450/0.00	428/-2.68	406/-7.25
550	523/+0.32	497/+0.86	473/0.00	449/-2.42	426/-6.53
575	547/+0.20	520/+0.75	494/0.00	470/-2.17	446/-5.89
600	571/+0.10	543/+0.64	516/0.00	491/-1.95	466/-5.23
625	595/+0.01	566/+0.56	538/0.00	512/-1.76	486/-4.83
650	619/-0.06	589/+0.46	560/0.00	533/-1.58	506/-4.38
675	642/-0.12	611/+0.40	581/0.00	553/-1.42	526/-3.98
700	666/-0.18	633/+0.35	603/0.00	573/-1.29	545/-3.62
725	689/-0.24	656/+0.29	624/0.00	594/-1.19	565/-3.31
750	713/-0.29	678/+0.24	645/0.00	613/-1.09	584/-3.08
775	736/-0.34	699/+0.19	665/0.00	633/-0.99	602/-2.84
800	759/-0.38	721/+0.14	685/0.00	652/-0.89	620/-2.60
825	781/-0.41	742/+0.11	705/0.00	670/-0.80	638/-2.38
850	804/-0.44	762/+0.08	724/0.00	688/-0.72	655/-2.18
875	826/-0.47	782/+0.05	742/0.00	705/-0.67	671/-2.03
900	848/-0.50	802/+0.02	760/0.00	722/-0.62	687/-1.88
925	869/-0.53	820/-0.01	777/0.00	738/-0.57	701/-1.75
950	889/-0.55	838/-0.03	794/0.00	753/-0.52	715/-1.64

Ballistic Coefficient = 0.0275

M.V. (fps)	Range (yards)				
	10 yds.	20 yds.	30 yds.	40 yds.	50 yds.
400	381/+1.53	363/+2.09	346/0.00	329/-4.93	313/-13.22
425	405/+1.19	386/+1.79	368/0.00	350/-4.42	334/-11.61

Ballistic Coefficient = 0.0275

450	429/+0.93	410/+1.48	390/0.00	372/-3.82	354/-10.27
475	453/+0.74	433/+1.31	412/0.00	393/-3.24	375/-8.87
500	477/+0.57	456/+1.11	435/0.00	415/-2.98	395/-7.80
525	501/+0.43	479/+0.97	457/0.00	436/-2.61	416/-7.09
550	526/+0.30	502/+0.84	479/0.00	457/-2.35	437/-6.33
575	549/+0.19	525/+0.74	501/0.00	479/-2.10	457/-5.73
600	573/+0.09	548/+0.62	524/0.00	500/-1.89	477/-5.17
625	597/+0.00	571/+0.53	546/0.00	521/-1.70	498/-4.68
650	621/-0.07	594/+0.45	568/0.00	542/-1.54	518/-4.25
675	645/-0.13	617/+0.40	589/0.00	563/-1.35	538/-3.84
700	669/-0.19	639/+0.18	611/0.00	581/-1.25	558/-3.51
725	692/-0.25	662/+0.28	632/0.00	604/-1.15	578/-3.23
750	716/-0.30	684/+0.22	653/0.00	625/-1.05	597/-2.99
775	739/-0.35	706/+0.17	674/0.00	644/-0.95	616/-2.74
800	762/-0.38	727/+0.13	695/0.00	664/-0.85	634/-2.51
825	785/-0.42	749/+0.10	715/0.00	683/-0.76	652/-2.29
850	808/-0.45	769/+0.07	734/0.00	701/-0.70	670/-2.10
875	830/-0.48	790/+0.04	753/0.00	719/-0.65	686/-1.95
900	852/-0.51	810/+0.01	771/0.00	736/-0.59	701/-1.81
925	873/-0.53	829/-0.01	789/0.00	752/-0.54	718/-1.69
950	895/-0.55	847/-0.04	805/0.00	767/-0.49	732/-1.57

Ballistic Coefficient = 0.0300

M.V. (fps)	Range (yards)				
	10 yds.	20 yds.	30 yds.	40 yds.	50 yds.
400	383/+1.50	366/+2.07	350/0.00	335/-4.88	320/-12.84
425	407/+1.16	389/+1.74	373/0.00	356/-4.37	340/-11.49
450	431/+0.90	413/+1.41	395/0.00	378/-3.78	361/-10.13
475	455/+0.73	436/+1.30	417/0.00	400/-3.06	382/-8.59
500	479/+0.55	459/+1.09	440/0.00	421/-2.94	403/-7.74
525	503/+0.41	482/+0.95	462/0.00	443/-2.57	424/-6.93
550	528/+0.28	506/+0.83	485/0.00	465/-2.30	445/-6.20
575	552/+0.18	529/+0.71	507/0.00	486/-2.06	466/-5.58
600	576/+0.08	552/+0.61	529/0.00	508/-1.85	487/-5.03
625	600/-0.01	575/+0.52	552/0.00	529/-1.67	507/-4/56
650	624/-0.08	598/+0.44	574/0.00	551/-1.50	528/-4.14

Ballistic Coefficient = 0.0300

675	648/-0.14	596/+0.38	596/0.00	572/-1.34	548/-3.75
700	671/-0.20	644/+0.33	618/0.00	593/-1.24	569/-3.43
725	695/-0.26	667/+0.27	640/0.00	614/-1.13	589/-3.18
750	719/-0.31	689/+0.21	661/0.00	634/-1.02	608/-2.92
775	742/-0.35	711/+0.16	682/0.00	654/-0.92	628/-2.67
800	765/-0.39	733/+0.12	703/0.00	674/-0.83	646/-2.43
825	788/-0.42	755/+0.10	723/0.00	693/-0.74	665/-2.21
850	811/-0.46	776/+0.06	743/0.00	712/-0.69	683/-2.04
875	834/-0.49	790/+0.03	762/0.00	730/-0.64	700/-1.89
900	856/-0.51	816/+0.00	781/0.00	747/-0.57	716/-1.76
925	877/-0.54	836/-0.02	798/0.00	764/-0.52	732/-1.63
950	899/-0.56	855/-0.04	815/0.00	780/-0.47	746/-1.51

Ballistic Coefficient = 0.0325

M.V. (fps)	Range (yards)				
	10 yds.	20 yds.	30 yds.	40 yds.	50 yds.
400	384/+1.48	369/+2.05	354/0.00	339/-4.86	325/-12.55
425	408/+1.13	392/+1.72	376/0.00	361/-4.33	346/-11.23
450	433/+0.86	415/+1.35	399/0.00	383/-3.76	368/-9.90
475	457/+0.72	439/+1.28	422/0.00	405/-3.16	389/-8.40
500	481/+0.54	462/+1.08	444/0.00	427/-2.84	410/-7.57
525	505/+0.40	486/+0.94	467/0.00	449/-2.54	431/-6.74
550	529/+0.28	509/+0.81	490/0.00	471/-2.26	452/-6.08
575	553/+0.17	532/+0.70	512/0.00	493/-2.02	474/-5.47
600	577/+0.07	556/+0.60	535/0.00	514/-1.81	495/-4.94
625	602/-0.02	579/+0.51	557/0.00	536/-1.63	516/-4.47
650	626/-0.09	602/+0.43	580/0.00	558/-1.45	537/-4.04
675	650/-0.15	625/+0.37	602/0.00	579/-1.32	557/-3.66
700	673/-0.21	648/+0.32	624/0.00	600/-1.21	578/-3.37
725	697/-0.26	671/+0.26	646/0.00	621/-1.10	598/-3.11
750	721/-0.32	694/+0.20	667/0.00	642/-0.99	618/-2.84
775	745/-0.36	716/+0.15	689/0.00	663/-0.89	638/-2.59
800	768/-0.39	738/+0.12	709/0.00	683/-0.79	657/-2.15
825	791/-0.43	760/+0.09	730/0.00	702/-0.72	675/-2.15
850	814/-0.46	781/+0.06	750/0.00	721/-0.67	694/-1.98
875	837/-0.49	802/+0.02	770/0.00	739/-0.61	711/-1.85

Ballistic Coefficient = 0.0325

900	859/-0.52	822/+0.00	789/0.00	757/-0.55	728/-1.71
925	881/-0.54	842/-0.03	807/0.00	774/-0.50	744/-1.58
950	902/-0.56	861/-0.05	824/0.00	790/-0.48	759/-1.46

Ballistic Coefficient = 0.0350

M.V. (fps)	Range (yards)				
	10 yds.	20 yds.	30 yds.	40 yds.	50 yds.
400	385/+1.46	371/+2.05	357/0.00	343/-4.76	330/-12.35
425	409/+1.11	394/+1.71	380/0.00	365/-4.22	352/-11.04
450	434/+0.89	418/+1.42	403/0.00	388/-3.52	373/-9.44
475	458/+0.70	441/+1.25	425/0.00	410/-3.14	394/-8.19
500	482/+0.54	465/+1.07	448/0.00	432/-2.76	416/-7.45
525	506/+0.39	488/+0.93	471/0.00	454/-2.48	438/-6.61
550	531/+0.26	512/+0.79	494/0.00	476/-2.22	459/-5.97
575	555/+0.16	535/+0.68	516/0.00	498/-1.99	480/-5.37
600	579/+0.06	559/+0.59	539/0.00	520/-1.78	502/-4.85
625	603/-0.03	582/+0.48	562/0.00	542/-1.63	523/-4.42
650	627/-0.09	606/+0.43	584/0.00	564/-1.40	544/-3.95
675	651/-0.15	629/+0.37	607/0.00	586/-1.30	565/-3.57
700	675/-0.21	652/+0.31	629/0.00	607/-1.19	586/-3.32
725	699/-0.27	675/+0.25	651/0.00	628/-1.08	606/-3.05
750	723/-0.32	697/+0.20	673/0.00	649/-0.98	627/-2.78
775	747/-0.36	720/+0.15	694/0.00	670/-0.87	646/-2.53
800	770/-0.40	742/+0.12	715/0.00	690/-0.78	666/-2.29
825	793/-0.43	764/+0.08	736/0.00	710/-0.72	685/-2.11
850	817/-0.47	786/+0.05	757/0.00	729/-0.66	703/-1.95
875	839/-0.50	807/+0.02	776/0.00	748/-0.60	721/-1.81
900	862/-0.52	827/-0.01	796/0.00	766/-0.54	738/-1.67
925	884/-0.55	847/-0.03	814/0.00	783/-0.48	754/-1.54
950	906/-0.56	867/-0.05	832/0.00	800/-0.44	770/-1.42

Ballistic Coefficient = 0.0375

M.V. (fps)	Range (yards)				
	10 yds.	20 yds.	30 yds.	40 yds.	50 yds.
400	386/+1.45	373/+2.05	359/0.00	347/-4.65	335/-12.19
425	410/+1.09	396/+1.71	383/0.00	369/-4.12	356/-10.90

Ballistic Coefficient = 0.0375

450	435/+0.88	420/+1.39	406/0.00	391/-3.45	378/-9.26
475	459/+0.68	444/+1.22	428/0.00	414/-3.13	400/-7.98
500	483/+0.53	467/+1.06	451/0.00	436/-2.71	421/-7.36
525	508/+0.38	491/+0.91	474/0.00	458/-2.45	443/-6.54
550	532/+0.26	514/+0.78	497/0.00	481/-2.19	465/-5.89
575	556/+0.15	538/+0.68	520/0.00	503/-1.96	486/-5.30
600	580/+0.05	561/+0.60	543/0.00	525/-1.76	508/-4.78
625	605/-0.04	585/+0.48	566/0.00	547/-1.60	529/-4.35
650	629/-0.09	608/+0.42	589/0.00	569/-1.40	551/-3.89
675	653/-0.16	632/+0.36	611/0.00	591/-1.29	572/-3.54
700	677/-0.22	655/+0.30	633/0.00	613/-1.18	593/-3.28
725	701/-0.28	678/+0.24	656/0.00	634/-1.07	614/-3.01
750	725/-0.33	701/+0.19	678/0.00	655/-0.96	634/-2.73
775	748/-0.37	723/+0.14	699/0.00	676/-0.85	654/-2.48
800	772/-0.40	746/+0.11	721/0.00	697/-0.76	674/-2.24
825	795/-0.44	768/+0.08	742/0.00	717/-0.71	693/-2.07
850	819/-0.47	790/+0.04	762/0.00	736/-0.65	712/-1.93
875	842/-0.50	811/+0.01	782/0.00	755/-0.58	730/-1.78
900	864/-0.52	832/-0.01	802/0.00	774/-0.52	747/-1.63
925	886/-0.55	852/-0.04	820/0.00	791/-0.47	764/-1.49
950	908/-0.57	872/-0.06	838/0.00	808/-0.43	780/-1.38

Ballistic Coefficient = 0.0400

M.V. (fps)	Range (yards)				
	10 yds.	20 yds.	30 yds.	40 yds.	50 yds.
400	387/+1.43	374/+2.02	362/0.00	350/-4.62	338/-12.15
425	411/+1.08	398/+1.72	385/0.00	373/-4.04	360/-10.80
450	436/+0.87	422/+1.38	408/0.00	395/-3.33	382/-9.11
475	460/+0.67	445/+1.20	431/0.00	417/-3.13	404/-8.14
500	484/+0.52	469/+1.04	454/0.00	440/-2.69	426/-7.32
525	509/+0.37	493/+0.90	477/0.00	462/-2.43	448/-6.49
550	533/+0.25	517/+0.78	501/0.00	485/-2.17	470/-5.83
575	557/+0.14	540/+0.67	523/0.00	507/-1.94	491/-5.23
600	582/+0.05	564/+0.59	546/0.00	529/-1.74	513/-4.71
625	606/-0.04	587/+0.47	569/0.00	552/-1.56	535/-4.26
650	630/-0.10	611/+0.42	592/0.00	574/-1.38	556/-3.82

Ballistic Coefficient = 0.0400					
675	654/-0.16	634/+0.36	615/0.00	596/-1.28	578/-3.51
700	678/-0.22	658/+0.30	637/0.00	618/-1.16	599/-3.24
725	702/-0.28	681/+0.24	660/0.00	640/-1.05	620/-2.96
750	726/-0.33	704/+0.18	704/0.00	661/-0.94	641/-2.68
775	750/-0.37	726/+0.14	704/0.00	682/-0.84	661/-2.43
800	774/-0.40	749/+0.11	725/0.00	703/-0.75	681/-2.20
825	797/-0.44	771/+0.07	746/0.00	723/-0.70	700/-2.03
850	821/-0.47	793/+0.04	767/0.00	743/-0.63	719/-1.89
875	844/-0.50	815/+0.01	787/0.00	762/-0.57	738/-1.74
900	866/-0.53	836/-0.02	807/0.00	781/-0.51	755/-1.59
925	889/-0.55	856/-0.04	826/0.00	798/-0.46	772/-1.47
950	911/-0.57	876/-0.06	845/0.00	815/-0.42	788/-1.35

APPENDIX D:

SOURCES FOR HUNTING REGULATIONS

Alabama

Alabama Department of Conservation and Natural Resources
64 N. Union St.
Montgomery, AL 36130
(334) 242-3465
www.dcnr.state.al.us/agfd

Alaska

Division of Wildlife Conservation
P.O. Box 25526
Juneau, AK 99802-6197
(907) 465-6197
www.state.ak.us/local/akpages/fish.game/wildlife

Arizona

Arizona Game and Fish Department
2221 W. Greenway Road
Phoenix, AZ 85023-4312
(602) 942-3000
www.gfd.state.az.us

Arkansas

Arkansas Game & Fish Commission
2 Natural Resources Drive
Little Rock, AR 72205
(800) 354-4263
www.agfc.state.ar.us

California

California Department of Fish & Game
1416 Ninth St.
Sacramento, CA 95818
(916) 227-2244
www.cfg.state.ca.us

Colorado

Colorado Division of Wildlife
1313 Sherman
Room 718
Denver, CO 80203
(303) 297-1192
http://wildlife.state.co.us/

Connecticut

Connecticut Department of Environmental Protection
79 Elm St.
Hartford, CT 06106-5127
(800) 424-3105
http://dep.state.ct.us/pao/

Delaware

Delaware Division of Fish and Wildlife
89 Kings Highway
Dover, DE 19901
(302) 739-4431
dep.state.ct.us/burnatr/wildlife

Florida

Florida Department of Game and Freshwater Fish
620 S. Meridian St.
Tallahassee, FL 32399-1600
(850) 488-4676
www.state.fl.us/gfc

Georgia

Georgia Department of Natural Resources
Wildlife Management Division
2111 Highway 278
Social Circle, GA 30025
(770) 918-6416
www.ganet.org/dnr/

Idaho

Idaho Department of Fish and Game
P.O. Box 25
Boise, ID 83707
(208) 334-3700
www.state.id.us/fishgame

Illinois

Illinois Department of Natural Resources
524 S. Second St.
Room 210
Springfield, IL 62701
(217) 782-2965
www.dnr.state.il.us/ildnr/

Indiana

Indiana Department of Natural Resources
402 W. Washington St.
Indianapolis, IN 46204
(317) 232-4080
www.dnr.state.in.us

Iowa

Iowa Department of Natural Resources
Wallace State Office Building
Des Moines, IA 50319-0034
(515) 281-5145
www.dnr.state.ia.us

Kansas

Kansas Parks and Wildlife
900 SW Jackson St., Suite 502
Topeka, KS 66612-1233
(785) 273-6740
www.kdwp.state.ks.us

Kentucky

Kentucky Department of Wildlife Resources
1 Game Farm Road
Frankfort, KY 40601
(502) 564-4336
www.state.ky.us/agencies/fw/kdfwr.htm

Louisiana

Louisiana Department of Wildlife & Fisheries
P.O. Box 98000
Baton Rouge, LA 70898
(504) 765-2980
www.wlf.state.la.us

Maine

Maine Department of Inland Fisheries &
Wildlife
285 State St.
41 State House Station
Augusta, ME 04333-0041
(207) 287-2571
webmaster_ifw@state.me.us

Make sure that you are complying with all state game laws when hunting with airguns.

Maryland

Maryland Department of Natural Resources
Wildlife Division
580 Taylor Ave., E-1
Annapolis, MD 21401
(401) 260-8540
www.dnr.state.md.us/huntersguide

Massachusetts

Massachusetts Department of Fisheries and
Wildlife
Field Headquarters
Westboro, MA 01581
(508) 792-7270, ext. 110
www.state.ma.us/dfwele/

Michigan

Michigan Department of Natural Resources
4590 118th Ave., Route 3
Allegan, MI 49010
(517) 373-1230
www.dnr.state.mi.us

Minnesota

Minnesota Department of Natural Resources
500 Lafayette Road
St. Paul, MN 55155-4026
(651) 296-4506
www.dnr.state.mn.us

Mississippi

Mississippi Department of Wildlife
2906 North State St.
Jackson, MS 39205
(800) 546-4868
www.mdfo.state.ms.us

Missouri

Missouri Department of Conservation
P.O. Box 180
Jefferson City, MO 65102
(573) 751-4115
www.dnr.state.mo.us

Montana

Montana Fish, Wildlife, & Parks
1420 E. Sixth Ave.
Helena, MT 59620
(406) 444-2535
http://fwp.state.mt.us/

Nebraska

Nebraska Game and Parks
2200 N. 33rd St.
Lincoln, NE 68503
(402) 471-5003
www.ngpc.state.ne.us

Nevada

Nevada Division of Wildlife
P.O. Box 10678
Reno, NV 89520
(702) 688-1500
www.ndw.state.nv.us

New Hampshire

New Hampshire Fish and Game Department
2 Hazen Drive
Concord, NH 03301
(603) 271-3211
www.wildlife.state.nh.us

New Jersey

New Jersey Division of Fish, Game, and
Wildlife
P.O. Box 400
Trenton, NJ 08625-0400
(609) 292-2965
www.state.nj.us/dep/fgw

New Mexico

New Mexico Department of Game and Fish
P.O. Box 25112
Sante Fe, NM 87504
(505) 827-7911
www.gmfs.state.nm.us

New York

New York Department of Environmental
Conservation
Wildlife Division
50 Wolfe Road
Albany, NY 12233
(518) 457-3521
www.dec.state.ny.us/

North Carolina

North Carolina Wildlife Resources Commission
512 N. Salisbury St.
Raleigh, NC 27640
(919) 662-4370
www.ncwildlife.org/

North Dakota

North Dakota Game and Fish Department
100 N. Bismarck Expressway
Bismarck, ND 58501-5095
(701) 328-6300
www.state.nd.us/gnf/hunting

Ohio

Ohio Division of Wildlife
1840 Belcher Drive
Columbus, OH 43224
(614) 265-6300
www.dnr.state.oh.us/odnr/wildlife/hunting

Oklahoma

Oklahoma Division of Wildlife
1801 N. Lincoln Blvd.
Oklahoma City, OK 73152
(405) 521-3853
www.odr.state.ok.us

Oregon

Oregon Department of Fish and Game
P.O. Box 59
Portland, OR 97207
(503) 872-5270
www.odfg.state.or.us

Pennsylvania

Pennsylvania Game Commission
2001 Elmerton Ave.
Harrisburg, PA 17110
(717) 787-4250
www.pgc.state.pa.us

Rhode Island

Rhode Island Fish and Wildlife
Oliver Steadman Government Center
480 Tower Hill Road
WakeField, RI 02879
(401) 789-3094
www.state.ri.us

Small game hunting with an air rifle is legal in many states. Be sure to consult with the appropiate state department for specifics.

South Carolina

South Carolina Department of Natural Resources
Wildlife Division
P.O. Box 167
Columbia, SC 29202
(803) 734-3843
www.dnr.state.sc.us

South Dakota

South Dakota Department of Game, Fish, and Parks
523 East Capitol
Pierre, SD 57501
(605) 773-3485
www.state.sd.us

Tennessee

Tennessee Wildlife Resource Agency
Ellington Agricultural Center
Nashville, TN 37302
(615) 781-6580
www.state.tn.us

Texas

Texas Parks and Wildlife
4200 Smith School Road
Austin, TX 78744
(512) 389-4820 or
www.tpwd.state.tx.us/hunt

Utah

Utah Wildlife Resources
1594 West, North Temple, Suite 2110
Salt Lake City, UT 84114-6301
(801) 538-4700
www.nr.state.ut.us

Vermont

Vermont Department of Fish and Wildlife
103 S. Main St.
10 South Building
Waterbury, VT 05671-0501
(802) 241-3700
www.dnr.state.vt.us\fw\fwhome

Virginia

Virginia Department of Game and Inland Fisheries
P.O. Box 11104
Richmond, VA 23230-1104
(804) 367-1000
www.dgif.state.va.us

Washington

Washington Department of Fish and Wildlife
600 Capitol Way N.
Olympia, WA 98501-1091
(360) 902-2464
www.wa.gov/wfdw

West Virginia

West Virginia Department of Natural Resources
Wildlife Division
1900 Kanawha Blvd. E.
Capital Complex, Building 3
Charleston, WV 25305
(304) 558-3380
www.wvdnr.state.wv.us

Wisconsin

Wisconsin Department of Natural Resources
Box 7921
Madison, WI 53707
(608) 266-2621
www.dnr.state.wi.us/

Wyoming

Wyoming Game and Fish Department
5400 Bishop Blvd.
Cheyenne, WY 82006
(307) 777-4600
http://gf.state.wy.us/

APPENDIX E:

BALLISTICS EQUATIONS

Those airgunners who enjoy calculating the ballistics of their particular air rifle/pellet combinations should find this section helpful. See Chapter 8 for more information, as well as the ballistics tables in Appendix C that eliminate the need for some calculations. The equations are numbered for easy reference.

The weight and diameter of a projectile are related properties. In order to express the relative weight of a projectile in terms of its diameter, a property known as the sectional density is determined. The function w/d^2 is defined as the sectional density, D.

$$D = \frac{Weight\ in\ pounds}{(Diameter\ in\ inches)^2} = \frac{w}{d^2} \qquad (16)$$

Bullets that are long and heavy relative to their diameter have a high sectional density. Such bullets penetrate the atmosphere (and, generally, the target) better than bullets having smaller values of D. However, penetration also depends greatly on bullet construction. Airgun pellets have very low sectional densities because they are usually very light for their caliber owing to their hollow interior. Also, when compared to long, pointed bullets used in centerfire rifles, pellets are not very streamlined.

How well a bullet passes through air is expressed by the number known as its ballistic coefficient. We have already mentioned that the sectional density is also involved. Therefore, the sectional density and ballistic coefficient of a bullet must be related characteristics. While we have not discussed it specifically, the shape of the projectile is also important.

The equation that relates the ballistic coefficient, sectional density, and the shape of the projectile can be written as:

$$C = \frac{w}{id^2} \qquad (17)$$

Since w/d^2 is the sectional density (D), the equation also can be written as:

$$C = \frac{D}{i} \qquad (18)$$

In these equations, w and d are the weight and diameter of the bullet, while i is the quantity that is related to the shape of the projectile and is the quantity known as the form factor. Since we want the projectile to have as large a value for C as possible, a large value of D and a small value of i are desirable.

The form factor (i) of a projectile is a number that is related to the shape of the projectile. It expresses the drag caused by air on the projectile relative to air drag on a projectile with a particular shape known as the standard projectile. The most efficient projectiles from a ballistic standpoint are those that are heavy for the caliber and sharp-pointed. Equations (17) and (18) show that if the pellet weight, diameter, and form factor are known, the ballistic coefficient can be calculated. Very streamlined bullets have form factors in the range of 0.40 to 0.60, while the values for blunt bullets (like wadcutter handgun bullets) range from 1.25 to 1.50. Also, pellets are very light for their diameters. A .22 caliber pellet normally weighs 14 to 15 grains, while a .22 rimfire bullet weighs 40 grains. Bullets for centerfire .22 caliber rifles frequently are in the range of 40 to 55 grains and have very sharp points. Therefore, form factors for pellets are much larger than those for bullets. For a .224 caliber pellet weighing 14.3 grains, the calculation of C, the ballistic coefficient, when $i = 1.5$ can be shown here:

$$C = \frac{\dfrac{14.3\ grains}{7{,}000\ grains\,/\,lb.}}{1.5\ x\ (0.224\ in.)^2} = 0.027 \qquad (19)$$

This value of C is very close to that known for certain .22 caliber pellets.

If C is known for a particular pellet, it is possible to use the same equation to calculate i.

$$i = \frac{\dfrac{Pellet\ weight\ (grains)}{7,000\ grains\,/\,lb.}}{C\,d^2} \qquad (20)$$

In the case of the .20-caliber Crosman Premier, which weighs 14.3 grains, the ballistic coefficient is 0.040, so the form factor for that pellet is:

$$i = \frac{\dfrac{14.3\ grains}{7,000\ grains\,/\,lb.}}{0.040\ x\ (0.200\ in.)^2} = 1.28 \qquad (21)$$

The Crosman Premier is a domed pellet of excellent shape and solid construction up front. In fact, it is one of the most efficient aerodynamic pellet designs, so it represents about the smallest form factor of any conventional pellet. At the other extreme, a very flat-nosed wadcutter that has a large interior cavity may have a form factor as large as 3.0 to 3.5. The vast majority of airgun pellets have form factors in the range of 1.2 to 3.0.

Here is an interesting aspect of these numbers. Suppose you are using a 14.3-grain, .22-caliber wadcutter design that has a value of i that may be in the interval from 2.7 to 3.0. We will now determine the value of C that would result for each of these values of i. The calculations are:

$$For\ i = 2.7,\ C = \frac{\dfrac{14.3\ grains}{7,000\ grains\,/\,lb.}}{2.7\ x\ (0.224\ in.)^2} = 0.0151 \qquad (22)$$

$$For\ i = 3.0,\ C = \frac{\dfrac{14.3\ grains}{7,000\ grains\,/\,lb.}}{3.0\ x\ (0.224\ in.)^2} = 0.0136 \qquad (23)$$

These results show that although an exact form factor value is not known, if it is in the 2.7 to 3.0 range, the ballistic coefficient will about the same anyway and in the range of 0.0136 to 0.0151. As we shall see, calculations using a ballistic coefficient of 0.0151 do not give results that are much different from those using a value of 0.0136. We do not actually need a highly accurate value for the ballistic coefficient in most cases and an approximate value is usually adequate.

Approximate values for the form factors of different types of pellets can be given as:

Pointed	Domed	Wadcutter or Hollow Point
1.3 to 2.0	1.3 to 2.5	2.8 to 3.4

These values are sufficiently accurate to allow the ballistic coefficient to be calculated with sufficient accuracy for most uses. Because air rifles are used at short ranges, calculated velocities and trajectories do not vary greatly even if the value for the ballistic coefficient is only approximate. This will be illustrated later in this section.

It is interesting to note that some of those wicked-looking pellets with sharp, angular profiles may actually have considerable drag in spite of the sharp points because there is a lot of turbulence behind the sharp corners. They are not very streamlined. A smooth profile without sharp corners like that shown in the Figure 7 works best.

In estimating the form factor for a pellet, use the smaller end of the range provided if the pel-

Because of their different profiles and weights, these pellets have considerably different form factors.

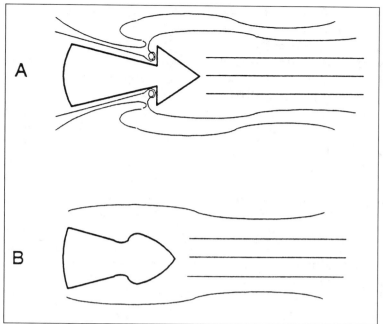

Figure A shows a pointed pellet that has a sharp angle where the head joins the body. These sharp angles cause turbulence that increases drag.

Figure B shows a pointed pellet with a streamlined profile that allows it to pass through the air without causing as much turbulence. Therefore, this pellet has lower drag than the other.

let has a smooth contour and the larger end of the range if the pellet has sharp corners. After the form factor is estimated, the ballistic coefficient can be calculated as illustrated above (equations 22 and 23). However, the best way to determine a ballistic coefficient is from actual firing data. In this way, the ballistic coefficient is determined from the velocity loss in a known distance interval. Most of the computer ballistics programs available are designed to perform this type of calculation. To use this procedure, the velocity is measured at two points (perhaps at the muzzle and at 30 yards) and the computer program then calculates C from the velocity loss.

We have already discussed the principle that the rate of velocity loss is higher for projectiles having low ballistic coefficients. Therefore, it is possible to calculate C from the velocities known at two distances along the trajectory (usually the muzzle and some longer range).

The equation used is:

$$C = \frac{R\,(feet)}{S_s - S_l} \qquad (24)$$

where C is the ballistic coefficient, R is the range in feet, and S_s and S_l are the values of the space functions corresponding to the velocities at the shorter and longer ranges, respectively. This is really a very simple equation to use because R, S_s, and S_l are just numbers. We know R and we

look up values for S_s and S_l. It works just like looking up how much tax you owe from tables arranged according to net income.

We will now show how this works with a real example. With my Crosman 2100 using 6 pumps, the 10.5-grain Crosman Premier pellet has a velocity of 590 fps at 5 feet from the muzzle, and the chronograph shows that at 30 yards (90 feet) it has an average velocity of 514 fps. From Ingalls' Tables, the value of the space function corresponding to the velocity of 514 fps is 24,947, while that corresponding to the velocity of 590 fps at 5 feet is 21,998. Thus, C is calculated as follows since the difference in ranges is 85 feet.

$$C = \frac{85}{24{,}947 - 21{,}998} = \frac{85}{2{,}949} = 0.029 \qquad (25)$$

This value agrees with the published ballistic coefficient for the 10.5-grain Crosman Premier pellet in .177 caliber. All that is needed is a chronograph and a set of Ingalls' Tables to get a value for S at the appropriate velocities. The problem is that Ingalls' Tables consist of about 15 pages of small print that do not need to be reproduced here. I prefer a single equation to a large table of data. Therefore, I derived an equation to calculate the space function when the velocity is known. That equation is:

$$S = 58{,}430 \times 10^{-0.0007816 \times v} \qquad (26)$$

where v is the velocity. We will now illustrate the use of the equation with the data given in the example above for the Crosman Premier shot from my Crosman 2100. For a velocity of 514 fps at the longer range (30 yards), the equation becomes

$$S_l = 58{,}430 \times 10^{-0.0007816 \times 514} \tag{27}$$

Multiplying in the exponent (-0.0007816 x 514) gives

$$S_l = 58{,}430 \times 10^{-0.3964} \tag{28}$$

Next use the $10x$ key on a scientific calculator to find the value of $10^{-0.3694}$. This is 0.4272, so the equation becomes

$$S_l = 58{,}430 \times 0.4272 = 24{,}962 \tag{29}$$

We now need the space function S_s for the shorter range corresponding to the velocity at 5 feet (which is 590 fps). Proceeding as before,

$$S_s = 58{,}430 \times 10^{-0.0007816 \times 590} \tag{30}$$

$$S_s = 58{,}430 \times 10^{-0.4240} = 58{,}430 \times 0.3767 = 22{,}012 \tag{31}$$

Now, making use of Equation 24, we calculate the ballistic coefficient.

$$C = \frac{85}{24{,}962 - 22{,}013} = \frac{85}{2{,}950} = 0.029 \tag{32}$$

This value agrees with that obtained by using the values of the space function taken from Ingalls' Tables. Therefore, we can now calculate the ballistic coefficient from velocities known at two points using Equation 26 just as well as from the elaborate tables.

If you have a chronograph and measure the velocity of a pellet at two distances, you can determine the ballistic coefficient of the pellet. Simply use a calculator and Equation 26 to determine the values of the space function and then use Equation 24 with the range or difference in ranges expressed in feet to obtain C.

Two things should be stated by way of explanation. First, Ingalls' Tables are not the only vehicle to determine the ballistic coefficient and other calculations not based on Ingalls' Tables may give slightly different results. Those that I have tried do not seem to give differences that exceed 0.004 in the value of C and usually no more than 0.002. A difference in C this small is completely negligible. Second, the ballistic coefficient is not strictly a constant because it varies slightly with projectile velocity. In view of these factors, the procedures described above are certainly adequate for airguns, even though they would not be adequate for long-range artillery.

Index

*An American air rifle is the perfect companion when exploring wide-open spaces—
or when you want to get away from it all for a relaxing shoot in the back yard or
basement. That's the real beauty of an air rifle.*

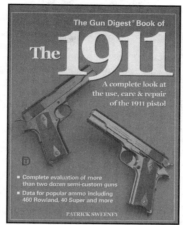
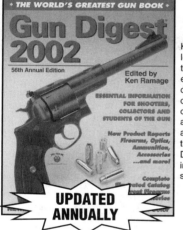
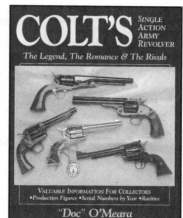
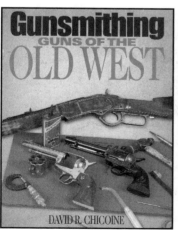
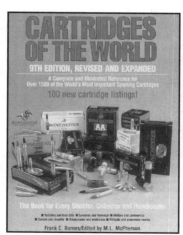

Top References for Top Shooters

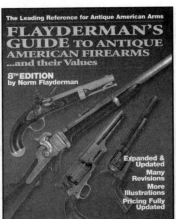
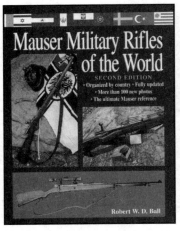

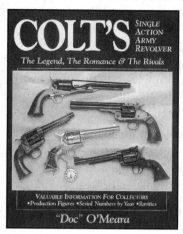

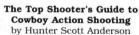

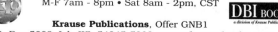

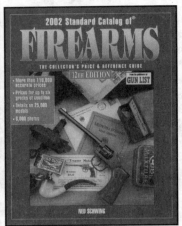
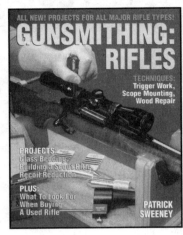
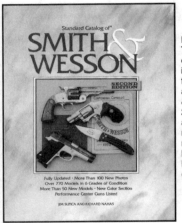